-90
Donated

P9-DDY-521

LA   Anderson, Stephen C.   25,571
2317
.E285 J.W. Edgar
A83
1984

DATE DUE

J. W. Edgar: educator for Texas
LA2317.E285A83 1   25571

Anderson, Stephen C.
     VRJC/WRIGHT LIBRARY

DEMCO

J. W. EDGAR

Educator For Texas

Stephen C. Anderson

EAKIN PRESS
Austin, Texas

All photographs are from the files of J.W. Edgar with the exception of
the dust jacket photo which was provided by Christianson Leberman,
Inc.

FIRST EDITION

Copyright © 1984
By Stephen C. Anderson

Printed in the United States of America
By Eakin Press, P.O. Box 23066, Austin, Texas 78735

ALL RIGHTS RESERVED

ISBN 0-89015-486-4

For Alice, William, and Stephen

CONTENTS

Preface and Acknowledgements

James Winfred Edgar took office as the first State Commissioner of Education in Texas on March 8, 1950. He served as commissioner for twenty-four years, a record for length of service which will probably never be broken. The purpose of this research has been to compile an in-depth study of Edgar and his influence on education in Texas — an influence which is not small, for he taught in country schools, supervised instruction and was a superintendent of schools prior to becoming Commissioner of Education. This study examines each segment of his life, usually with emphasis on his career, and critically analyzes it in terms of his influence on education. All of Edgar's career is interpreted from the viewpoint of his role in the proposal, passage, and implementation of the Gilmer-Aikin Laws of 1949. The study concludes with Edgar's retirement from the Texas Education Agency in 1974.

Edgar's career covers the period from 1923–1975, an era of significant change in education in the United States and Texas. The major world events of this era, the Depression of the 1930s, World War II in the 1940s, Korea in the 1950s, and the Vietnam Conflict in the 1960s and 1970s, shaped the course of education in the United States. Education in the United States during this time was transforming from village school to urban system.[1] Educators such as John Dewey and Horace Mann were congnizant that the functions of schooling were shifting in response to these modernizing patterns.[2] Throughout Edgar's career, which encompasses this era, four major trends influenced curriculum. At various times Edgar embraced all of them.

The *Humanists*, comprising one group, were steeped in traditional education ideas which were based on the power of reason. Three groups of reformers, each with distinct ideas of

---

1. David B. Tyack, *The One Best System: A History of American Urban Education.*)Cambridge: Harvard University Press, 1977), p. 5.
2. *Ibid.*, p. 8.

what knowledge should be embodied in the curriculum[3], were set against the humanists. G. Stanley Hall led the *Developmentalists*, a group who believed that the curriculum which should be taught ought to be based on the natural order of development of the child.[4] Joseph Mayer Rice spearheaded the *Social Efficiency Movement* which was to dominate American thinking in the 20th century.[5] This group proposed that education emulate the practices of private industry and be organized accordingly. Others of this group, such as Elwood P. Cubberly, William Torrey Harris, and Charles W. Eliot, were convinced that schooling should be more closely aligned with the practices of business, and that school administrators should serve the same functions as corporate managers in business.[6] Finally, the *Social Meliorists* saw the schools as a major force for social change and social justice. The social meliorists felt schools should have the power to create a new social order.[7]

Herbert M. Kliebard wrote the following concerning the four influences on curriculum during this era.

> The 20th century was to become the arena where these four visions of what knowledge is of most worth and of the principal function of schooling were presented and argued. No single interest group ever gained absolute supremacy, although general social and economic trends, the national mood, and local conditions and personalities affected the strength of each of these influences in different periods as the 20th century progressed. In the end, what became of the American curriculum was not the result of any decisive victory by any of the contending groups, but a loose, largely unarticulated, and not very tidy compromise.[8]

Edgar's own state of Texas experienced the same major world events as did the rest of the United States. The major educational events in Texas during Edgar's career both influ-

---

3. Herbert M. Kliebard, "Education at the Turn of the Century: A Crucible for Curriculum Change," *Educational Researcher*, January, 1982, p. 23.
4. *Ibid,* p. 18.
5. *Ibid.*, p. 20.
6. Milam C. Rowold, *The Texas Rural Schools Revisited, 1900–1929.* (Unpublished Dissertation, University of Texas at Austin, 1983), p. 5.
7. Kliebard, "Education at the Turn of the Century," p. 23.
8. *Ibid.*, p. 23.

enced him and were influenced by him. These events are rural aid, state leadership with local control, and federal aid.

Early in the 20th century the superiority of urban schools and independent districts over rural and common schools was evident.[9] The year 1911 marked the birth of rural aid which was the first of three major forces that would influence education in Texas during Edgar's career. The emphasis on rural aid to education was to last until 1949 with the passage of the Gilmer-Aikin Laws. Dr. L.A. Woods, State Superintendent of Education from 1933 to 1950, was a great champion of rural aid. Woods' greatest accomplishment was the large annual increase in the monetary appropriation for rural aid. This increase meant a reduction by half or more of the number of common school districts. This reduction greatly improved the quality and quantity of educational opportunity for rural children.[10]

The Gilmer-Aiken Laws introduced a period of state leadership in education with local control. This also marked the beginning of Edgar's leadership of education in Texas.

The third force in Texas education was the influence of the federal government. This began with the *Brown vs Board of Education of Topeka* case in 1954 and continued until Edgar's retirement in 1974.

Professional meetings in Texas were full of curriculum reform rhetoric during the early part of the 20th century. Much of this rhetoric was in favor of the social efficiency movement. The leaders of this movement in Texas singled out the rural school as an obstacle to their goal of reform.[11] Later the proponents of strong state leadership attacked and helped to change the established State Superintendency. Finally, the federal government intervened with money and laws which were not always well received. These influences characterize the Edgar Era in Texas educational history which parallels the same curriculum influences mentioned by Kliebard.

How important or valuable is a biography of J.W. Edgar? A.M. Aikin, former State Senator of Texas, said of Edgar, "I

---

9. Ed Yoes, Jr., "Texas," *Education in the States: Historical Development and Outlook*, Jim B. Pearson and Edgar Fuller, Eds. (Washington, D.C.: National Education Association of the United States, 1969), p. 1203.
10. *Ibid.*, p. 1209.
11. Milam C. Rowold, *Rural Schools Revisited*, p. 7.

ix

think he has a record that's been equalled by few and excelled by none . . . I think Edgar is one of the greatest public officials this state has ever had . . ." [12]

Edgar's career as an educator includes: five years as a country school teacher and principal in Burnet County; three years as Superintendent of Instruction for the school district in Victoria; and eighteen years as Superintendent of Schools in Mirando City, Orange, and Austin, Texas. These jobs gave him experience that prepared him for his appointment as Commissioner of Education.

Edgar came to national prominence for his work with Lanham Act funds during World War II in Orange, Texas. His dissertation is the only comprehensive study of the federal assistance to schools under the Lanham Act.

Edgar's involvement in the proposal, passage, and implementation of the Gilmer-Aikin Laws gave him direct input into the structure and creation of the Texas Education Agency as it became after he was made Commissioner. This greatly increased his importance in state educational circles. According to Senator Aikin, Edgar was a *unanimous* choice of the State Board of Education which was created by the Gilmer-Aikin Laws.

The position of Commissioner of Education was created in 1950. Edgar held that post for twenty-four of the thirty-four years since its creation. He was in charge of education in Texas through the turmoil and changes that took place during those years. In the brief span of ten years since his retirement, three persons have occupied the post of Commissioner of Education in Texas. These facts are a good illustration of his dominance of the Texas Education Agency and leave no doubt concerning the importance of Edgar to education in Texas and concerning the importance of this research about him.

A key part of this research employs the extensive use of taped interviews with Edgar. His life was divided into workable units, and he was interviewed one section at a time. The author employed the use of oral history through the technique of elite interviewing to accomplish the interviews.

Why the use of oral history? This technique is the closest

---

12. J.W. Edgar: School Man for an Era," unpublished speech, 1974.

thing to pure unaltered memory, and sometimes oral history has proven more accurate than manuscript sources.[13]

As Davis, Back, and MacLean state, oral history is not heresy. When conscientiously gathered, carefully processed, and critically examined, it contributes moderately to the quantity and uniquely to the quality of what we know about the recent past.[14] All of the interviews with Edgar used in this study were transcribed as close to verbatim as possible.[15] The same procedures were also used to interview people who know and/or worked with Edgar with the exception that these interviews have been indexed rather than transcribed due to monetary considerations.

The interviews were accomplished using the principles of elite and specialized interviewing as described in Dexter. An elite interview, according to Riesman, is an interview with any interviewee, who in terms of the current purposes of the interviewer, is given special, nonstandardized treatment. Nonstandardized treatment is defined as:

    1.   Stressing the interviewee's definition of the situation;
    2.   Encouraging the interviewee to structure the account of the situation;
    3.   Letting the interviewee introduce to a considerable extent his notions of what he regards as relevant, instead of relying upon the investigators notions of relevance.[16]

In other words, whenever possible, the investigator let the interviewee teach him what the problem, the question, or the situation was.[17] Another trait of an elite interview is that an exception, a deviation, or an unusual interpretation may suggest a revision, a reinterpretation or a new approach to the method of research.[18]

---

13. Cullom Davis, Kathryn Back, and Kay MacLean, *Oral History: From Tape to Type.*) Chicago: American Library Association, 1977), pp. 5–6.
14. *Ibid.*, p. 6.
15. Mary Joe Deering and Barbara Pomeroy, *Transcribing Without Tears.* (George Washington University Library: Oral History Program, 1976), p. 11.
16. Lewis Anthony Dexter, *Elite and Specialized Interviewing.* (Evanston: Northwestern University Press, 1970), p. 5.
17. *Ibid.*, p. 6.
18. *Ibid.*, p. 7.

The research is based on the historical method and is dependent on interpretation of data. This interpretation is subject to the bias of the researcher and puts limits on the work. Likewise, oral histories are subject to the limitation of faulty memory. Every attempt has been made, therefore, to verify all information by written document or by other interviews.

The author wishes to thank O.L. Davis, Jr., Gary R. McKenzie, Mark Seng, and Ricardo Romo who each helped in his own way with this work. Special thanks is due to J.W. Edgar who not only gave his time but helped in every other way possible. He was an inspiration. Thanks to my wife, Alice, who edited this book. Her unselfish help made this project progress smoothly. The Paul & Mary Haas Foundation and The University of Texas at Austin Graduate Studies Office deserve thanks for providing financial support which greatly eased the burden of this research. Finally, the author is especially grateful to Judge Thomas C. Ferguson for providing the financial assistance to make this book possible.

Stephen C. Anderson
Austin, Texas
May 29, 1984

1

Youth To Victoria:
The Rural Phase

This chapter describes Edgar's early life and his early
career from his first teaching job until he began his work as
Superintendent of Schools in Orange, Texas. This period covers thirty-five years — from before his birth in 1904 until
1939, the year in which he left Victoria, Texas, for Orange,·
Texas. This provides an explanatory foundation for what
happened later in Edgar's career.

EARLY LIFE: GRADE SCHOOL AND HIGH SCHOOL

James Winfred Edgar was born on September 15, 1904, in
Briggs, Texas, a small community about fifty miles north of
Austin in eastern Burnet County. His father, James William
Edgar, had come to Texas about 1886 from a little town called
Center Point in Henderson County, Tennessee. Edgar's
mother, whose maiden name was Sarah Miranda Morris, was
from a farm outside of Florence, Texas. Florence is located in
Williamson County about eighteen miles north of Georgetown
and about ten miles from Briggs. They were married in 1892.
Edgar was the third of four children. He had an older brother
(Robert Morris), an older sister (Mae), and a younger brother
(Donald).[1] Edgar's father had bought a general mercantile

store, which he ran until 1912, in Briggs. Both of his parents were Baptists; both were active church members. Their house was located about four or five blocks from the store and took up about one city block. A barn was located on the property near the house. James Edgar also owned a farm, located about four miles from Briggs, which he rented out.

Edgar had a good relationship with both of his parents. This relationship is evidenced in the following description Edgar gave about his family.

> He [my father] was the oldest member of his family. He had younger brothers and sisters and was sort of a father figure to them. All through their life and all through his life he sort of helped them, and worked with them. He was a very good family man. He provided very well for my mother and for the family. He was a quiet sort of person. He was religious, but I don't think he had quite as deep a religious conviction as my mother did. But he was a religious man.[2]

> My father's store [was] in Briggs. He'd been there about twenty-five years, and I think every farmer in that whole area owed him money. He carried them through the lean years, and the good years. So for some time after he sold the store and moved to Burnet, he would go out and visit these people on their farms in the Briggs area. He would take me with him, in the summertime, of course. We'd go on a buggy, from one farm to another, and try to collect a little money. We did collect a little money — enough to live on, I guess, with what he had saved previously. Sometimes we'd get money. Sometimes we'd get chickens or stove wood or something. Anyway, we'd spend the night, or camp out at night by ourselves. In that way I got to know him better than I guess I would [have] any other way. I came to understand him much better than I ever had.[3]

> My mother was a more intense person. She was, again, the oldest child of her family. She had seven or eight younger brothers and sisters. Again, she was sort of a mother figure to them, and helped them all along. She, of course, devoted full time to her own family . . .She was, I believe, sixteen years younger than my father. He was thirty-nine when he married her in 1892. And she was about twenty-three.[4]

> She was more aggressive than my father, especially with us children. I wouldn't say that she was dominating in any way, but she was pushy. She had a dream about what she wanted us to do, and some plans also. I think it was her influence probably that got me going in school.[5]

Edgar's parents had a good relationship with each other. Of their relationship, Edgar states:

> I would say a very good one [their relationship]. They were not demonstrative in any way with each other, but of course he was much older than she. I never heard her call him anything except Mr. Edgar. Finally through the years it developed into "Mistegar" . . .At the same time there was a cordial and compatible relationship between them. Certainly they never caused any of us children to think otherwise because we were very much in a fine family atmosphere.[6]

Young Edgar started school in Briggs when he was six years old in a three- or four-teacher school. Of his early schooling, Edgar said:

> No one has ever accused me of being a scholar. But I always enjoyed school . . .Particularly the reading. It just seemed like a way of life to me . . . going to school.[7]

After going to school two years in Briggs, Edgar's mother became dissatisfied with the quality of the school there. She had heard that Burnet had a good school system. Also, Burnet had a private school where students from all over the county attended. For the next few years they would rent a house in Burnet from September until May. Edgar's father would come to Burnet every weekend. Edgar's brother and sister attended the private school while Edgar attended the public school (beginning in the third grade) because his mother felt that his brothers and sister had not had a good basic educational foundation and she wanted them to have one. In 1912 Edgar's father sold the store in Briggs and moved to Burnet permanently because Mrs. Edgar wanted her children to remain in the Burnet schools.

Edgar remembers some of his time in grade school.

> I was in third grade. My teacher said there were some songbooks for sale to use in school — in the mornings for singing — and they cost eight cents. Any student could buy one, so of course I wanted one. So I told my teacher I'd buy one. I went home and told my mother. And she said I shouldn't have promised that eight cents without asking her. I thought that was a little conscripted, but I guess it taught me a lesson. Anyway, I got the eight cents and bought the songbook.[8]
> Also, I remember in about the fifth grade — I'm left-handed,

if you'll notice — a student asking the teacher what made people
left-handed. And she said, well, there's something wrong with
their brain. And I carried that with me for years . . . that there
was something wrong with my brain because I was left-handed.[9]
     But I remember sixth grade very well because I failed it and
had to repeat it[10] . . .Of course I was embarrassed. I suppose my
parents were too . . . I think my mother asked me why I did [fail].
I said well, I'd started school a year early, and I was younger, and
it didn't really matter because I had time. But I don't know how
she really felt about it[11] . . .I failed because I failed Arithmetic.
That was, of course, a major subject, so I was detained. Mathe-
matics was always very hard for me. I never really did learn it
until I started teaching it.[12]

At the time Edgar was in high school there were four
grades — eighth, ninth, tenth, and eleventh. When he reached
ninth grade, he loved high school. He enjoyed the association
with the other students. He tried out for all the athletic teams,
but was not well coordinated, and so usually was just on the
squad. When Edgar was in the ninth grade, the school superintendent offered him and two other students a chance to fin-
ish the last three years of high school in two years.[13] He tried it
and made it, but just barely. Gaining back this extra year enabled him to get back the year he had lost when he failed the
sixth grade. His senior year Edgar was president of his class.
At his graduation on May 24, 1921, he gave the class president's address. There were twelve students in his class — five
boys and seven girls.[14]

Judge Thomas Ferguson, a classmate of Edgar's all
through high school, said of him:

> Dr. Edgar was always a good student. I don't recall that he
> was flashy in any sense of the word. He was a sound student. And
> he was well liked.[15]

Edgar worked all through grade school and high school. As
early as 1912, he picked cotton in the fall and chopped cotton in
the spring. This continued for several years. In his last two
years of high school he worked after school and on Saturday in
a cleaning and pressing shop. When he graduated from high
school, the tailor gave him a tailor-made suit as a graduation
present.[16] This was an excellent gift for both college and teaching, as Edgar was soon to learn.

COLLEGE AND TEACHING AT LAKE VICTOR

After graduating from high school, Edgar faced the problem all high school graduates face — what to do next. His father had been in business, and his older brother had had a soda fountain in Burnet for several years. With this in mind, Edgar went to a business school the first year after he graduated from high school, 1921–1922. He recalls:

> We had bookkeeping and typewriting. I didn't have shorthand. [We had] business law or something like that. I realized pretty quickly, I think, at least during that year, that business was not my field as a livelihood. I did the work. What I learned, of course, helped me along in later years. But I never became attached to it or really interested in it too much.[17]

Edgar was not satisfied with business school nor was his mother. She wanted him to go to college, and she insisted that he did go. It was her ambition that Edgar graduate from college. She and his father got together enough money for him to go for one year. In the fall of 1922, he enrolled at Howard Payne College in Brownwood, Texas. This was a Baptist College about one hundred miles from Burnet with about six hundred students. Edgar felt his mother wanted him to become a Baptist minister but that she would settle for him becoming a teacher. So she told him to be sure and take the courses that were necessary in the freshman year to get a teaching certificate. He took the six hours of education courses required for a teaching certificate that would enable him to teach for two years in high school or four years in elementary school. At the end of Edgar's freshman year in college, the money for his education ran out. Consequently, he got a job teaching in Lake Victor, Texas, in the fall of 1923 at the age of nineteen. The job paid seventy-five dollars a month, of which he paid twenty-five for room and board. He lived in Lake Victor with a family. Sometimes he would go home on the train that ran from Lampasas to Burnet. He would leave on Saturday morning and return on Sunday afternoon. Edgar recalls:

> You were supposed to be around to attend church. The history of the community, I guess, was that teachers were supposed to be Sunday school teachers. But I always avoided that responsibility if I could. And I managed successfully, I think. But I did

attend church occasionally. I don't want to give the impression that I'm not religious. I am. But it's very casual.[18]

Edgar began teaching in a room with the fifth, sixth, and seventh grades in it. He fell in love with teaching from the first day.

> From the first day I was hooked on teaching, and I never wanted to do anything else. I think I discovered a brand new world, and I thought I owned it or something because it enveloped me. It didn't take me very long, maybe a year or two before I began to think about what I wanted to do in teaching. And I determined pretty early that I was going to be a school superintendent. And that's all I really ever wanted to be was a school superintendent.[19]

Teaching for Edgar was not easy. On the first day he realized that he was not really prepared to teach. He had not had enough training, background, or preparation. At this point, he realized he had a problem.

> So I realized I had a problem to face. I think I began to try to look at these youngsters as individual people and not just a class of students. I guess this was my first idea of individualizing instruction . . . by looking at each pupil and trying to find out what his skill and knowledge was, and working with them individually. I think I was able to develop some programs that were helpful. In other words, when we would have a reading class, we'd have all twenty of [the students] in the same class. Fifth graders would be reading sixth grade books, and sixth graders would be reading fifth grade books to learn where they were. The brighter students would help the slower, or the older students would help the younger students.[20]

Edgar learned very fast that just the schoolroom activities were not enough to develop the skills and interests of his students. Some students were old enough to begin to get tired of schooling. So he began to supplement his class work with other activities, some of which were sponsored by Texas' University Interscholastic League. Some of these activities involved writing essays, participating in spelling contests and declamation. These were a means to get the students interested in building and advancing outside interests. Another activity Edgar promoted at Lake Victor was field trips. He continued and advanced this activity all throughout his career.

The first year Edgar taught at Lake Victor, S.P. Cowan was in the sixth grade. Following are some of his recollections:

> I was in Dr. Edgar's class in a three teacher rural school the first day he taught. I was in the sixth grade . . .He was a strong teacher in my opinion. The thing that I remember about him so well [is that] he just never was absent; he was always there. Sometimes he might not feel well. He might have an extreme cold or something. But he would read sometimes on those days very interesting stories . . .He was not one that would ever let you by with anything. He was a strong disciplinarian but was never harsh . . .You'd always remember him as a friend and respect him. He tried to get me to say a declamation which would have led on to the district meet. He couldn't persuade me. I wouldn't do it . . .One time when they organized a band, he'd come and sat on the seat beside me — "don't you want to get in the band?" [21]

In the spring of 1924 Edgar finished his first year of teaching at Lake Victor. He told the school board that he did not want to come back because he was planning to go to school. A short time later, however, he realized that a lack of money would prevent him from returning to school. After the school session at Lake Victor was out for some time, the Bethal School Board asked Edgar to be the Principal of their school. Their school was a two teacher district located about eight miles from Burnet and five miles from Lake Victor. The Bethal School District was part of the Lake Victor community. Edgar accepted the job as principal. It paid one hundred dollars per month for a seven month school year. The school at Bethal had nine grades. Edgar taught the last four grades while the second teacher taught the first five. Edgar had about twenty students in his class. This school session finished in the Spring of 1925.

In the early part of the summer of 1925 the Lake Victor School Board called Edgar and asked him to go back to Lake Victor as principal. He accepted and began teaching in September of 1925. The school was still a three teacher school with ten grades. Edgar taught the high school grades and was also the coach, as he was the only man there. He was paid one hundred and twenty dollars per month for an eight month school session. As Principal at Lake Victor, Edgar was obligated to live in the community. He did not have much supervi-

sion of the other two teachers. He taught eighth, ninth, and
tenth grades.

Dr. M.G. Bowden attended school in Lake Victor in 1926–
1927. His teacher was a Miss Robinson. He remembers:

> I lived three miles from school. My sister and I traveled to
> and from school on a horse. We put her in a horse stall that was
> school owned. The school itself had an auditorium upstairs and
> four classrooms downstairs, with a little cloakroom in between
> two of the classrooms called a library. It must have had ten or
> twelve books in it . . . There were as many as one hundred chil-
> dren in the school . . . My first recollection of meeting him [Mr.
> Edgar] was that his face would flush when meeting new people.
> He would act like he was embarrassed. He was a very shy sort of
> quiet, easy-going person. He was much more tense than we kids
> ever realized . . . [Once] when Miss Robinson went on the train to
> Lampasas, Mr. Edgar took over our class . . . We were always in
> awe of him because he was a man and always looked very serious,
> although he wasn't as serious as he appeared. He had a better
> sense of humor than he appeared to have had then.[22]

As principal he had reports to fill out and was responsible for
the maintenance of building and grounds.

The school building at Lake Victor was in poor condition
for it had seriously deteriorated over the years. A movement
which wanted to build a new school existed in the community.
Some people, however, were not in favor of a new school building. The Lake Victor School Board decided to sponsor a bond issue. They brought S.M.N. Mars, the State Superintendent of
Public Instruction, to speak to the community. Edgar recalls
this well.

> He came up out of Burnet . . .The county superintendent
> brought him up for an evening to speak in the church house. This
> was my first contact with the State Superintendent of Public In-
> struction . . . and a very fine one, incidentally. He was very, very
> generous to us. I always thought he made a wise talk. Instead of
> getting up and urging people to support the bond issue, he out-
> lined the pros and cons and facts on both sides. He kind of left it
> with them. I was very much impressed with him.[23]

The bond issue passed and the new school was built for the
next school year (1926–1927). Edgar again told the school
board he wanted to go back to school in the fall of 1926. They
asked him to stay and pointed out there would be a new build-

ing, the addition of the eleventh grade, and four teachers instead of three. He agreed to stay.

The same school board that had been so eager to have Edgar stay, terminated him at the end of the 1926–1927 school year. The termination resulted indirectly from Edgar meeting his future wife, Sue Oakley, late in the summer of 1926 before school started. One night he decided to go to a dance at the opera house in Burnet. He did not have a date. When he arrived, he met one of his high school classmates who did have a date. Along with his date was Sue Oakley whose family owned a ranch in northern Burnet County. She was teaching at Elm Grove School, a small one teacher school about five miles from Lake Victor. Edgar's high school friend introduced them and they danced. Edgar's wife has a different version of how they met.

> We don't agree on when we met, but it was the same summer, I'm sure . . . He says we met at a dance. I say we met at a swimming party.[24]

Regardless of how they met, they began seeing each other in the fall of 1926. The girl that Sue was with the night of the dance was her niece. Her niece was twenty-three years old, one year older than Sue. In the fall of 1926, one of Edgar's high school students began going with this niece. At Thanksgiving Edgar, Sue, Sue's niece, and this high school boy went to Burnet to a dance. Some people from Lake Victor were there. The Lake Victor School Board learned of this outing and met with Edgar about it. The board told him that they felt it was not proper to dance. (Lake Victor was a community of strict Baptists and Church-of-Christ people.) Edgar had the following comments:

> I had my first invitation to meet with the school board after that. They told me they didn't think it was proper for me to dance . . . I knew my future was sealed as far as Lake Victor was concerned . . . the main sin was dancing. It wasn't an original sin, but it was way up on the list, particularly for a school teacher.[25]

In spite of the dancing problem the 1926–1927 school year was successful. Edgar coached the basketball team which won the county championship. S.P. Cowan was a member of that team. The spring of 1927 concluded Edgar's teaching career at

Lake Victor. The school board hired another teacher and Edgar
prepared to return to Howard Payne full time in the fall of
1927 as a married man.

MARRIAGE AND HOWARD PAYNE: 1927–1928

In the summer of 1927 Sue Oakley was in Baylor College
at Belton and Edgar was in Howard Payne at Brownwood.
They knew that Sue was going to teach in Atascosa County be-
low San Antonio and that he was going to return to school in
the fall of 1927. They decided to get married anyway. Edgar
had this to say about the proposal:

> We just talked about it and finally agreed. I didn't get down
> on my knees.[26]

The wedding ceremony was a small private one, just family and friends. They planned it that way because they knew
they would be separated. They had no honeymoon due to lack
of money. During the 1927–1928 year, Edgar and Mrs. Edgar
saw each other at Thanksgiving, at Christmas, and once during the spring when one of their mutual friends died. Throughout the year they wrote to each other almost every day.

Edgar figured by going to school the summer of 1927, the
1927–1928 school year, and the summer of 1928, he could graduate. He knew he would need financial help, so he got three
jobs. The first job was as the janitor of the first floor of the
administration building. This involved mopping and sweeping.
The Biology Department was located there and he was sup-
posed to clean all the equipment. There was a maintenance director who would tell Edgar what he wanted done, and Edgar
would do it. His second job was a part-time job in the Bursar's
Office; he ran errands and was a clerk. The third job was grad-
ing themes for one of the English professors. This job was time
consuming and required much work. Edgar remembers:

> The job of grading the English themes was time consuming.
> I would do that at night as well as whatever studying I had to do
> . . . I enjoyed it because I had enjoyed teaching the English part to
> the kids at Lake Victor, and I worked. Outside of being lazy and
> dreading it, overall I enjoyed it.[27]

The year at Howard Payne went well for Edgar. Mr. Peter
Marchek, a freshman at Howard Payne in the fall of 1927,
wrote about Edgar:

Dr. Edgar returned to Howard Payne College to complete his work for a degree. This was my freshman year at Howard Payne College. We roomed across the hall in the "Old Horse and Mule Barn," that was our reference to the men's dormitory. We became friends. My roommate and I tormented him every opportunity we got, like stacking his room. Somehow, he knew each time this happened who did it. As freshmen we received our reward — so many licks for every occasion as far back to the time we met. However, we liked him and came back for more. I remember him as a very nice person — intelligent, quiet, warm, willing to share his experiences.[28]

Edgar received his degree in the summer of 1928 as planned. In the spring of 1928, he began searching for a superintendent's job. He had thought,

Well, I'm just ready to be a superintendent. And surely with a degree I won't have any trouble just stepping out and getting a job in one of the smaller school districts.[29]

Four or five school boards interviewed Edgar. The interviews would go well until the boards found out that Edgar was only twenty-three years old. He realized that nobody was looking for *him* to be superintendent. This early failure led to his first job as superintendent at Heidenheimer, Texas.

HEIDENHEIMER: 1928–1929

It was May of 1928 and Edgar still did not have a job. In addition to finding himself a job, he also wanted to find a job for Sue because they wanted to teach together. Before Edgar began summer school, he went to Bell County which is where Temple is located. He spoke to the county superintendent and asked him about any vacancies. The superintendent told Edgar that a couple of schools needed superintendents. One of them was Troy, just north of Temple. The other was Heidenheimer, southeast of Temple. Edgar went to Troy first and spoke to several members of the school board; they did not show any interest. Edgar then went to Heidenheimer:

I was going back down to Heidenheimer, and I stopped at a garage . . . the first place I came to in Heidenheimer that was open. As luck would have it, the school board was meeting in that garage. I went ahead and met with them.[30]

Their eleven grade school had been burned the year before, but

they had rebuilt an eight grade school. This was not specifically what Edgar was looking for, but at that point he was not
in a position to be choosy. Sometime in the early part of June,
a member of the Heidenheimer School Board called Edgar and
told him that both he and Sue had jobs.

Edgar's job at Heidenheimer carried the title of Superintendent. The school district had two schools and five teachers.
There was a Black school with one Black teacher, and a White
school with four White teachers. Heidenheimer was a community of Czech and German farmers. They were very responsive
to Edgar. The Edgars lived in a teacherage, which was a house
the school system provided. Two other teachers lived in rooms
in the house. Edgar's salary was one hundred and fifty dollars
per month for a nine-month school session. Sue's salary was
eighty-five dollars per month. Edgar taught the seventh and
eighth grades. The other three teachers divided up the first six
grades. Sue taught the third and fourth grades.

The first time Edgar had worked with a Black school was
during his year at Heidenheimer. The school had twenty or
twenty-five students, most of them young. The older students
had withdrawn from school. About the Black school, Edgar recalls:

> If I had had my way, I would have packed them all up and
> brought them back to the other school, but of course we couldn't
> do that because it was against the law in those days. So I tried to
> be as helpful as I could without seeming to dictate or interfere too
> much with them . . . the relationship was very cordial.[31]

In addition to being superintendent, in the White school Edgar was also principal. He organized a football team that played
against some of the other schools. He supported the Interscholastic League contests. Edgar and Mrs. Edgar were also involved
with the community. Edgar describes this involvement:

> The community . . . we were involved with them. We organized
> a Dramatics Club and gave some plays. I had to direct those plays. I
> thought I was pretty good, but I really wasn't. I was pretty sad. But
> I did get a chance to work there with the community people.[32]

Heidenheimer had a seven member school board. The secretary of the board was a farmer named J.C. Edds. Edgar felt
J.C. Edds was important to his career:

He was interested in schools. He would have made a good school superintendent too. He really taught me a lot about how to work with the school boards . . .He's dead now. He had a large family. He and his wife were interested in school. They were interested in us. He had been on the school board a long time. He'd come up to the school and talk to me about what was going on — not in a dictatorial or proprietary way at all, but just in a friendly counselling type of relationship. I learned quite a bit from him on that basis.[33]

Edgar was well thought of in Heidenheimer. Mr. J.A. Marshall did not attend school in Heidenheimer, but his family owned a store in Heidenheimer in 1928. Marshall recalls,

> We used to play basketball together. He was a teacher and I was a student. We had a grocery store at Heidenheimer. So we were real well acquainted with him because we saw him every day . . .I knew a fellow that worked for us who I talked to twenty or thirty years later, and [we] talked about Mr. Edgar. He talked about him being a fine gentleman . . .His name was Tom Marshall [no relation] . . .He had a very high regard for Mr. Edgar.[34]

During the 1928–1929 school year, Edgar was looking for a better superintendency. He enjoyed Heidenheimer but wanted something a little more challenging. He learned of a teaching placement agency in Abilene, Texas, run by a man named W.A. Bynam. If Mr. Bynam got you a job, you would pay five percent of your first year's salary to him. Edgar contacted Mr. Bynam and asked him to look for a job for him. Late in the spring a superintendency in Mirando City opened up. Edgar applied.

Meanwhile, during the summer of 1929 Edgar stayed in Heidenheimer. One of Sue's brothers had a thrasher — to thrash grain. He gave Edgar a job which paid two dollars and fifty cents per day to work with him thrashing grain. Edgar worked at that job half the summer. Sue spent the summer in Heidenheimer, with her family near Lampasas, and with Edgar's family in Burnet. During the early summer Mr. Bynam had told Edgar the job in Mirando City had been filled. About the middle of August, Mr. Bynam wrote Edgar that the man who was chosen as superintendent at Mirando City had resigned. Edgar called the president of the school board in Mirando City and told him that he was still interested in the job. About a week later, Edgar received a wire from the school

14 *J.W. EDGAR: Educator For Texas*

board in Mirando City saying that the board had elected him as superintendent. They asked him if he could report by September 1, 1929.

Edgar knew he was going to have to resign at Heidenheimer and that it was very late in the year to be resigning. He called Ed Lamb, a friend of his who had gone to Howard Payne with him and who needed a job. Ed's wife also needed a job. When Edgar met with the Heidenheimer School Board for the purpose of resigning, he had his replacement set up. The board hired the Lambs and the Edgars were on their way to Mirando City in the fall of 1929.

MIRANDO CITY: 1929–1936

Edgar left Burnet in his Model-A Ford Roadster and arrived in Mirando City right on September 1, 1929. Sue had gotten a teaching job but joined Edgar later. His salary was $2,400 for twelve months. In addition to being Superintendent, Edgar was also Tax Accessor Collector. This was a unique situation. The Magnolia Petroleum Company, which later became Mobil Oil, paid most of the taxes. Edgar had no problem in carrying out both jobs at once. This combination of superintendency with tax collector was the only situation of its kind that Edgar, during his long career, ever heard of.

Mirando City, Texas, was located thirty-two miles east of Laredo, Texas, in Webb County in the desert. It was an oil town with a population of about one thousand people. The political fathers in Laredo had allowed the district to be founded as an independent school district, but they contained it almost in the exact area of Mirando City. Mirando City was the southwest headquarters for the Magnolia Petroleum Company.

Edgar jumped right in. He found a good school system in Mirando City. The previous superintendent had died. Six teachers taught three hundred students through the tenth grade. About one-third of these students were Mexican-American. The first and second grades were separated for language purposes. Mirando City had a Black school with about eight children in it. Edgar tried to give them as much help as possible:

> Again, I would have liked to have brought them all into the same school district, and should have, but could not.[35]

The years Edgar was at Mirando City were Depression years. These years were tough, as Mrs. E.J. Lunz wrote:

> The thirties were difficult times for most people, but in some ways we were fortunate. Ours was a small independent school district with oil companies paying most of the taxes. How that came to be, I have no idea because Aguilares, about twelve miles west of us and Oilton and Bruni to the east, were under the domination of the Webb County Superintendent. There we sat in the middle, so to speak, of Webb County with oil money which Laredo obviously coveted . . . But money was not plentiful. We were always scrimping for something. Jack Fulbright and my husband promoted the first Mirando City carnival, which endures to this day, to get funds for the football team.[36]

Edgar found no organized high school in Mirando City. He began right away to talk to people to learn what kind of schools they wanted. He found that people were receptive and wanted to improve the schools:

> The first thing we did was to form a Parent-Teacher Association . . . We got the community support through the Parent-Teacher Association work . . . This was the first one I'd ever tried to form. You had to work it out through the state machinery . . . through the Parent-Teacher machinery. So we did that.[37]

Mrs. Bettina Charles Rosett, a student throughout Edgar's tenure at Mirando City, wrote:

> Dr. Edgar's success lies in the fact that he was a born leader, and knew how to get important things accomplished. When he became Superintendent for the 1929–1930 school year, he was twenty-four years of age, and at the time Mirando School had only six teachers. He realized that the most important thing in a small town is for everyone to participate in all school activities, and that year he investigated the organization of the Parent-Teacher Association. That same year the first edition of Mirando Panther [school newspaper] was published.[38]

During the 1929–1930 school year, Edgar held conferences on developing a high school program. Forming an organized high school meant building a high school building. Everyone in Mirando City was behind the idea. Consequently, a bond issue was passed for ten thousand dollars. Federal money was available through a program which matched the funds that Mirando City raised. The federal part of the money became bogged down with standards that Mirando City could not meet. Meanwhile, the school board had hired an architect from Laredo named Ernest Page. When Mr. Page learned that the federal part of the funds were tied up, he told the school board that if the board gave him the ten thousand dollars from the bond issue, he could build the new high school. So he did. In the spring of 1930, the new high school was completed. The first high school session began in the fall of 1930.

The only thing the new high school lacked was accreditation, which was the next project Edgar tackled. Edgar recalls:

> Our job then, during the year of 1930–1931, the first year we were in the building, was to get state accreditation of the high school. This was something I'd never done. I don't think any of our teachers had gone through that process. But we got some help from the State Department — some consulting help. We began to develop a teaching program, an activity program that would meet the requirements of the state accreditation. It did take us a couple of years, but we did get the high school accredited.[39]

Edgar hired Mr. J.E. Fulbright to teach at the high school and to assist him with the job of accreditation. Mr. Fulbright came to Mirando City from Abilene, Texas. He remembers:

> To me it [Mirando City] was quite a letdown from Abilene, but I, being hardheaded, was determined to make a good hand. That was the first time I met J.W. and his wife, Sue. Immediately they didn't look too bad. J.W. said, "Young man, as you can see, we are going to start from scratch. We want an accredited school and as you will learn (with a small grin) that means a lot of work." [40]

Edgar taught some classes during the 1929–1930 and 1930–1931 school years. Those years were the last years Edgar would teach. After that time, his concentration was focused on the administrative aspects of his job. In Mirando City, Edgar's relationship with the school board was always good. Edgar remembers the school board:

> The school board was a good school board. They said, "Here it is. It's your job. Run it. We'll help you when we can." That was pretty much their position all the time I was there. They helped me set policy and turned it over to me. If I got into trouble, they helped me out. I had an excellent school board all the years I was there. I didn't have any problems with the school board.[41]

Edgar and the school board undertook a project in 1931 which did not work out. An oil-field school, called the Aviators School District, existed to the south of Mirando City. Their high school students came into Mirando City. Edgar and the school board decided early in 1931 to consolidate Mirando City and Aviators School District. They went to the Aviators School Board and learned that their community also wanted to consolidate. An election was called. The day before the election, however, the district judge issued an injunction against the school board holding an election. Edgar explains:

> This goes back to the political machinery of Webb County . . . They had carved out a very small area for the Mirando City School District. They [Webb County] didn't want it enlarged. They wanted to keep the rest of the county in the common school district that they could control from the County Superintendent's Office. Now it is my understanding that you can't issue an injunction to prevent an election, but this district judge did issue it. Our school district didn't want to fight it because they had representatives of the Magnolia Petroleum Company on our school board, and they had to get along with the political machinery . . . So we just dropped it.[42]

While Edgar was superintendent at Mirando City, he still had the desire to be a school superintendent in a larger school district. In the summer of 1932 he began work on his Master's degree in School Administration with a minor in Journalism at The University of Texas at Austin. He moved to Austin for the summer. Sue went along and she studied music at the Texas School of Fine Arts. Edgar worked on his Master's degree every summer until he finished it in 1938.[43]

Meanwhile, Sue had quit teaching in 1934 in order to start a family. Ruth was born October 15, 1935, Sally on April 21, 1939, and Susan on January 25, 1943.

It was while Edgar was at Mirando City that he began to realize there was an organized education profession on both a national and state level. Edgar used his membership in these associations to broaden his horizons and strengthen his perception of what could be accomplished in the role of school administrator. He joined the Texas State Teachers Association (TSTA) and the American Association of School Administrators.[44] In 1934 he and three other superintendents attended their first professional meeting at the annual convention of the American Association of School Administrators. Edgar recalls:

> It was held in Cleveland, Ohio, and we drove up there. Like to froze to death . . . I almost took pneumonia . . . took a real bad cold . . . we spent one night in Chicago at a hotel. Other times we stayed in what they called "tourist homes." [45]

In addition to beginning his participation in professional organizations, Edgar also began to associate with other administrators in Mirando City through the Gulf Coast School Administrators Association. This association met monthly and extended from Laredo to Corpus Christi. Edgar's first assignment in a professional association was in 1936 for the Texas State Teachers Association. The president appointed him a member of the Teacher Retirement Committee. The committee's job was to propose recommendations, which they did, for establishing a state retirement system. This work with professional organizations was both rewarding and challenging for Edgar as was his work at Mirando City.

Edgar stayed in Mirando City for seven years until the end of the 1935–1936 school year. During the seven years he was there, the school system stayed about the same size. Edgar felt good about his work in Mirando City:

> It was my understanding that . . . everybody that was there — that is, the Anglo people who would come in with the oil — they felt like they were there temporarily. I think that [was] the reason they hadn't done more with their schools before I had gotten there. Even with that feeling, they were willing to dig in and give their support. And we developed a good school system. The kids had a wonderful morale and [a] wonderful spirit. They were responsive. We just felt like one big happy family. [46]

Bettina Charles Rosett supports this statement with a similar one:

> He [Dr. Edgar] was a doer and an organizer . . . things others only dreamed of, he brought into being. He came to this small little oil town that was made up of people from all walks of life and united us all. [47]

At the end of the 1935–1936 school year, Edgar felt he had been at Mirando City long enough and that he had accomplished his task there. No problems existed and everything was running smoothly. He began to think of leaving.

In 1934 the State Superintendent of Public Instruction, Dr. L.A. Woods, along with Dr. Otto, from The University of Texas at Austin, had established a statewide curriculum revision program. Edgar became interested in it and began to see himself as a curriculum person. He had become friends with Porter Garner who had worked at Robstown, Texas, and Kingsville, Texas. They had met through the Gulf Coast School Administrators Association. It was Porter Garner who offered Edgar a job in Victoria, Texas.

VICTORIA: PRELUDE TO ORANGE, 1936–1939

In the spring of 1936 Edgar was offered the job of Assistant Superintendent of Instruction and Personnel in the Victoria, Texas, School System. Porter Garner was Superintendent at Victoria and he wanted Edgar for the job. In July, 1936, the Edgars moved to Victoria. Edgar felt he had gotten the "curriculum bug" and he wanted to work in curriculum for a while to gain some experience in this field and to see if he liked it.

The Victoria School System had two thousand students. It was a community with a large Catholic population. A junior college came under the direction of Edgar with respect to its curriculum. The junior college had about one hundred students and was totally academic (rather than vocational). Edgar's main responsibility was to work with teachers on planning. When he got to Victoria, he along with the teachers began building teaching units and developing strategies for individualizing instruction. Some of the older teachers at first resisted the change which Edgar was initiating, but almost immediately he began to get loyalty and respect from almost all of the teachers. He worked under Porter Garner and never met with the school board.

At the beginning of the 1938–1939 school year, Dr. M.G. Bowden became principal of the Mitchel Elementary School in Victoria. He describes Edgar's activities as Curriculum Director:

> While he [Dr. Edgar] was there, he was very strongly oriented toward curriculum, which is kind of unusual to find an Assistant Superintendent who knew anything about curriculum in the first place, and second, who was willing to do anything about it if he knew anything about it. And he was . . . In Social Studies he appointed a committee to look at Social Studies . . . He wasn't satisfied with the content . . . so we rewrote the curriculum for

VERNON REGIONAL
JUNIOR COLLEGE LIBRARY

the third, fourth, fifth, and sixth grades in the elementary school
. . . the medieval history . . . we tried to be very objective about
those things because Mr. Edgar was very concerned about it . . .
the objectivity . . . The kids seemed to like it . . . He did this in all
areas. In fact, he had faculty committees. And that [was] kind of
unheard of in those days . . . We incorporated a lot of ideas of Har-
old Rugg in Social Studies. Rugg was trying to implement the
University of Chicago thesis that what you learned you could do.
Learn by doing . . ., Dewey's philosophy. We heard a lot about
Dewey and we also heard a lot about making things practical and
realistic.[48]

Victoria was a good experience for Edgar but he really did
not enjoy his work there. He found out that he did not know as
much about curriculum as he thought he did and that his major ambition was in being a school superintendent, not a school
curriculum expert. Part of this dissatisfaction may have come
from the general circumstances of the job at Victoria. Edgar
summarizes the whole experience:

Because of the large enrollment in the Catholic schools, community support was split between the Catholic and the Public
school system. The public schools were sound academically, but
were very conservative in their philosophy. The previous superintendent and school board had permitted the school plant and
curriculum to be outgrown and outdated. Mr. Garner was brought
in to modernize the plant, equipment, and curriculum. He was
ideally suited for this kind of work, but it required that he spend
his full time developing community support rather than working
on inside matters. Thus, he felt the need for an assistant to work
on the school instructional program. When I left three years later,
bond issues had been voted, new buildings were in place or under
construction, and Mr. Garner had more time for inside work. He
did not fill my place. He left in 1940 and entered business in Laredo, Texas. When industry and military establishments came to
Victoria during the forties and the population grew, the school
system was ready to develop along with the growth because of Mr.
Garner's earlier leadership.[49]

Edgar's dissatisfaction with his job in Victoria did not affect his relationship with Porter Garner at all. Mr. Garner
helped Edgar get the job as Superintendent of Schools in Orange. When Edgar told Mr. Garner he was interested in the job
at Orange, Mr. Garner had some people he knew in Victoria
get in touch with some people they knew in Orange. Mr. Gar-

ner also recommended Edgar to one of the leading citizens in Orange whom he knew. Edgar felt if he was going to be a superintendent of a large school district, he had better get prepared. This meant doing everything he could to get ready, including getting his doctoral degree. So he went back to summer school at The University of Texas at Austin in the summer of 1939 to start work on his doctorate. While in school, he ran into W.E. Lowery who was also in school. Mr. Lowery was Superintendent of Schools at Orange; however, he had just been elected as Dean at Sam Houston State College in Huntsville, so he was leaving Orange. Edgar asked him what kind of man the board was looking for to replace him. Mr. Lowery told Edgar the board was looking for someone like Edgar.

Edgar immediately sent in his credentials and an application which had references of everybody he could think of, all different kinds of people. [This, according to one of the Orange School Board members, helped him get the job.] Edgar had made two trips over to Orange to speak with the school board; he spoke with them individually. The first time he went was just to get acquainted. Seven members comprised the Orange School Board and two of them were women. This was Edgar's first experience with women board members. After a while he decided he would push the board a little with respect to his potential job there. Consequently, he went to Orange again. After this, he felt he had gotten a pretty good reception and that things looked promising.

Edgar returned to Victoria in August. He had contracted with a man to rent a house that this man was building. When Edgar arrived in Victoria, he called this man to tell him that he was ready to move into the house. The builder told Edgar that he had heard that Edgar was moving to Orange. He refused to rent the house to someone who might be leaving at any time. Thus, the Edgars were forced to stay in a motel for about a week. Finally, in late August of 1939, a member of the Orange School Board called Edgar and told him that the board elected him Superintendent of the Orange School System.

This election marked the end of the first part of Edgar's career. He was almost thirty-five years old. The first part of his career had had many significant aspects which laid the foundation for his upcoming success.

CONCLUSION

This period in Edgar's life — beginning with his early home life through until he left his position in Victoria — was a foundation for what was to occur later in his career. During this period events of a *specific* nature were influencing Edgar. These specific events were: failing the sixth grade; being terminated by the Lake Victor School Board; his early decision to be a school superintendent; his choice to be a professional educator; and his decision to go to Victoria. Also events of a *general* nature were significantly influencing Edgar. These general influences were: the prodding of his mother; his methodical evolution of working with school boards; and the expansion of his general knowledge of how to work with people involved in every aspect of education, from children to administrators.

One of the specific events which influenced Edgar's life was his failing the sixth grade. First, this gave him an early knowledge of what it means to not succeed. This knowledge gave him a greater understanding of students' problems. Certainly it is easier to understand a student's failure when you have experienced failure yourself. Secondly, the way in which Edgar handled the failure was significant. Although the failure embarrassed him, he went right along with his schooling. When the opportunity presented itself in high school to cover three years of school in two, he did so, and thus compensated for the year he lost in sixth grade. This taught Edgar the meaning of failure, how to work through it, and how to conquer it.

A second specific event which was important in Edgar's early career was his termination by the Lake Victor School Board for dancing and being seen socially with a student. This was the only time in Edgar's long career that he would be terminated. The significance of this occurrence is twofold. First, it made Edgar aware of the nature of school boards and made him realize the importance of working closely with them. Secondly, Edgar's participation in the dance showed character. Edgar knew in the back of his mind that by dancing he was placing himself in a less than secure position. He went ahead and did what he felt was right. It's easier to see this second point if one remembers Edgar did not do anything wrong. Another factor is that he was dancing with his future wife. This gave the event even more significance.

Another specific factor which influenced Edgar's career was his ambition early in his career to be a school superintendent. This ambition provided stability and focus to his career. This focus helped him time and again in making definite decisions that had specific direction in his career. For example, he constantly sought better jobs as evidenced by his decisions to take the superintendent jobs at Heidenheimer and Mirando City.

The fourth specific factor which was meaningful to Edgar's career was his decision that he wanted to be a professional educator and continue his education, working toward an M.A. and Ph.D. Once Edgar became aware of the existence of professional organizations, he began joining them. Edgar's association with these groups proved invaluable to him throughout his professional career. Edgar describes this well:

> I finally recognized that I was a member of a profession — national and statewide. That's one of the reasons I broadened my horizons and strengthened my perception of what could be done in the role of administrator.[50]

A final specific factor which was important to Edgar's early career was his decision to go Victoria. This job in Victoria ensured that Edgar would gain experience in a larger, more urban school district. Victoria was to be a stepping-stone to greater responsibility.

The general events which influenced Edgar's career were broader in scope. These factors were having a constant influence on him.

The first of these general events was the influence that Edgar's mother had on him throughout his early life. She was highly conscious of the advantages a good education could offer. She prodded Edgar along and forced him to stay on track. This drive on the part of Edgar's mother began when she had the family move to Burnet so that the children could attend good schools. It was Edgar's mother who wanted him to go to college, to become a teacher. It was she who advised Edgar to take education courses that would lead to a teaching certificate that first year at Howard Payne College. Her influence on the direction that young Edgar followed is undeniably a considerable one.

The second general event which was to lay a good foundation for Edgar's later career was the methodical way Edgar evolved his understanding of and ability to work with school boards. This began with his termination by the Lake Victor

School Board. At Heidenheimer he worked with J.C. Edds who patiently provided him with a counselling type of relationship. By the time Edgar left Mirando City, his expertise with school boards was well along the path toward full development. This paved the way for Edgar's eventual success in working with the Texas State Board of Education.

A final general factor which significantly prepared and aided Edgar for his later success was the expansion during this time of his ability of how to work with people involved in every aspect of education, from students to officials. Edgar describes his work at Lake Victor, Bethal, and Heidenheimer:

> I think each year I was adding to my knowledge and under-standing — particularly of how to relate to young people of differ-ent ages. Also [I was learning and understanding more about] whatever administrative duties I had with the pupils throughout the whole school, and their parents. I think I was trying to de-velop a technique of working with the pupils and their parents on a one-to-one basis as much as possible . . . I understood how to work with the community, how to work with the parents, how to work with the school board, and how to relate to the pupils.[51]

The specific and general events in the early part of Edgar's career can be called the "rural phase" with the exception of Victoria which was a transitional phase. The rural phase con-sisted of Edgar's early life, his jobs at Bethal, Lake Victor, Hei-denheimer, and Mirando City. This phase bred familiarity in Edgar with all of the workings of a rural school system: he taught; he was a principal; he was a superintendent. There was not any part of a rural school system that Edgar did not know intimately.

Victoria was the transition between Edgar's rural begin-ning and his urban phase. In Victoria, although he never met with the school board, he learned how to relate to large num-bers of teachers and students. He needed an experience of this nature before he could move to a large district like Orange. It is also significant that the curriculum was the vehicle which Edgar chose to make the transition from rural to urban. Edgar describes it well:

> It's bound to have enlarged my horizon and point of view. I'm sure I changed quite a bit during those three years. At least up until that time I had never worked in a school district that was

more than eleven or twelve teachers. That broadened my vision a little bit, I guess. It was really a pretty good stepping stone . . . from a small superintendency at Mirando City to a larger one . . . And Victoria was a much broader curriculum than I had ever worked [with], in particular the junior college.[52]

Finally, Edgar gained this knowledge and built this educational foundation during the first part of his career without alienating anyone, with the possible exception of the Lake Victor School Board. In fact, he gained the admiration and respect of both students and teachers. Bettina Charles Rosett, a student the entire time that Edgar was at Mirando City, wrote:

> His success came because he was able to create miracles from absolutely nothing and because he never became discouraged . . . I realize that the main reason for Dr. Edgar's success is that he really cared.[53]

Peter Marcheck, a teacher at Mirando City and classmate of Edgar's at Howard Payne, wrote:

> He was a man of vision, firm in his convictions, and firm in his judgment.[54]

In addition to Edgar's professional success, Edgar was also successful in building a strong family life of his own. This was a natural continuation of the strong family life he had had with his parents, brothers, and sister. Mrs. Pauline Berry, Edgar's former sister-in-law, said:

> Usually on holidays, and always on Sunday, if they were near, the Edgar family would meet at their family home and we'd have lunch after church.[55]

Edgar's success, both professional and personal, during this rural phase of his career demonstrate his ambition which fully prepared him to succeed as Superintendent of Schools in Orange, Texas, and in Austin, Texas.

2

Orange and Austin:
The Urban Phase, 1939–1949

J.W. Edgar's work as Superintendent of Schools in Orange, Texas, and in Austin, Texas, provided him with valuable experience in two urban settings. The Orange School District changed from a small urban school district to a large urban one while Edgar was at Orange. Edgar's work at Orange made him well known throughout Texas and the country. The Austin School District was located in the capital city of the state of Texas. The job of Superintendent of the Austin Independent School District was one of the most sought after superintendencies in the state. These two jobs, each in their own way, provided Edgar with a base of experience that would serve him well as the first State Commissioner of Education in Texas. In Orange, Edgar showed what he was capable of accomplishing. Austin placed him close to the center of power.

EDGAR AT ORANGE: 1939–1947

Orange, Texas, is located on the Sabine River, the boundary line between Texas and Louisiana, in the Piney Woods. Historically, Orange was a lumber/saw mill town which was populated by French descendants from Louisiana, Italians, and Anglos. During the latter part of the nineteenth century, a family by the name of Lutcher moved to Orange from Pennsylvania. They bought a large area of forest acreage in Louisiana and Texas. Oil, and later sulfur, was discovered on the land. As a result of the discovery, the Lutcher family became very wealthy. This original family had two daughters: one married a man named Stark; the other married a man named Brown. The Stark daughter had one son named H.J. Lutcher Stark. The Brown daughter had four children, and of these, one lived in Orange. His name was Edgar Brown, Jr. Since the Brown children had divided their part of the Lutcher fortune four ways, Edgar Brown Jr.'s wealth was less than that of his cousin, Lutcher Stark.

When Edgar arrived in Orange, Lutcher Stark owned a paper mill and two small shipyards. The Depression had ravaged the whole community and many store buildings in the business section were empty. Orange was economically depressed and in poor condition when Edgar arrived in the fall of 1939.

The Orange School Board, 1939

Immediately after the Chairman of the Orange School Board called Edgar and told him he had been elected superintendent, another member of the Orange Board called to ask Edgar if he would accept a one year contract. Edgar told him that in case the board did not like him or he did not like the board, he would accept a one year contract. Edgar's salary was three thousand dollars per year. He and Mrs. Edgar rented a big two-story house for fifteen dollars a month, and Edgar settled into his job as Superintendent of Schools in Orange.

The school board makeup presented an interesting set of problems for Edgar. Mrs. Lutcher Stark was a member of the school board. Three of the other members of the board worked for the Stark interests. Two of the remaining three members were indebted financially to Lutcher Stark. The Chairman of the Orange Board, Hunter Beaty, was its only independent member. The Starks did not control Hunter Beaty as they did the other board members; at the same time, however, Hunter Beaty was not against the Starks.

In the fall of 1939, Mrs. Lutcher Stark died. This caused Lutcher Stark to be especially difficult to get along with. Edgar felt that if he was going to succeed in Orange, he had to find a way to work with Lutcher Stark. Edgar describes this very well:

> It was just a fact of life that I had to establish the right kind of relationship with Mr. Stark. I couldn't give into him always. He couldn't run the school. That wouldn't have been proper. But at the same time, you couldn't ignore him. Fortunately, he as a man, all he wanted was the best school system in the world.[1]

Edgar was aware of Lutcher Stark's relation to the schools.

> He was so involved in the school program. Of course, people used to say to me, "Don't pay any attention to that Lutcher Stark. Don't let him run the school." I would say, "Well, I'm going to run it but according to the way the school board wants it run. But at the same time, I'm going to try to work a harmonious relationship with Lutcher Stark because I think its necessary for the welfare of the schools" . . . [I'd] let his interest continue, as active as it was, but keep it in the proper perspective, and not let him get over into dominating the school.[2]

Edgar learned the dynamics of the school board soon after his arrival in Orange. This understanding helped him throughout his stay at Orange. Dr. Frank Hubert, band director at Orange from 1938–1944, spoke about Edgar's ability to work with the Orange School Board:

> He was a master at board relationships. J.W. had an excellent rapport with his board of trustees. He brought to them timely information [and] good recommendations. I don't know of a single occasion when any recommendation he made to the board during his tenure there was not accepted unanimously.[3]

It is evident that Edgar's board experience prior to Orange served him well there.

Orange, 1939–1941

Edgar found that the people in Orange were enthusiastically supportive of the schools. They were responsive and wanted to work to develop good schools. In 1939, Orange had about two thousand students who were contained in: two White elementary schools; a White four-year high school; and a grade one through eleven Black school with approximately three hundred and fifty students. The principals of all four schools were women. In addition to the principals, the staff included a man who worked as bookkeeper and tax assessor/collector. Edgar did not have a secretary in his office.

The principal of the high school, Miss Helen Carr, had been principal for years and was highly respected in the community. She was a bit suspicious of Edgar in the beginning, and had not gotten along well with the previous superintendent. Edgar felt he had to prove himself to her:

> I began to develop . . .I didn't exactly court her or anything like that . . . but I began to work with her in such a way that she began to understand that I wasn't going to interfere in the operation of the high school . . . that she was going to be the high school administrator and I was going to support her and work with her in that way. It didn't take but a very little while and we became the closest of friends and were all the time that she was there.[4]

Some of the other teachers were like Miss Carr in that they had been teaching in Orange for many years and were not sure of Edgar. He felt he had to prove himself to these teachers also; he did so with few problems.

Edgar found that school conditions in Orange were generally good. Most of the buildings and equipment were old but were in good condition. The curriculum was generally acceptable but needed some development and some reorganization. Edgar set up some study groups within the faculty to examine what specific areas needed to be strengthened, expanded, or curtailed. The schools had no physical education program and just a semblance of a vocational program. The academic subjects were all right, and particularly good, well-developed speech/drama and music programs existed.

The music program at the Orange High School comprised a special situation. Lutcher Stark had been a Sunday school teacher at a Presbyterian church in Orange during the Depression. He wanted to interest the Sunday School students in Sunday school activities, so he formed a band. He purchased all the musical instruments and other equipment. Eventually this band became the high school band which was run by Lutcher Stark and which was only a quasi part of the high school since Stark did not turn the band over to the school. He continued to sponsor it. He formed a corporation called "Lutcher Stark's Boys and Girls, Incorporated." He had a boys band called the

Bengal Lancers and girls marching corps called the Bengal Guards: both were excellent. Frank Hubert was the director of the boys band and a Mrs. Hustmyvae directed the girls marching corps. They were on Lutcher Stark's staff rather than the schools; he paid their salaries. Frank Hubert comments on this situation:

> At no time did I feel that Lutcher Stark tried to pull any strings to direct or push the music program in a way which was not in the best interest of the Orange Independent School District.[5]

Edgar supports this account:

> Lutcher Stark managed the music department. We had it on the grounds of the high school in a building. He had furnished a building with thousands of dollars worth of equipment . . .This was a real unusual situation that I had never been faced with before. Here was a man, a multimillionaire, actually going out on the drill field to help drill the Bengal Guards. He got close to the situation. He didn't try to interfere, particularly, with the rest of the school system. But he was a constant presence there in the school system because of his responsibility with the Guards and the Band.[6]

Edgar did not feel threatened by Lutcher Stark, but he felt the need to inform Stark of his own view:

> I told him one day that he might own that music department, but it was also mine because it carried the name of the Orange Public Schools, and I was going to be interested in it. Well, that kind of please him, I think.[7]

Lutcher Stark would take the students on special trips. They went to Chicago, among other places, by train. Stark made sure the students were lacking for nothing and even took nurses on the trips with them. In spite of the inconveniences, Edgar saw the value of these activities:

> The thing that I learned very quickly [was] that the kids were really getting a good sound musical education; also, excellent character training, discipline, and health. I felt like I could put up with some of the inconvenience as long as the kids were profiting by it.[8]

The music department was excellent and unique; Edgar gave it special consideration.

During Edgar's first year at Orange, Lutcher Stark came to him and said he would like to build a new football stadium for the school. His adopted twin sons were going to be seniors in high school during the fall of 1940, and he wanted them to have a new stadium to play in. He told Edgar he would build the best stadium money could buy, and that he wanted to be left alone while he built it. After the stadium was finished he would then turn it over to Edgar and the school district.

In the fall of 1940 the stadium was finished and ready to be used. Since Stark's boys were on the team, he wanted to buy the best equipment available. He bought all the best equipment any coach would ever need, including formal uniforms. The coach was being paid jointly by Lutcher Stark and by the school. The night before the first game the coach decided it would be a good idea to have a dress rehearsal so that the players could get used to the feel of the uniforms. He took the players, with the new equipment, out on the field to let them get used to the stadium. Lutcher Stark learned of this incident and became irate because he had not yet turned the stadium over to the school and also because he had wanted to be the one to give the go ahead to use the new turf. He called Edgar the night before the first game and told him that the football team could play the next day but that there would be no Bengal Lancers or Bengal Guards at the game. The team lost the first game. The whole town became upset. The high school students went on strike. They paraded around town, carrying signs that said, "We Are Stark Mad." Edgar, Miss Carr, and the Chairman of the Orange School Board met and decided to just ignore the strike. The students came to school the next day. The football coach resigned. His assistant was put in charge. The team lost most of its games that year. The townspeople settled down and the incident, though it was forgotten, had made headlines all over the state. For years Edgar was kidded about getting out on the grass at Orange. Edgar explains Lutcher Stark's role in the incident:

> Again, although I could have surely shot the man, again, I had to realize his purpose was good. He wanted a good school. He wanted things perfect, too perfect, of course . . . I was told that as long as Mrs. Stark was alive, that Lutcher didn't have these tendencies to jump the gun.[9]

Edgar stayed in Orange the summer of 1940. He was still
organizing and getting acquainted with the community. He
and Mrs. Edgar were very happy in Orange and wanted to stay
there. Edgar was trying to get ready for the new school year. In
the fall of 1940 the school had a new football stadium. About
the first of October, news arrived that there was to be a big
shipyard located in Orange to take advantage of the deep
water port. The size of the population was sure to climb. Edgar
realized there had to be some kind of community planning
done. The federal government had instituted a defense program which called for the rationing of building supplies which
restricted any business development that would ordinarily
raise tax revenues. Rents were also frozen. The shipyard would
bring in large numbers of people but would not be on the tax
roll. Edgar was caught in a dilemma: on the one hand, he had
the prospect of a huge increase in population with government
housing being built; on the other hand, he had no means of increasing tax revenues. Edgar went to the federal government
for help.

The Lanham Act Of 1941

Edgar's work with the Lanham Legislation was to give
him state and national exposure. With the aid of the Lanham
Legislation, the Orange School District was able to cope with
the changes that took place before and during World War II.
These changes centered around a large increase in population
for Orange and the Orange School District.

In the fall of 1940 when Orange heard of the impending
changes in their schools, groups in the Orange Chamber of
Commerce were planning courses of action. During the Depression, a former mayor of Orange, named Lea, had been a successful Washington D.C. lobbyist in getting federal money for
the Orange area. When someone suggested that Mr. Lea
should go to Washington, Lutcher Stark said that Mr. Lea
should not represent the schools. He felt school matters should
be handled by school people — the Superintendent and the
School Board. As a result, Edgar and the Chairman of the Orange School Board, Hunter Beaty, went to Washington to see
what they could learn.

In Washington Edgar first went to the U.S. Office of Education's School Administration Division. H.F. Alves, the Director of the School Administration Division, was from Texas. He had worked at the State Department of Education at one time and later went back to Texas and was a Professor of School Administration at The University of Texas at Austin. He helped Edgar and told him that the President had asked Congress to consider developing a law for providing aid to community facilities in war/defense areas.

Mr. Lanham was a representative from Fort Worth. He was Chairman of the House Committee on Public Works. He immediately began work in his committee to develop legislation to enact the Community Facilities Assistance Program. This initiation of committee work was what the first trip to Washington accomplished; it gave everyone some hope.

Edgar made a second trip to Washington. During this trip he met Mr. Ralph Hood, from New Brunswick, Georgia, in Mr. Alves's office. Mr. Hood's school district was also in a war/defense community and he and Edgar were faced with the same set of problems. As Edgar recalls, he and Mr. Hood began to organize:

> We got together, trying to figure out what we could do to help. We decided we would organize a nationwide organization of school superintendents from the various defense areas of the nation. So we wrote and alerted them to the probable legislation that was being developed in Washington — to get behind it and start supporting it through their congressmen. That was the beginning of the effort of the school superintendents throughout the country to promote the Lanham Act — what finally became the Lanham Act.[10]

At first the Lanham Act emphasized the facilities, buildings, and construction.[11] Later it emphasized programming. The Works Progress Administration (WPA) and the Public Works Administration (PWA) were used to administer the Lanham Act beginning in the Spring of 1941. Edgar and Mr. Hood had gone to see Mr. Lanham about letting the school part of the Lanham Act be administered by the United States Office of Education. Mr. Lanham said that was not practical or politically feasible since the act was also going to cover health and other community services.

In the fall of 1941 the PWA began their program, called

the Maintenance Operations Program, for the Lanham Act. Edgar got approval for whatever it took to operate the schools — the difference between what the school district got on both the local and state levels and what the district needed in order to be fully operational. The PWA approved this amount all through the years that the Orange School District needed it. Edgar gained national prominence for his work with the Lanham Act. Not only did he gain personal prestige, but Orange itself had a school district which became a model for other districts throughout the country. Agnes E. Meyer, who made a survey of all of the defense installations at the time, wrote about the town of Orange in April 1943:

> It [Orange] was a sleepy little town of 7,500 people in 1940. Now it is the center of a population of 35,000 owing to the activities of the Levingsten, the Consolidated, and the Weaver Shipyards, and the presence of a naval training station. Two Navy housing projects, amounting to some 1,700 family units, 500 dormitory units, and vast numbers of private and public trailor communities make the original town hard to find.[12]

Mrs. Meyer also describes Edgar's school facility:

> The structure itself, of ultramodern design, has a capacity of 3,000 and is intelligently adapted to the use of the very primitive population which it serves . . . In addition to the usual classrooms it has a beautiful combined gymnasium and auditorium with a large stage. There is an excellent library, some 65 feet in length. Among the vocational rooms is one for shorthand, another for typing, bookkeeping, a big carpenter shop, and agricultural room, and a homemaking department containing sewing machines, laundry, kitchen, dining and living room, as well as a personal improvement room . . . I was delighted with the diversified occupation department where the pupils who have jobs can get mechanical training.[13]

The Lanham Act had two ways of financing buildings. They would match funds and turn the whole thing over to the local school district to run and then get out of the picture. Or they would put one hundred percent of the money into the building, supervise the construction, and keep property rights to the building. Edgar made applications for two large elementary schools using the one hundred percent financing program; both were approved.

An extensive community services program existed as part

of the Lanham Act. Counselors handled personal, recreational, educational, and vocational needs. A nutritional service showed people how to eat balanced meals. Four nursery schools existed: one for sleeping fathers who worked at night; one for working mothers; one as a laboratory on campus; and one for Black children. A kindergarten was open from 6 a.m. to 6 p.m. for children from five to six years of age. Edgar was the Chairman of the Child Welfare Committee which worked on every aspect of the youth program.

Using the Lanham Act, Edgar organized the schools in Orange to handle the large growth in population and ensure that the city's school children would be affected as little as possible by the war/defense effort. Edgar's use of the Lanham Act funds was nothing less than brilliant. Relying on his creativity and ingenuity, he managed to create a completely unique system. Mr. C.O. Chandler, principal of one of the two elementary schools Edgar had built, wrote of some of the new programs Edgar started:

> Through his foresight and persuasion, programs were developed for Orange school children that were to become models for schools of the future. Some of the programs he initiated that are found today in most schools are: summer school recreation programs; kindergarten; school nurses; libraries in all schools; dietitians and lunchrooms for all campuses; assistant principals; and well organized maintenance programs.
>
> As a result of the innovative programs Mr. Edgar devised, the Orange schools began to receive national attention. Soon Orange began to have visiting college people, school administrators, and teachers from far and near to see the new things being done in Orange.[14]

In addition to implementing the Lanham Act, Edgar continued his job as Superintendent of the Orange Schools.

Orange, 1941–1944

Edgar's work on the Lanham Act was spaced around his duties as Superintendent of the Orange School District. His primary task was to get a new high school funded and built. In June 1941, the school district had one hundred and twenty-five thousand dollars and the government provided another three hundred and seventy-five thousand dollars for a new high school. In addition, Edgar applied for temporary buildings called "hutments" while the new building was being constructed. These hutments were little fabricated square buildings that were placed on the high school grounds during the 1941–1942 school year. Each hutment was large enough for a classroom.

One of the most crucial jobs Edgar was responsible for was the hiring of teachers. A general shortage of teachers existed, and this was particularly true in the war/defense areas. There simply were not enough teachers available in Texas, so Edgar turned to Louisiana for help. He found that Southwestern Louisiana University at Lafayette and Louisiana State University at Baton Route had potential teachers available. Edgar began recruiting heavily from Louisiana teachers, most of which were just out of college with no experience. Recruiting from Louisiana went on for about a year or two. Then Edgar began having problems with the school people in Louisiana. He recalls:

> Finally . . . I had gotten so many teachers out of Louisiana that the Governor of Louisiana wrote all those teachers in Orange [wrote each one of them a letter] and pointed out to them that Louisiana had paid for their college and university training . . . their teacher training . . . and that they were indebted to the state of Louisiana, to come back home and teach in that state. Some of them did; some of them didn't. But anyway, that killed my source of supply in Louisiana.[15]

Recruiting teachers was a continual problem for Edgar, as was teacher housing. He solved the problem of teacher housing by having the school district contract for rooms and apartments and guarantee the owner full time payment twelve months a year. This way housing was always readily available for the teachers. When teachers occupied the space, the teachers paid the rent; when the space was vacant, the school district paid the rent.

In the fall of 1941 Edgar hired an assistant superintendent and a supervisor of teachers. Edgar hired the assistant superintendent to help him run the schools while he was out of town or otherwise occupied. Edgar hired Mr. T.W. Ogg for the job; he was a principal from Vidor, Texas. Edgar talks about how he hired Ogg:

He just walked into my office one day and said, "Is there any way I can help around here? I'd be interested in trying to help if I can." I must of said, "There sure is a way you can help," because I hired him immediately.[16]

Mr. Ogg was energetic and was just the right person for the job. The job of supervisor of teachers was a job that consisted of supervising the new teachers who came into the school district. Edgar hired a professor from North Texas State University named Epsie Young. People whom Edgar had talked to about her told him she would be perfect for the job if she were interested. Edgar remembers:

> So I went up to North Texas State and got a hold of Miss Young. I talked to her and she began to respond to me. She liked the idea, I guess, of contributing to the war program — the defense program as it was then. Anyway, she was agreeable to come. Of course she saved my life.[17]

In addition to Mr. Ogg and Miss Young, Edgar now had a secretary, Vivian Leigh, and some other office help.

During the 1941–1942 school year Edgar established and operated the War Industry Training School for the training of shipyard workers. The shipyards had a great need for welders. The need for shipyard workers was so great that the school operated for twenty-four hours a day to accommodate a maximum number of people. The War Industry Training School operated twenty-four hours a day for years. The manpower that the school fielded was invaluable to the success of the defense program.

The senior high school (mentioned in the previous section) had been under construction but wasn't completed at the start of the 1942–1943 school year. The construction company agreed to let the school be occupied a section at a time. The school was named Stark High School for Lutcher Stark. A problem arose with the location of the high school. Edgar talks about this:

> We had decided the location of the building on the high school campus. The architect had outlined the boundaries on the ground. In one part at one end of the building, in one of the wings, there were some trees on the ground. One day one of the janitors came to me and said, "I need some firewood, could I cut one of those trees down?" And I said, "Well yeah, we're going to have to

cut them down. The building is going to have to be built there." So
I gave him permission to cut it. After a while my telephone rang,
and it was Lutcher Stark. He had driven by and had seen this guy
cutting this tree. And he said, "Only God can make a tree, but any
blankety blank S.O.B. can cut one down." And I said, "What in
the world are you talking about?" He told me. I said, "That's
where the building is going to be." He said, "Move the building."
So we got the architect and adjusted the building to save the
trees. This is the kind of guy he was.[18]

The new school was Edgar's pride and joy. It had a complete vocational wing and a cafeteria. A personal improvement
room, which Edgar was especially proud of, also existed as part
of the building. Edgar describes this:

> In the homemaking suite, we had a personal improvement
> room which was equipped with everything that a girl needs —
> sewing machines, hair curlers, hair wash — to wash your hair,
> makeup, cosmetics, everything. These girls, many of them that
> were coming in with their families, just had nothing in their
> homes for this kind of thing. They'd come into the improvement
> room, even during the summer, and wash their hair and so forth
> and so on, makeup and curl their hair.[19]

The new high school was complete by the spring of 1943.
In the summer of 1943 Edgar remodeled the old high school to
be used as a junior high school. The junior high school was
named Helen Carr Junior High School after Helen Carr, the
principal of the high school who was eventually transferred to
the central office.

Edgar was not involved only with the implementation of
the Lanham Act and carrying out his duties as Superintendent
of the Orange School District. He was also actively involved
with professional organizations.

The Texas Association Of
School Administrators,
1940–1943

Edgar had continued being active in the Texas Association of School Administrators (TASA) during his time in Orange. In 1940 he was elected Vice-President of the organization for 1940 and 1941. The TASA had a policy of promoting
the vice-presidents to president; thus, in 1942 Edgar was

elected President of the TASA for 1942–1943. Early on during his presidency, Edgar was confronted with the problem of what to do about the lack of gasoline for the transportation of athletic teams in Texas.[20] The Texas High School Coaches Association was interested in trying to get some relief from the gasoline rationing. Since one of the big interests promoted during the war was physical fitness, Edgar decided that the competitive athletic program could be included as part of the physical fitness program. So the Texas High School Coaches Association and the University Interscholastic League proposed that the TASA appoint a committee to go to Washington to seek relief. The two associations gave Edgar a fifteen hundred dollar grant to investigate the problem. Edgar appointed a committee called the Physical Fitness Committee. In March of 1943, Edgar and several members of this committee went to Washington. They met with the War Production Board, which dealt with the rationing of gasoline. Mr. Alves of the Office of Education was at the meeting. Edgar describes the meeting and its results:

> We had the hearing. The War Production people were very interested and very cooperative, but they finally said to us, "Well, now look, we need these buses for war transportation purposes. We don't need them for transporting football teams, and we can't help you. But why don't you see if you can work out a plan for using private automobiles — for transporting your football team — and perhaps we can give you some relief on the rationing of gasoline for that particular use." Well we came back to Texas and did develop a plan for the use of private cars, and took it back up there, and they approved it.[21]

The Office of Price Administration proposed an increase in the gasoline mileage from four hundred and seventy miles to seven hundred and twenty miles per month for holders of "B" Ration Books. This became official in May of 1943.[22]

A second problem Edgar confronted was the dilemma of school bonds. After World War I, several areas of Texas had booming oil fields which were accompanied by a predictably large increase in population. These oil areas needed large sums of money in order for their schools to function adequately. In most cases these communities had voted for forty-year bonds at five or six percent interest. When the Depression came, many school districts were forced to default payment of both interest and principal on these bonds. This problem continued into the Forties. Edgar appointed a Bond Committee to work on the problem. The State Board of Education did not encourage the committee and, in fact, disapproved of its work. The committee came up with a plan that would set a lower interest rate for the many school districts in Texas that had sold long-term school bonds at high rates of interest without option of payment before maturity. The committee had a bill prepared which went to the House Education Committee of the Texas Legislature. This bill would have reduced the interest rate on all bonds owned by the State Board to three percent. The bill passed both the Texas House and Senate. Governor Coke Stevenson vetoed the bill just hours before it would have become law.[23]

Edgar left the office of the President of the Texas Association of School Administrators in 1943 but continued to be active in its affairs. Gradually the tremendous wartime pace of the job at Orange began to wind down.

Orange, 1943–1947

During the 1943–1944 school year Edgar continued running the Orange School District which he had so brilliantly created to handle the war/defense effort. By then he had employed additional personnel. In the spring of 1944 Lutcher Stark came to tell Edgar that he was turning the whole music program over to the school. Frank Hubert, the band director, was going into the Navy and Lutcher Stark was getting tired of the music business. Lutcher Stark would never again be as actively involved in the schools as he had been in the past.

In 1945 Terrel Ogg, Edgar's assistant superintendent, had taken a job as superintendent elsewhere. Edgar had hired C.O. Chandler to be an elementary school principal. When Mr. Ogg left he promoted Mr. Chandler to Assistant Superintendent and Business Manager of the Orange School District. Mr. Chandler succeeded Edgar as Superintendent of the Orange School District. Of his appointment by Edgar to the assistant superintendency, C.O. Chandler writes:

> Soon after this promotion, I barged in on Mr. Edgar to ask his advice on the wording of a complicated federal application. After listening to me for a few minutes he said to me, "O'Hara,

what do you think we are paying you the wages of a Business Manager for? This is part of your assignment, not mine."
Later I mentioned to him how disappointed I was that he did not help me. He replied, "I saw potential in you and your ability. If I had helped you instead of your helping yourself, you would have little chance for professional growth." He had a statement that, "I want every administrator working for me to want my job . . . but I want them to know how to get it." [24]

Also in 1945 Edgar's secretary, Vivian Leigh, was forced to leave due to her husband's illness. Mary Smithheisler became Edgar's secretary. She describes what it was like working for Edgar:

> He was a perfectionist, number one. You were on time for meetings. You did your work as you were expected to do. No excuses. He was rigid. I learned the best working habits that you could imagine . . . He was always there when I got there at 8:00. He was out of town a lot . . . He was a very great favorite with his contemporaries. With the people who worked for the District in the offices, teachers, principals, he was all business. He had a very dry sense of humor . . . you had to listen to each word he said or you [might] miss the humor that [was] in it. [He was a] marvelous person to be with; [I] really enjoyed working for him. He was very strict. You learned by working with him. [25]

Mrs. Smithheisler was also Edgar's secretary in Austin.
During the summer of 1943 Edgar began attending The University of Texas at Austin to work on his doctorate. In 1944 he began attending the University during the regular school session. He would go to Austin on Friday night, go to school on Saturday, and return to Orange on Saturday night. He finished his doctorate in 1947 but did not receive his degree until 1948.
In 1946 Edgar was appointed by the State Board of Education to the State Textbook Committee. It was an advisory committee that reviewed all the books and reported their recommendations to the State Board. The State Board did not have to take the recommendations of the State Textbook Committee, but it had to consider them. Edgar served on the committee until 1948.
Edgar began to get job offers because of his exceptional work during his early years at Orange. One of these offers came from Richmond, Virginia. He visited there but was not interested. Another offer came from Columbus, Georgia. He

went there and looked into the job, but did not take it. The
Houston School Board invited Edgar to apply in 1944. Edgar
was interested in the Houston job but the board gave it to the
Deputy Superintendent of the Houston School District. The
President of the School Board of Tyler wrote Edgar a letter
asking him to go there, but Edgar was not interested in Tyler.
The superintendency of the Austin Independent School District was the job that really interested Edgar. The Austin
School Board invited three people to interview for the job. Edgar was one of these three.[26] The others were S.M. Brown of Tyler and W.B. Irwin of Highland Park, Texas, a wealthy Dallas
suburb. Mr. Irwin was not very interested in the job, but Mr.
Brown was interested as was Edgar. Edgar was anxious to interview for the job in Austin. He knew that Austin was the center of power for the whole state of Texas. In the spring of 1947
he eagerly began his effort to seek the job of Superintendent of
Schools in Austin.

EDGAR AT AUSTIN: 1947–1950

In 1947 Austin, the State Capital of Texas, had a population of about one hundred and twenty-five thousand people.
The Austin Independent School District had had a long-term
superintendent, A.M. McCallam. He had been superintendent
in Austin for over thirty years. In 1944, he died, leaving behind
him a good school system. Although Mr. McCallum was a great
educator and a great leader, as far as operation of the schools
went, he overlooked many details. He was running things from
his office with only the help of his secretary. He negotiated
with each teacher on that particular teacher's salary; he had
no pay schedule. When a new teacher was needed, his secretary would often pull an application from the application file
and that person would be hired. A school system run in such a
manner begins to develop weaknesses after a while. The school
board, after McCallum's death, had elected his assistant superintendent, Dr. Russell Lewis, as superintendent. About this
time the community decided that changes in the school system
were necessary. A group of men and women who supported
these changes ran for the school board. Five of them were
elected. The new board worked with Dr. Lewis for about three

years. After that time, they decided that they could no longer work with him. The board terminated Dr. Lewis at the end of his contract. This paved the way for the hiring of Edgar.

The Make Up Of The Austin School
Board And The Hiring Of Edgar

The Austin School Board was a seven-member board. Mrs. Hal Bybee and Mr. Gus J. Moos were the two remaining board members from the McCallum era. The five new members were: R.W. Byram, President; Paul Bolton; Fred S. Nagle Jr.; W.I. Kocurek; and Mrs. O.D Weeks. These were the people charged with the task of hiring a new superintendent. The board became interested in Edgar through Mr. Byram as Mrs. O.D. Weeks, a board member, relates:

> One of the board members, Ronald Byram . . . was very interested in the schools. He had a child coming up and he wanted to be sure things were going to be good for her. So he started going around to different places to meetings. The superintendents had these annual meetings . . . and [he] listened to some of those fellows talking and he was particularly pleased [with] and admired J.W. Edgar. He came back, Mr. Byram did, from this trip to Houston, where he had met so many of these fellows. And he didn't come back with two or three names, he just came back with one [J.W. Edgar].[27]

After receiving the intitial phone call from Mr. Byram and notifying the Austin School Board of his interest in the job, Edgar sent his credentials in March of 1947.[28] He went to Austin and talked to each member of the board. He went back to Austin a second time and spoke to each member of the board again. The board had almost made up its mind on hiring Edgar, but Mrs. Bybee was not sure. The board wanted her to be satisfied. Mrs. O.D. Weeks relates this situation:

> They said, "We'll have him [Edgar] come up and see the rest of the board." And so he came up and had a visit . . . She [Mrs. Bybee] was delighted with him. She was never crossways with us. She just wondered if maybe we shouldn't stay in our own system and we said, "No. We want fresh meat." We wanted somebody that would be so good that nobody would be sorry that we hired him . . . And so after we'd [had] several discussions, we met in Mr. Byram's office and said, "Now what shall we do." And somebody

spoke up and said, "Well, I'm for just calling him and offering him the job right now." And Mr. Byram said, "Well that's interesting because I've had him come up from Houston and he's down at the hotel." And so we called him and he came up there and we asked him a lot of questions about how he would go about things. And it all just sounded so good. And I think he must have gone right back to Orange, Texas, then and started packing his bags, but he was packing his thoughts too.[29]

Mrs. Bybee was highly respected by the other board members. Prior to the final meeting she hadn't told them how she felt. Still, she was never against the election of Edgar. All of the board members were pro-Edgar board members as Willie Kocurek confirms:

> Dr. Edgar came from Orange. Our feeling was that he was capable of doing for Austin what he had done for Orange. And Austin was a fast growing much in-need community. So Dr. Edgar fit the bill for Austin needs . . . it was not at all controversial. It was unanimous. The board as a whole felt that he was the man that would fit into the area of our need.[30]

Mr. Paul Bolton, Austin Board member, relates what happened when Edgar was offered the job:

> I know Byram and I were present at the time . . . We said we offer you so much to be our superintendent of schools and he [Edgar] said, "You're faded", [i.e. your bet is covered — meaning he would take the job].[31]

The entire board felt very strongly that Edgar was the right man for the job. They felt Austin was similar to Orange before World War II, and what Edgar did for Orange, he could do for Austin.

Edgar called his wife, Sue, and asked her if she wanted to move to Austin. She said, "I might as well. You spend all your time up there anyway." [32] So the Edgars left Orange in late June to start work in Austin for July 1, 1947.

Austin, 1947–1948

Before Edgar and his wife moved to Austin in late June, they came up to Austin and bought a house on Parkway. This house is the first and only house they have ever bought with the exception of a cottage on Lake Buchanan. The Austin School Board gave Edgar a three-year contract paying seventy-five hundred dollars the first year, eight thousand dollars the second year, and eighty-five hundred dollars the third year.

The Austin Board was ready to go when Edgar arrived in Austin. A short time earlier the board had sponsored a bond election. The people of Austin had voted seven million dollars in bonds for new buildings and remodeling. The school board took twenty-three thousand five hundred dollars and employed a planning engineer, Jac Guebbles, to guide them in their task of locating and planning new schools. Mr. Guebbles made a survey of Austin, forecasted the population growth for the next ten years, and located fifteen new sites for schools. When Edgar arrived in Austin in 1947, the school board had already begun construction on several sites. Most of the sites, however, were still to be planned and built.

The Austin School Board was organized into three standing committees: the Building Committee, the Budget Committee, and the Personnel Committee. Edgar spoke about these standing committees:

> After Dr. Lewis was dismissed, the rumors got around over the state that this board had just moved in and started running the schools. They bypassed the superintendent, and finally fired him. I came in with that kind of rumor. I found the board just anxious to get out of it. They told me the reason they had gotten pretty heavily involved — particularly in the building program — [was that] they weren't satisfied with the way Dr. Lewis was working. So I said to them, "Well, I think the general practice now is not to have standing committees — work with the committee as a whole, and then have temporary committees if you need a certain job to be done. But I don't want you to make any changes cause I'm going to need the help of these committees while I get oriented in this situation." [33]

Edgar got seven copies of a publication on school board organization issued by the American Association of School Administrators. The publication advocated no standing committees. With the help of the report, Edgar had no problems in reorganizing the board into a full committee and getting away from the standing committee practice.

In addition to the board, the Austin School District had a good staff. On the staff were a Business Manager, a Director of Instruction, a Pupil Personnel Director, and a Secretary. The board had also employed an architect named Mr. Harris.

One of the first jobs on Edgar's agenda was to get familiar with the construction program and establish some plans for the building which had not yet been planned. Edgar began to form faculty committees for the purpose of planning the functions that were to take place inside the school buildings. They planned the architectural arrangement of the buildings around the activities that would be taking place inside of them. This way the architectural arrangement would serve the purpose of the school. This kind of planning and building was new to the architect. Although Mr. Harris was in favor of the idea he could not get used to it, so he resigned. Edgar liked the idea, so he hired a new man for the job:

> To me, this was the only way to plan a school building. It certainly gave the teachers an opportunity to help see and be sure that the inside of the school building was planned properly. Anyway, I knew one of the principals here, [one of] the elementary principals. His name was Temple Mayhall . . . I'd been in school with him at the University. I knew that he got his Master's degree in School Administration . . . But he also had his degree in Architecture. He was a licensed architect . . . I talked to the two board members that were on the Building Committee . . . They were agreeable. So I . . . made him Director of School Planning and Director of School Maintenance and Operations. It worked out very well.[34]

Mr. Mayhall was used to working with teachers and viewing the school buildings from an educational viewpoint. He also was familiar with the architectural viewpoint. In Mr. Mayhall, Edgar had found both sides of the same problem. Mr. Mayhall helped in alleviating the task of planning and constructing new school buildings. The problem of building new schools consumed much of Edgar's time the three years he was in Austin.

Another situation arising during the construction of schools occurred in Edgar's first year in Austin. The planning engineer's report had located an elementary school on a hillside and into a ravine. The property belonged to an elderly lady named Mrs. Bowman. She did not want to sell it. Edgar began condemnation proceedings on her land. He remembers:

> We finally started condemnation proceedings . . . this was not a popular thing to do . . . particularly to Mrs. Bowman because she was an old-timer here. We didn't want to do it.[35]

Right in the middle of the proceedings, a woman who was a friend of Mrs. Bowman and owned the property near her, said she would sell her property to the school district if the school district would release Mrs. Bowman's property back to her. The woman's property was level and was actually a better site. The site was located on Exposition Road. Casis School was built on that site.

Another of Edgar's responsibilities he faced his first year in Austin was the hiring of new teachers. The practice had been that Miss Gray, Mr. McCallum's and Dr. Lewis' secretary, would keep a file of applications. When a teacher was needed, she would find an application, give it to the superintendent, and he would employ the applicant. Edgar called a meeting of all the principals to get them involved with the hiring of their own teachers:

> I said to them, "You've got to help me in finding the teachers that you want and need, and help me locate them, and recommend them to me. If I find they're acceptable, we'll employ them." I said, "Here's the file. You know what teachers you need. Here are the applications. If you don't find what you need in here, we can began looking somewhere else . . . When you find the people you want, come to me and we'll work out their employment." [36]

Dr. Lee Wilborn, Principal of Allen Junior High while Edgar was the Austin Superintendent, supports Edgar's statement:

> I was, at the time, Principal of Allen Junior High School. I remember the first principals meeting we had with him. It was late in August, and at that time we had some teacher shortage problems and we had some vacancies in the Austin schools that had not been filled at that time, although we had an extensive file of applications. The principals had not had any voice in the selection of teachers up to that time. A teacher would be assigned to a certain school from central administration, and the only time the principal knew about it was when that person showed up. So at the first principals meeting we told Dr. Edgar of some of the vacancies we had . . . At that point he said, "The meeting is over. We have some work to do. You fellows get into the applications, study them, and make some recommendations to me." And that's what we did . . . We had a responsibility and he gave us room to function.[37]

This method for employing teachers was a new practice for the principals. They immediately took an interest in the hiring process, and this renovation of the old procedure was established.

Another innovation Edgar made was the establishment of a routine whereby representatives of the faculty could meet with him on a regular basis. A plan was set up where each school would select their own representative who would go to Edgar's office about once a month. These representatives and Edgar would exchange information and ideas. Edgar relates this:

> We'd meet about once a month, I guess. I'd tell them what was going on. They would tell me their needs and express points of view . . . we just exchanged information and ideas.[38]

As soon as possible Edgar began visiting each building and talking to the teachers individually. He would go into a room and anyone who wanted to talk to him could do so. He was trying to inform himself. The principals and teachers were in favor of it. Dr. M.G. Bowden, Principal of Woolridge School at the time, spoke of these meetings:

> I'd get an idea and we'd talk it over with teachers . . . I would go down to Mr. Edgar, but I had to make sure I had my plan well developed and he would put me through this sort of third degree . . . what about parents . . . Then I would think, "I've lost that bout." Then he would say, "Okay, you can put it in next year if you want." He said, "All I want now is for kids to come out learning. And if they don't learn, let's abandon it before we waste any more time.
>
> One time I did not think through my idea very well. And he said, "Go back and rethink this and then come back." And I walked into his office about a week later all prepared . . . and he said, "Bowden, give me the paper and I'll sign it." [39]

These meetings helped to encourage the already good rapport that Edgar had with his principals and teachers.

In the summer of 1947 the elementary school teachers came to Edgar and expressed a desire to change their system of teaching. They were operating on a departmental program where the children went from room to room. Many of the other school systems in other areas at this time were using a system based on self contained classrooms. The self-contained classrooms had one teacher handling the same group of students all day, teaching all subjects to them with some help in the specialized fields. This was exactly what teachers wanted; so in the fall of 1947, all elementary schools were run on a homeroom, self-contained basis. Edgar speaks of his view of the decision:

> I think the teachers, most of them, were favorable to that, but you can imagine, that it was sort of upsetting. The principals felt that was the way to do it; they could handle it . . . it went very well.[40]

The decision may have created some feelings of uncertainty among some teachers, but Edgar felt it was the right one to make.

Another dilemma that the Austin School Board wanted Edgar to solve during his first year in Austin was a problem concerning high school fraternities and sororities at Austin High School. Austin High School was the only White high school, with over three thousand students in a building designed for two thousand students. Fraternities and sororities had existed for many years. In some respects, the organizations were good, but they had become controversial. Many parents felt this was not an egalitarian process to expose high school students to at that age. The parents in favor of the organizations wanted the fraternities and sororities to continue; other parents wanted the organizations stopped. Edgar solved the problem by writing a letter to the parents of each child in the ninth grade who would be coming to high school the next year. In the letter Edgar explained the fraternity and sorority program and asked the parents to write to him if they did want their child to be in one of these organizations. Edgar received only one or two positive replies out of hundreds of letters that he had sent out. On the basis of this poll of ninth grader's parents, Edgar recommended to the board that the fraternity and sorority program be discontinued. The already established members of the fraternities and sororities protested some, but otherwise the decision went over well. The next year the Texas Legislature passed a law outlawing fraternities and sororities in public high schools.

Edgar's first year in Austin was an extremely active year. He felt uncomfortable about all of the changes he had made so rapidly. He suspected that there was some resistance even among faculty and staff. At this time Charles Green, editor of the *Austin-American Statesman*, came out with a column related to Edgar and his work. Edgar describes this column:

> He [Charles Green] was very complimentary . . . He said that there was a growing respect for my leadership in Austin, that I had proved myself as an able administrator by, as he put it, careful planning and not shooting until I could see the whites of their eyes. He said the schools are costing more now, but nobody is complaining, and everybody is happy with what's going on.[41]

Edgar felt that the column was a good endorsement; however, the schools were costing more money which was due to the school tax election which Edgar initiated.

The School Tax Election
And Mayor Tom Miller, 1948

By 1948 Edgar began to look at the school programs. He wanted to make some plans on determining what the future needs of the school program would be. He began by working through the principals and faculty members. In this way Edgar developed a list of needs with attached priorities. Edgar came out with a report called, "Seven Problems Facing the Austin Public Schools." [42] He presented it to the Austin School Board and they readily approved it. The report was printed and distributed publicly. In order for the program to be implemented, a fifty to sixty percent raise in maintenance taxes would be needed. The school board did not back off; they supported Edgar all the way. The main cost of this program was the development of a salary schedule for teachers and administrators with the base being a minimum of twenty-four hundred dollars per year. Edgar knew he had to cushion this increase in some way, so he developed the idea of putting the teachers on a ten month pay plan instead of a nine month pay plan. The teaching year was extended from one hundred seventy-five days to one hundred eighty days. Edgar developed what he called "Curriculum Days" during the school year. These were five days when the teachers would be on duty during the year without the students. Also, five days were added on to the teaching year for teachers only both at the beginning and end of the school year. This change required much planning in order to keep the teachers busy. The school board appointed a Citizen's Advisory Committee made up of private citizens from the community. The committee was to study the seven problems outlined in the report in any way they wanted to. The Citizen's Advisory Committee studied the seven problems and approved them all. Edgar asked the school board to call an election to increase the tax rate.

Edgar was for this election, but one thing that worried Edgar was the schools' relationship to the city. Austin, at the time, had a mayor, Tom Miller, who had served a long time and was highly respected. The school board told Edgar they wanted to have a school election but did not want the city to have an election also. They felt as soon as Tom Miller learned of the school election he would call a city election as well. Thus, the board suggested that the election should be kept quiet. Edgar relates part of this story:

> They didn't specifically instruct me not to say anything to Tom Miller, but the more I thought about it, the more I realized that you didn't treat a man like Tom Miller that way whether he's mayor or not. He was a member of the community. One afternoon I made an appointment and went to see him. I told him our plans. Then I told the board I'd done it. They didn't fire me, but I'm sure they wanted to at the moment.[43]

As soon as Tom Miller found out about the school election, he called a city election for the same day. On the day of the election the school tax increase won out; the citizens of Austin had spoken out in favor of the school tax increase. The city's proposals were defeated. Most of the board members agreed later that Edgar was correct in telling Tom Miller about the election.

The school tax increase which the citizens of Austin voted for in the election helped the Black schools in the Austin Independent School District. Edgar made a small move for integration in the Black schools. This kind of action was unusual for this period of time in Austin.

The Black Schools In Austin, 1947–1949

Edgar had always responded to the needs of the students in Black schools that were under his jurisdiction. He was generally held back, however, by the law and by the current feeling of the era. In Austin in 1947, Edgar made a small statement in favor of integration.

During this time Edgar was not much in favor of needless meetings, so he was not much in favor of faculty meetings. He felt they were a waste of time unless they were short and specific.

Dr. James Jeffery, a teacher in Austin in 1949, said that one time in a faculty meeting at about eleven o'clock a.m., Edgar said to everyone that if they needed to go to the bathroom, then they needed to get the meeting over with.[44] Although Edgar would meet with faculty members for some specific problem, he never did have a regular schedule for meeting with them.

Edgar did, however, have a regular schedule for meeting with his principals. In spite of his feelings toward meetings, Edgar held meetings every two weeks with the principals. On Mondays he would meet with the White principals; on Tuesdays he would meet with the Black principals. There were four Black principals. This seemed to Edgar to be an unnecessary duplication of effort. One day he told the Black principals to attend the meeting with the White Principals:

> So one day I said to the Black principals, "At the next meeting, I want you to come on Monday and meet with the White principals. I don't want you to say anything about it to anybody. I'm not telling the White principals you're going to go. Just come on in and sit down. Let's have the meeting, and get together and cut out this foolishness of having separate meetings.[45]

At the next meeting the Black principals came in and sat down. The White principals were very surprised. Friendly R. Rice was one of the Black principals and has this account of the change in meetings:

> When we first met the principal meetings were separate. The meetings were equalized under his supervision. He called a meeting one day and that was that . . . It was a big change.[46]

Mr. Rice was the supervisory principal of the Black principals and said the change worked out smoothly. Mr. Rice felt Edgar treated everyone equally. Edgar visited the Black schools regularly and took an active role in their development.

Mary Frances Winston, a Black teacher, can also attest to the fairmindedness of Edgar. She was teaching in the Black junior high at the age of twenty. Discipline problems arose in her class, so she turned in her resignation. Edgar did not accept her resignation. He talked to her and asked her not to resign. Instead of teaching junior high school, he suggested she try teaching elementary school. Mrs. Winston had gone to Detroit. Edgar sent her a telegram with a job offer. She accepted the offer and then taught fourth grade for thirty-four years.

Once when Mrs. Winston became pregnant her principal wanted her to leave her job early. Edgar intervened and she was permitted to continue teaching until the baby was due.[47] Mrs. Winston admired Edgar a great deal. She felt he was very fairminded to all people.

Dr. E. Marie Gilbert, the former Black owner of a Black business college, also knew Edgar. She opened a Black business college in Austin in 1947. The college was accredited and was the only business college in Austin owned and operated by a Black person. Dr. Gilbert participated in many of Edgar's seminars and workshops. She felt Edgar made many contributions to education in Austin.[48] As Edgar started his second year in Austin, he had the support of the entire community.

Austin, 1948–1950

At the end of Edgar's first year in Austin, he was not at all certain about how well he had done and how well he was accepted. The changes he had had to make in one year were changes that would have normally taken two or three years. The editorial by Charles Green had helped ease these feelings, but the school board offered Edgar the real evidence. The Austin Board tore up Edgar's contract and gave him a new one at twelve thousand dollars per year. Edgar felt he had had his trial period and that the Austin Board had approved him.

During his first year as Superintendent in Austin Edgar had been involved with the Austin schools' relation to The University of Texas with respect to the operation of the model elementary school program. The model elementary school program was a project of the University. By 1948 the program, which had been located at Woolridge School on 24th street, was moved to the new Casis Elementary School. This project was run by Dr. Henry Otto, a professor of School Administration with a specialization in Elementary Education. Dr. Otto wanted to add a model program in Special Education. He got the University to build a wing onto the Casis School that was to be owned by the University. There was just a little connecting link between the main building and the Special Education wing. Dr. M.G. Bowden, Principal of Casis at the time, describes the new wing:

Then the University had the big idea of having a University

Laboratory School. And Dr. Henry Otto, who was at the School of
Education, and Dr. Edgar had thought of the idea of improving
the lab school . . . It was going to be the Casis School . . . And they
built Casis School and I was going to be the principal. I'd just returned from winning the war in Germany and so I was principal
first of Woolridge School while the new Casis School was being
built. Mr. Edgar was very helpful in setting that up. It was the
first real development in Special Education involving both Special Education, Gifted Education, and Regular Education in one
building.[49]

The experience was very helpful for Edgar and he learned a
great deal from the programs Dr. Otto and Dr. Bowden instituted.

At the beginning of his second year in Austin, Edgar
made a decision that was to have great significance later in his
career. He added to his staff the position of Director of Personnel. He brought in a man by the name of Warren Hitt. Mr. Hitt
had taught in the Fort Worth Public Schools, and was working
with the Federal Works Agency handling the public school finance allocations to war affected schools.[50] This was the program part of the Lanham Act. Edgar had met Mr. Hitt in his
duties involving the budget program and applications regarding the Lanham Act. Edgar felt he needed someone who could
be a troubleshooter for him. Edgar wanted someone that had
his confidence and that he could depend on. Warren Hitt was
this man. Mrs. Warren Hitt remembers when Edgar called her
husband:

> His [Warren Hitt's] father had died and we were in Denton.
> And Dr. Edgar called him and said, "I want you to come down to
> Austin and be my personnel man." And he [Hitt] said, "Guess
> who that phone call was from," and I said, "What are you going to
> do?" . . . And I could tell there wasn't any use in us talking about
> it. But we talked . . . He wanted back in Education, but never
> dreamed of coming to Austin. He said, "I'm tired of moving, but
> Austin would be a good place to bring up a child because UT is
> right there and I enjoy Dr. Edgar." [51]

Mr. Hitt was to be Dr. Edgar's right hand man until he died in
1970.

During the latter part of Edgar's tenure in Austin, he was
involved with organizations outside of the Austin School District. In 1948 Governor Beauford Jester through the Lieutenant

Governor, Allan Shivers, appointed Edgar to the Board of Trustees of the Teacher Retirement System of Texas. Edgar had known Lieutenant Governor Shivers in Orange. Shivers was State Senator from Orange while Edgar was there. The teaching members of the Board of Directors of the Teacher Retirement System nominated three candidates for the position. Edgar got it. He served on the Board of Trustees of the Teacher Retirmeent System until he became State Commissioner of Education. Edgar discusses the reason for his leaving the board:

> At the end of my first month in the office [State Commissioner], the Comptroller called me and said, "If you want your paycheck for April, you'd better resign from the other job because the Constitution says there cannot be a conflict of interest of jobs." [52]

Though it was an honor for Edgar to be appointed to the Board of Trustees of the Teacher Retirement System, it also required hard work because the board supervised the staff and the director, and invested all the money.

In 1949 Edgar was appointed to the Yearbook Committee of the American Association of School Administrators. He had joined the group in 1940 and had gone to their national convention in St. Louis that year. Their theme in 1949 was public relations with the schools. By now this was a familiar theme to Edgar.

There was one other appointment that was given Edgar while he was Superintendent in Austin that was vital to his career. In 1947, Lieutenant Governor Shivers appointed Edgar to the Gilmer-Aikin Committee. His work on this committee would pave the way for his job as the first State Commissioner of Education for the State of Texas.

Edgar was appointed as the first Texas State Commissioner of Education on February 3, 1950. He planned to stay in the Austin Superintendency until he actually took office; however, when the news of his appointment hit the papers, people from all over the state began to come to the Austin School Office to see Edgar about state business. Finally Edgar told the Chairman of the Austin School Board that his appointment was causing problems and that he should resign; he did.

The superintendency jobs at Orange and at Austin which comprised the urban phase of Edgar's career had been very beneficial to him. He had learned much from both jobs, and the jobs had set a firm foundation for him to become the first Commissioner of Education in Texas.

CONCLUSION

Edgar's work in Orange and in Austin gave him the experience and the recognition he needed to become the first State Commissioner of Education in Texas. These jobs comprised the urban phase of his early career. Several parallels in Orange and Austin can be drawn which gave Edgar invaluable experience during his career as State Commissioner: (1) his continued improvement in his ability to work with school boards; (2) his ability to accomplish much in a short period of time due to the rapid growth both Orange and Austin were experiencing; (3) his resourcefulness when it came to raising much needed money in Orange (through the Lanham Act) and in Austin (through the school tax election); and (4) his continued involvement in outside professional organizations increased his reputation statewide. A few differences also existed between the Orange and Austin jobs: (1) in Orange Edgar worked closely with the federal government, while in Austin, the mechanisms of his work were local in nature; and (2) when Edgar left Orange things were winding down; when he left Austin, they were winding up. The similarities as well as the differences of the Orange and Austin superintendencies helped to give Edgar a firm ground of experience on every level that would surely serve him well as State Commissioner of Education.

The first similarity which existed between the Orange and Austin superintendencies was the refinement of Edgar's expertise in working with boards. In Orange, Edgar was faced with the Lutcher Stark/Edgar Brown Jr. dilemma. His ability to sense out a board was impressive, as was his choice of actions concerning boards. This is evidenced by Edgar's description of what he did with his money after arriving in Orange:

> They had two banks there [Orange]. One of them belonged to Edgar Brown, Jr.; one of them belonged to Lutcher Stark. I opened an account in Lutcher Stark's bank, and siphoned off a little bit and put it over in Brown's bank in my wife's name. I didn't have to do that, but it seemed like maybe the thing to do. Because of the dominance of the Stark interest, I didn't want to alienate

Edgar Brown, Jr. because he had some resources and he could help out.[53]

In Orange the school board was dominated by two men. Edgar saw this and worked through it. He never had any difficulties with the board in Orange (see reference 3, chapter 2). Likewise, Austin was similar. When Mrs. Bybee was not sure of whom she wanted to elect as superintendent, Edgar went and spoke with her. She was won over to his side. In Austin Edgar carried his board expertise a step further. He became skilled at running the board meetings through hard work. Both Mrs. O.D. Weeks and Dr. Clyde Colvert have accounts of Edgar's skill in working with school board members and in running school board meetings in Austin. Mrs. Weeks, an Austin School Board member, relates what it was like working with Edgar and meeting with him:

> I'm telling you, I have never worked so hard for pay as I did for him . . . I believe we almost had a meeting every night or every afternoon for the first year. It wasn't that bad but it seemed that way. He asked the board, "I'd like to know what expectations you have of me?" Mr. Byram said, "Now Dr. Edgar, we are inviting you to come and take care of the Austin schools and make them the best in the state." . . . One time he really gave it to us. He started explaining some project and he said on page so and so in your agenda. And he started talking about it. And the board members started asking questions. And it was rather evident from these questions that they were not very much in favor of what it was he was going to promote. And so he just closed up his copy of the agenda and said to the board, "When you have had time to study this agenda we'll take it up at another meeting" . . . We just didn't get the point of what he was trying to do . . . Next time he said, "I think I have reworked this material in a manner that would be more pleasurable for you to study" . . . And they went right through it.[54]

Dr. Colvert, head of the Junior College Program at UT at the time, describes how Edgar taught him a lesson about boards:

> He taught me a very valuable lesson about dealing with boards. He would have an agenda and all the board members would have an agenda to carry on and Dr. Edgar would have all the papers and stuff about the program. He'd bring up the item on the agenda and if he found that they weren't going to do it or didn't understand it, he'd say. "Well, gentlemen, I see you don't

understand that very well. I'll just save it for another time . . . He
didn't try and brow beat them. And so he taught me a valuable
lesson in dealing with boards and I appreciated it.[55]

Edgar's adeptness in working with these boards prepared him
well for his eventual work with the State Board of Education.

The second similarity between Edgar's Orange and Austin
jobs was his ability to accomplish a lot during a short period of
time due to the growth both places were experiencing. In Orange over a period of three to four years, Edgar skillfully managed a fourfold increase in the number of students in his district due to the defense and wartime efforts that were
underway in Orange. Edgar was instrumental in the development of the Lanham Act. Through the implementation of the
Lanham Act, Edgar built new schools and aided many people
with all kinds of problems which they were experiencing due to
the war effort (for example, the sleeping father's day care program where the children of parents in which the mother
worked all day and the father worked at night, and so slept
during the day). Many people whom the author interviewed
first heard of Edgar while he was at Orange.

In Austin, Edgar increased this recognition and experience. Most of what he accomplished was in the span of one
year. Mr. Guebbles, the planning engineer the Austin Board
had hired, found fifteen sites for new schools. Edgar planned
new buildings, organized administration and staff, created
new programs, and overall set a good foundation for the growth
of Austin schools. Edgar never tired of his work in Orange and
in Austin; he was able to accomplish all his goals.

The third parallel of Edgar's Orange and Austin jobs was
his resourcefulness when it came to raising money. In Orange
Edgar was able to raise hundreds of thousand of dollars
through the Lanham Act, which he had helped to develop.
Through the Act, he brought in money for school buildings and
school programs as well as for community programs. Edgar's
work at Orange became known throughout not only Texas, but
the rest of the country. In Austin, Edgar successfully raised
school taxes to over fifty percent of what they had previously
been. In a city wide maintenance tax election which involved
taxes for both the schools and the city, the citizens of Austin
overwhelmingly supported the school tax and did not support

the city tax. Edgar had gained the confidence of the people in both the Orange and Austin school districts.

The final parallel in Edgar's Orange and Austin superintendencies was his continued involvement in outside professional associations which furthered his reputation. In Orange Edgar was President of the Texas Association of School Administrators. While he held this position, he was able to solve the transportation problem for sports teams which existed due to gas rationing. To solve this problem, he had again turned to the federal government. In Austin, Edgar was appointed to the Board of Trustees of the Teacher Retirement System of Texas. This appointment was an honor for him. A more important appointment, however, was his appointment to the Gilmer-Aikin Committee in 1947; this would alter his career forever. His involvement with these committees gave him recognition in the political arena in Austin. Edgar's outside involvement with organizations and committees in addition to his continued work on his M.A. and Ph.D. degrees firmly set him as a professional educator.

One of the differences between Edgar's work in Orange and his work in Austin was that his work in Orange was federally oriented while his work in Austin was locally oriented. Through implementation of the Lanham Act in Orange, Edgar learned the intricacies of working with the federal government. He made several trips to Washington. This federal experience would serve him well during his Commissionership when the federal government began to play a more dominant role in education. In Austin, the mechanisms of Edgar's work were different. His work was locally oriented and involved the citizens of Austin voting for money, not the federal government appropriating it. In Austin, Edgar was also under the eyes of the powerful politicians of the state of Texas. State politicians watched as Edgar skillfully carried out his work in Austin. When persons were being considered for the job of State Commissioner of Education, Edgar's accomplishments in both Orange and Austin were working in his favor.

Another of the differences between Edgar's superintendencies in Orange and Austin was the pace of things when Edgar left. When Edgar left Orange, the pace of his work was winding down. The money had been gotten and the schools had been built. World War II was over and the great system Edgar had created in Orange would now diminish. In Austin, the pace of Edgar's work was winding up. He had the money to build the schools and create the programs, but much of the actual work was left to do. Edgar describes his experience at Orange and at Austin:

> [In] Austin probably more than any other place I'd been, I had to create solutions to problems that I never had faced before, and never heard of any similar problems or solutions . . . I pulled solutions out of the blue, particularly this problem with sororities and fraternities. So I know that it expanded my knowledge of administration. And I believe it developed a depth of understanding that I had not had before . . . In Orange we had to use some ingenuity to cope with the war program, but that was a different kind of situation. In Austin I had an established community with a long tenured superintendent before me.[56]

The time that Edgar served in both Orange and in Austin comprised the urban phase of Edgar's early career. Most of the tasks he performed in both places were similar to those he had performed previously in other places. The tasks were a bit more complicated and involved more students, more schools, more money, and more responsibility. After Edgar managed to accomplish all he did at Orange and at Austin, he felt he was prepared to handle any job. He had gained much confidence in his ability to deal with people and situations on all levels of school administration. Though his purpose in life was still singular — that of being a school superintendent, Edgar's outstanding work in Orange and Austin, which gained him state and national recognition, would set him up as the number one choice for the State Commissionership of Education in Texas.

J.W. Edgar's parents, James William and Sarah on their wedding day, December 14, 1890, in Georgetown, Texas.

J.W. Edgar (age six months) with his older brother, Morris, and older sister, Mae, in 1905.

Edgar family and family home in Briggs about 1907. J.W. (age 3); his father and mother; sister, Mae, and brother, Morris.

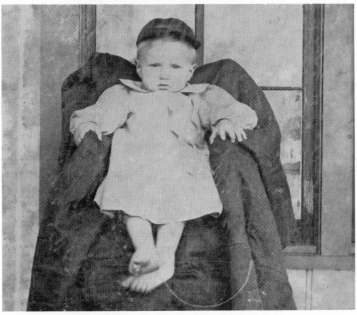

J.W. Edgar at one year of age in 1905.

J.W. (bottom left, age three) Morris and Mae.

J.W. on horseback at age five about 1909.

School house in Briggs in the early 1900s. J.W. attended school here.

J.W. Edgar (in the front row, third from right) in the first grade at Briggs, Texas in 1911.

J.W. (third from left, seated) in the sixth grade, about 1917.

J.W. in high school about 1920. He has his face covered with a book. Thomas Ferguson is top right.

J.W. Edgar as coach of the Lake Victor basketball team (J.W. is top right). Selmon(S.P.) Cowan is third from the left, second row from bottom.

J.W. Edgar's eighth, ninth and tenth grade class in Lake Victor about 1926. J.W. is standing at the top right.

Miss Sue Oakley in 1926 about one year before she married J.W.

J.W. while he worked in Victoria about 1937.

J.W. and Sue Edgar with daughter, Ruth, age six months, in 1936 while working in Mirando City, Texas.

J.W. and Sue Edgar at their farewell party in Orange, Texas with Master of Ceremonies, Howard Peterson (standing) in 1947.

Photo J.W. sent with his credentials when he applied for the job as superintendent at Austin, 1947.

Edgar family portrait, Sue; daughter Susan; J.W.; daughter, Sally; daughter Ruth. February 4, 1950, just before he took office as Commissioner of Education.

J.W. receiving the keys to the city of El Paso, Texas, from Mayor Dan L.P. Duke on October 25, 1950. This was part of Edgar's attempt to visit every county in Texas his first year in office as commissioner.

J.W. Edgar, Sue Edgar, Dr. Bascom B. Hayes and Mrs. Donna Hayes enjoying an outing at Barton Springs, Austin, Texas, in May of 1956.

J.W. and Sue Edgar as he receives the Freedom Foundation award in 1963.

J.W. and Sue Edgar at a dinner in Victoria, Texas in 1963.

Harry Ransom, J.W. Edgar and C.O. Chandler at a school dedication in Victoria, Texas, in 1969.

J.W. Edgar (far right) with Lyndon Baines Johnson (LBJ) at a meeting of LBJ's Task Force on Education in 1966.

VERNON REGIONAL
JUNIOR COLLEGE LIBRARY

J.W. and Sue Edgar celebrating their birthdays in September, 1963.

J.W. and Sue Edgar at Edgar's retirement party held by his staff in 1974.

J.W. and Sue Edgar receiving a standing ovation at his staff retirement party in 1974. With them are Dr. Dana Williams and Mrs. Lou Williams.

J.W. Edgar with Senator A.M. Aikin at Edgar's retirement party in 1974.

J.W. Edgar at his famous clean desk in 1974.

J.W. and Sue Edgar and friends with their new 1975 Oldsmobile given to them by the school administrators. They also gave the Edgars over eight thousand dollars in cash. All from donations.

Three Texas Commissioners of Education (from left) Mr. Alton O. Bowen and wife, Mary Bowen; J.W. and Sue Edgar, and Dr. M.L. Brockette and wife, Mary Brockette.

J.W. Edgar at his home in Austin in June 1984.

3

The Proposal and Passage of The Gilmer-Aikin Laws

Edgar's appointment to the Gilmer-Aikin Committee came at the same time he was hired as Superintendent of Schools in Austin. He worked on the committee for eighteen months, from July of 1947 to December of 1948. Four factors concerning his role with the Gilmer-Aikin Laws directly influenced his selection as the first State Commissioner of Education in Texas: (1) Edgar saw the need for change in Texas education, and through his activities with the Texas Association of School Administrators he would initiate ideas and propose changes in the educational system which would lead to the formation of the Gilmer-Aikin Committee; (2) Edgar's work on the Gilmer-Aikin Committee was directly related to the administrative job of State Commissioner of Education; (3) when the Gilmer-Aikin Bills were under debate for passage, Edgar assumed a passive, background role in support of the bills; and (4) the opposition of Dr. L.A. Woods to the Gilmer-Aikin legislation worked in Edgar's favor. These factors made Edgar visible in the political arena and made his selection as State Commissioner more probable than it otherwise would have been. That Edgar would be chosen to serve on the Gilmer-Aikin Committee was not surprising due to his excellent reputation as a professional educator.

THE TEXAS ASSOCIATION OF SCHOOL
ADMINISTRATORS AND THE ORIGIN OF THE
GILMER-AIKIN COMMITTEE

Nineteen hundred and forty-seven was an important year
for education in Texas. This was the first year since before the
beginning of the Depression through until after World War II
that the Legislature could meet and consider the needs of the
schools. The schools were facing the erosion of their school
buildings and equipment. They were also facing a predictable
tremendous amount of growth in population over the next two
decades. The power structures in Texas were in agreement
that some action had to be taken concerning the predicted
growth of population and the expansion, and perhaps restruc-
turing, of the public schools. At the regular session of the Fif-
tieth Legislative Session, Representative Dallas Blankenship
of Dallas introduced a bill which incorporated a plan of the
Texas State Teachers Association (TSTA) for raising teacher
salaries.[1] This bill was harmonious with the views of Dr. L.A.
Woods, the State Superintendent of Public Instruction. The bill
proposed the establishment of a fifty-five dollar per capita payment to all schools based on the number of students that they
had registered on their census (i.e. the number of students liv-
ing in the school district *not* the number of students that attended school). Previously, the per capita apportionment had
been based on whatever the available school funds had earned.
The TSTA wanted to set a floor and guarantee a fifty-five dollar per capita payment from the omnibus tax bill, an emer-
gency fund, if necessary. Representative Claud Gilmer spoke of
this incident:

> This fellow, Dallas Blankenship, who had opposed me for the
> Speakers Office . . . had a bill in the Legislature, in the House, to
> increase the teachers salaries. The mechanics that he had em-
> ployed to do it was that he was going to appropriate a lump sum
> of money out of the state treasury.[2]

In the middle of the legislative session, Senator James E.
Taylor and Representative Gilmer introduced a counterplan.
This plan set up the same minimum salary schedule as the
Blankenship Bill but provided that the state should contribute

aid above per capita only to those schools which could show
need.[3] Edgar described the struggle between these two bills.

> It was a very intense battle on these two points. Along in the
> spring of the year [1947], it just looked like there wasn't going to
> be any reconciliation on the different points of view. Finally the
> fifty-five dollar floor did prevail [TSTA plan], but it left a lot of
> people dissatisfied with what had taken place.[4]

The Blankenship Bill passed the Legislature. Governor Beauford Jestor simply let them become law without his signature.
The Gilmer-Aikin Committee originated, in part, out of this
conflict. Evidence shows that Edgar played an important role
in the origin of the Gilmer-Aikin Committee.

The Gilmer-Aikin Committee grew out of planning ses-
sions held by members of the Texas Association of School Administrators (TASA). In the fall of 1946, Dr. R.L. Williams,
President of TASA, formed a Committee on Educational Policies. Edgar was the chairman of this committee.[5] During the
month of November, 1946, the committee polled all members of
the TASA. After considering the views of the members, the
committee created Policy Statement Number One entitled,
"Legislative Policies for 1947." The first statement called for
strong, cohesive leadership at the state level. This dealt with
the State Board of Education and the manner by which they
were appointed. It also dealt with the executive officer of the
board (the State Superintendent), this officer's qualifications,
and his relationship to the board.[6] Edgar describes the Educational Policies Committee which gave birth to the report:

> That report had been developed by a committee — the Edu-
> cational Policies Committee of the Texas Association of School
> Administrators — of which I was Chairman. It had been set up in
> 1946. We used to meet on weekends, when we ought to have been
> home with our families, and sit around and try to visualize what
> could be done to improve education. So we finally arrived at a se-
> ries of policy statements. These statements showed the need for a
> full study of the schools . . . I think we met probably here in Aus-
> tin. It was a central point . . . We had a series of [meetings] in the
> fall of 1946 . . . Hollis Moore was on the Committee . . . [The pol-
> icy statement] got transmitted to [the] Legislature. I think it gave
> birth to the formation of [Gilmer-Aikin]. We took credit for it.[7]

Hollis Moore was a superintendent from Kerrville, which

was Claud Gilmer's legislative district. Moore was working on his dissertation which had to do with school financing.[8] He took the report of the Policies Committee to Representative Gilmer. Edgar gave an account of this.

> Claud Gilmer was the representative in the House of Representatives. There was a superintendent of schools in his district from Kerrville, which is about one hundred miles from here [Austin]. His name was Hollis Moore. One day Hollis Moore took a report, which we had developed . . . on school need, to Claud Gilmer and showed it to him. He was from Rocksprings, but he was in the Kerrville Legislative District. The proposals in that report showed the need for further study which could be made by having the Legislature and the Governor set up a committee to study the public schools and to make recommendations to the next session of the Legislature.[9]

Claud Gilmer recalls the same story.

> As it happened, there was a superintendent of schools in Kerrville, which was my legislative district . . . and I would go to Kerrville every time I went to Austin and every time I came back . . . and he saw some publicity about the Blankenship Bill and got in touch with me. Of course he was a school man, being Superintendent of Schools in Kerrville. He was in the process of doing a lot of research. He was getting his doctors degree . . . and writing a thesis on public school education. He had gotten material from other states and he'd conferred with educators, pro and con, and he had a lot of real solid, basic, well you called them theories then, as to how you'd go about improving our public school education in Texas. So I drew a lot of ideas from him and from discussions with him, and wound up proposing a bill that would be in lieu of or a substitute for the Blankenship Bill.[10]

Since Edgar was Chairman of the Policies Committee of the TASA, and since it was this committee's proposals that Hollis Moore took to Claud Gilmer, he played a key role in the origin of the Gilmer-Aikin Committee. With the information from Hollis Moore, Representative Gilmer set out to propose the formation of the Gilmer-Aikin Committee. Edgar would play a key role on this committee as well.

THE GILMER-AIKEN COMMITTEE, 1947–1948

In the spring of 1947, bills in the House and Senate were passed which created the Gilmer-Aikin Committee. Edgar relates what transpired:

> Claud Gilmer then introduced a resolution in the House of Representatives calling for the study . . . in the wording of his resolution, he said . . . "a committee to investigate the schools." This didn't go well with anybody, the school people particularly. Finally Senator Aikin over in the Senate, who was carrying the fifty-five dollar per capita legislation, told representative Gilmer that if he would take out the word "investigate" and substitute the word "study," that he [Senator Aikin] would sponsor the resolution in the Senate. Claud Gilmer rewrote the resolution to make it more of a study [and] soften it up some. He sponsored it in the House. Aikin sponsored it in the Senate, calling for the appointment of a two-year study committee.[11]

Senator A.M. Aikin confirms this story:

> Claud Gilmer, he'd never been pushing for the schools too much. He felt like they pretty well just busheled it out. That's the reason I held up his resolution. I agreed to ask the [legislative] committee to report it if he'd change the word "investigate" to "study" and put a little money in there for the committee [Gilmer-Aikin] to do something with, and then to agree to serve on the committee, and to attend the meetings . . . he came back just two or three days before the Legislature adjourned and said, "I'm going to agree." [12]

The House and Senate passed legislation which called for the formation of a committee to study education in Texas. The committee was made up of eighteen members: six appointed by the Governor; six by the Lieutenant Governor; and six by the Speaker of the House.[13] Gilmer relates how the Committee got its name.

> Someone is the committee raised a question: "Well, we think it ought to have a name too." About that time, Governor Jester walked in there to have his picture taken. Somebody turned around and said, "Governor Jester, we're thinking about having a name for this committee." [He] said, "What ought we to name the committee?" Just right back like that, before you could think, he said, "Why it ought to be called the Gilmer-Aikin Committee." Well they had asked him and he had told them.[14]

Lieutenant Governor Shivers appointed Edgar to the Gil-

mer-Aikin Committee. Shivers had been Edgar's senator when
he was at Orange. Governor Shivers spoke of how he knew Edgar.

> I knew him when he was Superintendent of Schools in Orange. I lived in Port Arthur, represented Orange . . . I knew him
> real well . . . We thought Edgar was one of the outstanding school
> superintendents in Texas.[15]

The Gilmer-Aikin Committee was organized into subcommittees: one on School Administration; one on Finance; and
one on Personnel. Edgar was appointed Co-Chairman of the
Subcommittee on School Administration. Senator Taylor,
Chairman of the Gilmer-Aikin Committee, discussed Edgar's
work on the Committee.

> We had a good many meetings . . . We would go up to Kerrville and have our informal sessions for a day or two at a time.
> And then we'd come back down to Austin and have our formal
> meetings to confirm what we had done up there. We got pretty
> well acquainted with each other in those informal sessions that
> we had . . . He was a retiring sort of a guy. He wasn't aggressive
> . . . Dr. Edgar would kind of sit back in the background and he'd
> answer questions if they'd ask him. But he'd very seldom volunteer much comment. He felt all the time that he was on there because of his professional standing. He was more interested in the
> committee doing a good job than he was in projecting any ideas
> that he might have had. I don't even remember him getting into
> any sort of an argument. We had all sorts of those.[16]

Betty King (formerly Betty Dunlavey), Secretary of the Texas
Senate, was the Secretary of the Gilmer-Aikin Committee. She
remembers Edgar on the Committee as being low key, and a
good operator.[17]

When the Gilmer-Aikin Committee was first formed,
members of the committee asked Dr. Larry Haskew to work
with the committee as a Technical Consultant since he had
worked with similar situations to their own previously in
Georgia. Consequently, Haskew came to Texas in 1947. Edgar
recalls the committee's decision to hire Haskew and his work
on the committee:

> I had gone to the Chairman, Senator Taylor, and told him
> about Dr. Haskew and suggested to him that we use Dr. Haskew
> with the Committee as Chief Consultant, which they did. And so
> Dr. Haskew came into prominence, rightfully so, in the forming of

the Committee report and the legislation . . . I want to stress here
the importance of Dr. Haskew to the Gilmer-Aikin Committee,
particularly in furnishing ideas and devising strategies. So far as
I know the Financing Plan, that is the Minimum Foundation
School Program, was his. Hollis Moore . . . made some important
contributions also.[18]

Haskew became closely involved with the Gilmer-Aikin Committee and with Edgar. Haskew recalls Edgar's role in his selection to the Gilmer-Aikin Committee.

> One of those activisms was a thing called the Southern
> States Workshop Conference which aimed at improving educa-
> tion with the Southern states . . . It met at Daytona Beach, Flor-
> ida, once a year in June. It was there that I first became ac-
> quainted with Dr. Edgar . . . [Edgar sent me] a clipping from the
> paper [in Austin] . . . He was at the time Superintendent here . . .
> in Austin . . . It listed the names of the Committee members and
> what the committee was about . . . So I immediately wrote to Dr.
> Pittinger, who also was a member of the committee, and asked
> him if I should know more about that committee and what it was
> up to . . . Dr. Pittinger very nicely wrote back and said he didn't
> think I needed to worry myself about that. That was just a show-
> piece sort of thing that wasn't going to amount to anything . . . I
> called Dr. Edgar . . . He said it might be a chance that this com-
> mittee might really do something . . . Dr. Edgar called and said,
> "I'm sitting here with the Chairman, James Taylor, of the Gil-
> mer-Aikin Committee. We've had three meetings now. And most
> of us agree that we're not getting anywhere. We're just going
> round and around. And so I told him about your previous experi-
> ence . . . He would like to meet you and talk with you." I said,
> "Why sure, of course" . . . We met and I outlined this kind of pro-
> cedure that had proved to be highly successful in arousing citi-
> zens interest and getting them ready to revolutionize, if neces-
> sary, a setup . . . The next morning James Taylor called and said,
> "I've just been talking with three or four others of the committee
> and they want me to call a special meeting of that committee to
> get you to tell them just about what you told me." Of course I
> jumped to it. So I went down and Dr. Edgar made it impossible for
> me not to be received well by his own stature and confidence. So
> that's what I did and that's the way I got in . . . It was a great
> show . . . But just the status of Edgar himself meant that the
> great pull of Texas superintendents finally turned in that direc-
> tion [of Gilmer-Aikin].[19]

As soon as Haskew joined, the committee began to work.

Edgar began to work within his own Subcommittee on
School Administration. The other Co-Chairman of the subcom-
mittee was Wright Morrow from Houston. Edgar describes Mr.
Morrow and the work of the subcommittee.

> Our Co-Chairman was Wright Morrow from Houston. He
> was casually interested, but he really didn't want to take the time
> to dig into it, so I did most of the Chairman's work on the School
> Administration Subcommittee. It was our job to look at the differ-
> ent levels of school administration and make recommendations
> with respect to any changes that we thought might be needed.
> [Changes in the] State machinery for public schools, the County,
> and the local machinery. We started at the State level. I felt like
> here was really the heart of our problem, perhaps.[20]

When the subcommittee began its investigation of Texas
school administration, they found what Edgar described as "a
three-headed administrative monster organization at the state
level." This consisted of the State Board of Education, the State
Superintendent, and the Legislature. The State Board of Education was appointed by the Governor, and the members were
designated by law for exclusively handling certain parts of the
educational program. The State Superintendent was elected by
the people in a general election. He was charged with the responsibilities of certain other aspects of the law. The Legislature, through its Audit Committee, oversaw certain functions
of the State Superintendent.

The State Superintendent, as time had gone by, administered the financial program through the school districts. The
only thing the state furnished to the districts was the per capita apportionment based on the census. In the smaller rural
districts, in addition to the per capita apportionment, the
schools received funds from what was called an Equalization
Fund that the Legislature proportioned.[21] The State Superintendent, who at that time was Dr. L.A. Woods, helped to dis-
tribute the Equalization Fund through his deputy superintendents.

Woods had established a system of deputy superintendents
strategically located all over the state. Since Woods' office was
an elected one, he had to run for office every two years. In order
to do this, he had to keep up a political apparatus to help him
with the job of reelection. His deputies served that purpose,

having two distinct functions, one political and one educational. Mr. Preston Hutchinson, who was an auditor for the Legislative Accounts Office at the time of Woods, talked about the deputies:

> Dr. Woods . . . in order to perpetuate in office [had deputies working under him] . . . the people working under him wanted to keep him in [office] so they could keep their jobs. So before the thing finally came to a head, he had twenty-four deputies covering the entire state, supposed to be supervising, which they were not doing effectively. It got to be too much politics.[22]

Gradually, through the deputy superintendents located all over the state, the administration of the Equalization Program had begun to be questioned to the point where the Legislature had lost confidence in their fair administration of the program. Consequently, the Legislature asked the Legislative Audit Committee to intervene. This committee was a standing committee of both senators and representatives and the members supervised the State Auditor. In turning over to this committee the responsibility of supervising the administration of the Equalization Fund, the Legislature was demonstrating their lack of confidence in State Superintendent Woods to do so.

The job of State Superintendent was just one aspect of the investigation of the School Administration Subcommittee. Edgar comments on the superstructure that the subcommittee investigated:

> So here we had the State Board of Education appointed from one source, the State Superintendent elected from another source, and then the Legislature through its Audit Committee . . . three distinct individual groups performing state administration.[23]

The subcommittee found that Woods had performed as Executive Officer of the State Board of Education as well as he could. Gradually through the years, however, their relationship had eroded. The board had taken away from Woods the power they had previously delegated to him. One of the powers the board stripped from Woods was the management of Vocational Education. Edgar states:

> [There was] a federal law which required that there be a state board for vocational education, and Texas had designated the State Board of Education as that board. They just separated Dr. Woods from having anything to do with the Vocational Edu-

cation Program, and set up their own director, who was responsible directly to the board.[24]

The State Board did have their own power.

One of the responsibilities that the State Board had was
the responsibility for adopting textbooks. Some members of the
board had come into public criticism because they were ac-
cused of soliciting funds for the Governor's race from textbook
publishers. Ottis Lock, a member of the Gilmer-Aikin Committee, agreed that improprieties between the textbook companies
and the State Board existed prior to Gilmer-Aikin.[25] The
School Administration Subcommittee found the State Board to
be under suspicion and lacking in public confidence as was
Woods. The School Administration Subcommittee wanted to
try to develop a plan for strong, unified, professional educational leadership at the state level. Edgar did not work with
the Subcommittee on Finance, which was developing the Minimum Foundation Program, but he kept up with it enough to
know that the success of the financial program would heavily
depend on what his subcommittee did as far as the administration of it. Dr. John Stockton, Director of the Bureau of Business
Research at The University of Texas, and responsible for constructing the Minimum Foundation School Program economic
index, said of Edgar:

> Dr. Edgar was the educational expert . . . He was always in
> the background and always supportive. He didn't pretend to be a
> statistician.[26]

The Finance Subcommittee's Minimum Foundation Program
would need strong unified state level leadership to succeed.
Edgar knew that the Legislature would never turn the financial program over to the administrative conditions with divided leadership which existed prior to Gilmer-Aikin. Edgar
comments on the direction his subcommittee took:

> I felt like there had to be a way found to bring all of these
> three state administrative elements together in some strong,
> nonpolitical type, professional type State Department of Educa-
> tion. That was the direction which I asked our subcommittee to go
> to look at. I thought the elements of such a unified set up would
> require whoever sets educational policy . . . to be responsible di-
> rectly to the people; and whoever administers that policy should
> be a professional type leader; and that the State Department of

Education itself should be a professional group of people. So from all of that we developed the idea of an elected board who would in turn appoint the state superintendent (or the Commissioner of Education, as it was called). The Commissioner of Education would be Executive Officer of the Board and would have the responsibilities for operating the State Department of Education. That was the recommendation we finally made to the full committee. It was accepted.[27]

The state structure which the School Administration Subcommittee recommended to the full committee was one that was already in existence in the local school districts. They recommended that the State Board be elected and that the members of the board appoint the State Commissioner. This plan at the state level was one people were already familiar with on the local level. Edgar's subcommittee recommended a nine member board, which was the number on the already established State Board. The board would be elected by specific districts which would be created by the Legislature. The Commissioner would be appointed by the State Board for a probationary period of three years and then be on indeterminate appointment.[28] In September of 1948 the Gilmer-Aikin Committee made a report to the people.[29] This report clearly showed the great amount of grass roots support the Gilmer-Aikin Committee had all over the State of Texas. Edgar and the Gilmer-Aikin Committee finished up their work in December of 1948. The Legislature came into session in January of 1949 and immediately began considering the proposals of the committee. Edgar's role in the passage of the Gilmer-Aikin Bills would be considerably less active than his role in the committee, but no less important.

THE PASSAGE OF THE GILMER-AIKIN LAWS

The period between January 1949 when the Legislature came into session and June 1949 when the Gilmer-Aikin Bills were signed into law was one of feverish activity to ensure passage of the bills.[30] Edgar remained in the background. Although he did not appear before any committee for giving testimony or for lobbying, he did make a few speeches around the state about the program and the legislation. Rae Files Still wrote about one panel discussion which Edgar was scheduled to attend but did not:

The first statewide protest against the Gilmer-Aikin Bills took the form of a panel discussion scheduled by Dr. Woods for the annual midwinter conference of the Texas Association of School Administrators on January 6, 1949, at Austin, Texas. The six speakers listed on the program for the discussion included two who favored the plan — Senator James E. Taylor and Dr. J.W. Edgar — and four who opposed it . . . Unfortunately, Dr. Edgar was ill, which left Senator Taylor as the only defender of the program.[31]

Edgar said of his illness:

That's the most fortunate illness I've ever had.[32]

Although he stayed in the background, Edgar did support the bills in his own way. Miss Waurine Walker, who worked on the Gilmer-Aikin Bills, spoke of Edgar's support of the bills:

Dr. Edgar was never one to get out and make a lot of speeches . . . Dr. Edgar, you might say, worked in the background helping to formulate and plan ideas which then would be brought to the public through other individuals . . . At that time the superintendents all went to Atlantic City for a big national meeting of superintendents throughout the United States. And they went by train. And on those trains, I remember that year there were little groups all up and down all the cars: the groups who were for [the Gilmer-Aikin Bills] and the groups who were against it. That year the whole train was nothing but a discussion group about the coming legislation. A great deal of the work was done at that time. And again, Dr. Edgar wasn't the one who went up and down the coaches. He was the one that they'd come back and say, "I think you better talk to so and so," Then [Edgar] would arrange and go up the coach, find whoever the individual was, and sit down. They'd get into a discussion. But he talked individually to superintendents. But left, shall we say, the organizing of the meeting and the platform speaking to others . . . It was a natural role with him.[33]

In addition to speaking to individuals, Edgar also indirectly got involved with the passage of the Gilmer-Aikin Bills in another way. In the Spring of 1949 he let Warren Hitt get involved in the deliberation. Hitt took a leave of absence from the Austin School District and went with the Texas State Teachers Association. He became very much involved in the legislative deliberation. L.P. Sturgeon, a member of the Executive Committee of the TSTA, recalls the hearings on the bills:

TSTA did not take a position of support for this new program until after the legislation was already in Austin and the bills had been introduced. I was on the Executive Committee at the time and we met in February. The Legislature had come to town the second Tuesday in January. At that meeting we took a position for the program. From that time forward we crusaded across the state in favor of it. We had many meetings of teachers in all sections of the state. We got citizens involved and we began to get support for the program. Now, we had division in our own rank . . . But the emphasis of leadership was in support of the program. By the time the bills reached the hearing stages, superintendents and teachers from all over Texas came in to testify in support. There was also a group who came in and testified against, and Mr. Woods handled that part of the opposition. But in 1949 after the February meeting, TSTA set up some gigantic meetings. I know I was in a meeting in San Antonio attended by more than five thousand people. There were both viewpoints represented there. But at the conclusion of the meeting, when different ones had spoken and explained, a vote was taken that overwhelmingly endorsed the program.[34]

Hitt worked inside of the TSTA to overcome the opposition to Gilmer-Aikin; his efforts were successful.

As the individual reports of the Administration, Finance, and Personnel Subcommittees of Gilmer-Aikin went through the Legislature, compromises with respect to Edgar's report and the other reports were made. Senate Bill 115, which created a nine member board, came under criticism. The members of the House of Representatives subjected it to rigorous debate. The Legislature did not want to create nine additional board districts and have to decide on an individual basis if each district was large enough to be represented or not. Consequently, the districts that were established for the election of the board members were the same as those already established districts for the election of congressmen. Since twenty-one congressional districts existed, a twenty-one member board was automatically created. Edgar comments on this board:

Well I think that was generally accepted, although some of us had some concern about such a large board. None of us had any experience working with that size board. Our reservations were minor. I think in the long run, it proved to be a strength to the board to have that large size, particularly covering the state with good representation.[35]

This change from proposal of a nine member board to passage of a twenty-one member board proved to be a good one.

Another change from the administrative plan proposed and the administrative plan passed was that the Senate would confirm the State Board's appointment of the Commissioner. The board would appoint the Commissioner for a four year term. This was not exactly what the school people wanted. Edgar spoke of this compromise:

> But again, I think it proved to be all right because if you don't have the confidence of the Senate, and you're Commissioner of Education, you might as well not be there. I never did have any trouble with confirmation. I was confirmed seven times by the Senate. It turned out to be a really good move. Perhaps better than our original recommendation.[36]

One of the amendments added to Senate Bill 116 was one which protected the Catholic schools. Senator Gus Strauss, a Catholic member of the Gilmer-Aikin Committee, wanted to ensure a smooth transition to Gilmer-Aikin for the Catholic schools. A special provision provided for a larger number of teachers for the 1948–1949 school year than for the following years to give the parochial schools a period of adjustment since the bill radically changed their teacher allotment.[37] No one objected to this amendment.

One amendment which Edgar did not agree with was the so called "Haskew Amendment." When Haskew joined the Gilmer-Aikin Committee and helped direct its work, strong opposition existed by Woods and his supporters to what he was doing. They charged that the idea of appointing a State Commissioner was created so that Haskew could be the Commissioner. Consequently, Woods' supporters pursuaded the House Committee to add an amendment to the Gilmer-Aikin Bills which stated that the Commissioner of Education had to be a resident of Texas for five years previous to his appointment.

One recommendation of the Gilmer-Aikin Committee concerning finance which was not accepted was that the per capita apportionment be defined as the number of children in an average day's attendance at school (Senate Bill 116). The larger school districts had depended on a set amount of money based on the school census, the number of school children from six to seventeen that lives in that school district, and were leery of the average daily attendance funding. The Rio Grande Valley schools were also opposed to average daily attendance funding because they had a large Mexican-American population, many of whom did not enroll in school; a vast gap existed between their census and their attendance, and they could see that their school districts would lose money. Many districts that depended on the funding of their large census count did not have faith in the equalizing provisions of the Minimum Foundation School Program to make up the difference between census count and average daily attendance. Thus, the definition of per capita based on average daily attendance was abandoned in the Legislature. The per capita apportionment remained based on census. (This was later changed in favor of the average daily attendance plan after confidence in the equalizing powers of the Minimum Foundation Program grew.)

Edgar worked to influence members of the Gilmer-Aikin Committee to have two other provisions added to the bills. The first was a minimum teacher salary of twenty-four hundred dollars a year based on a ten month school year for teachers and a full one hundred and eighty days of instruction for students. This plan was originated in Austin by Edgar and did pass the Legislature. Edgar felt this idea paid off in terms of public relations with the business and industrial interests because they would be more apt to agree with the upcoming expenditures for the implementation of the Gilmer-Aikin Bills. Secondly, Edgar wanted the financial plans that the State allocated to the school districts each year to be continuous so that local administrators would know years ahead of time how much money they could count on from the State. One of the bills (Senate Bill 117) provided that whatever the cost of the Foundation Program, it would have priority in the General Fund of the State each year. If the Dedicated Education Per Capita Fund of the State did not provide enough money, then the Foundation Fund would have the first priority on whatever money was in the General Fund. That established the continuity of financing in the local school district and the opportunity for the school boards to plan for the schools years in advance. Edgar was satisfied on both points:

At last the state had said to the local school districts, "Here's a plan. Now you develop your programming, your school building needs, and everything on the basis of this plan. You can depend on it, year in and year out. There may be some modifications, but basically this is what the state is going to do. You know how much now, five years from now, that this is going to be." This was the main thing that was needed by the school districts: some kind of a stabilizing base for financing that they could use for a long range development.[38]

The Gilmer-Aikin Laws were proposed in the form of three senate bills — Senate Bills 115, 116, and 117.[39] All three bills passed both houses of the Legislature by April 28, 1949. From there they went to a Conference Committee to work out compromises on the objectionable amendments. Governor Jester signed Senate Bill 115 on June 1, 1949. He signed Senate Bills 116 and 117 on June 8, 1949. The Minimum Foundation Plan became effective as soon as Senate Bill 116 was signed. The State Auditor, C.H. Caveness, began employing people immediately because the Foundation School Program was to go into effect in September of 1949. This was the first of the bills that would put Woods out of a job to which he had been elected every two years since 1932.

EDGAR AND DR. L.A. WOODS

Dr. Littleton A. Woods was born in Newton County in East Texas, the son of a preacher. He taught school in that part of Texas and in 1919 received his B.A. from Baylor University. In 1932 Woods campaigned all over the state for the office of Superintendent of Public Instruction; he was elected and would serve as State Superintendent until 1950 when Edgar replaced him. Up until this time when Woods started campaigning, the office of State Superintendent was considered nonpolitical.[40] Over the years Woods built up a reputation as a good educator; however, he had lost favor with some school people because of the political nature of his job: he had to run for office every two years. They began to feel he was more concerned with his politics than his job. Mr. E.L. Galyean, one of Woods' deputy superintendents for Fort Worth and Denton, describes Woods:

> Dr. Woods made a great contribution to education. Particularly rural education. He is more or less the father of rural aid which provided certain funds for the smaller and rural schools . . . Originally there was practically no funds except the per capita

funds and local taxes to run the schools. Dr. Woods sponsored the plan to provide legislation appropriation in addition to the per capita to be used to help the smaller rural schools that did not have the tax wealth. They didn't have a base upon which to collect much taxes. So they needed state aid and that was his program. And it was a great program for the rural schools. At that time there were a lot of those rural schools.[41]

Edgar expressed his opinion of Woods:

The present superintendent, Dr. L.A. Woods, he was a good educator and a good leader, and he did some very fine things educationally. He also had to run for office every two years. He had to keep up his political appartus if he was going to stay in office.[42]

Dr. Dana Williams, who taught in East Texas, expressed an opinion of Woods which reflects the political nature of his job:

I started teaching school in the rural schools of East Texas in 1935. I remember the big event of the year was the time that the so called Deputy State Superintendent would come visit with me because we depended rather heavily in this little two teacher school on something called rural aid . . . They had broad authority to allocate rural aid funds to the schools. I presume they had a limit but they could either give you whatever you needed to carry you through the year or they could give you less. And one of the things that was good for you was to stay in the know with the deputy superintendent.

Dr. L.A. Woods grew up in the Piney Woods of East Texas . . . We always knew Dr. Woods as a personable sort of fellow. I always thought of him as a fair sort of person. Yet all during the latter years of his administration, there was strong tones of unfairness in the selection of textbooks. Basically through the people who served on the State Board of Education . . . One of the problems with managing schools in those days was that we had an elected State Superintendent and the Governor appointed the State Board members . . . And the board members had very little to do with making policy . . . If they told the man in office to do something, he didn't have to do it . . . [Woods] did his job well. He had some strong people around him . . . There was always these political overtones. Woods was a great politician. He got out ánd campaigned heavily. It was hard to beat him. He had a good name with the electorate and he met people well. And he was always swept into office . . . They would never vote L.A. Woods out of office.[43]

When the Gilmer-Aikin Bills were proposed, Woods was against Senate Bill 115 which would mean an end to his job.

He actively fought the bill around the state and in front of the Legislature. Whether or not Woods could have been the first State Commissioner of Education had he supported the bill is open to debate. L.P. Sturgeon, who ran the Minimum Foundation Program, felt Woods could have gotten the job had he supported the bills:

> Dr. Woods had a good political machine across the state. Every State Superintendent of Education built up a machine as do other politicians. And he had very good friends. Dr. Woods made major contributions to the improvement of Texas education . . . The record shows that he was the first to start consolidation . . . The state owes him a great debt of gratitude for his leadership and ability. But for some reason he was just opposed to change. He was a man of strong conviction. He took a position and he did not change . . . It's fairly well known that Mr. Woods could have been the first Commissioner of Education had he not so bitterly opposed the new program. Although perhaps not recorded, there were visits made to Mr. Woods and legislative leaders did offer to recommend that he be the first Commissioner of Education. This would have been done by the newly elected board, but I believe the board would have gone along with the idea. So it was really the obstacles that were set up because of the battle that was fought, and the position that Dr. Woods took of complete opposition and nonacceptance of any of the ideas that were thrown in.[44]

Dana Williams did not think Woods would have gotten the job:

> That was discussed that maybe he might have been the Commissioner but I doubt it because I happened to be one of the young superintendents at that time and was sort of in the know on what the general feeling was. There was a general feeling that it was time to make a change. However, Dr. Woods did fight hard. I don't believe he could have been Commissioner at all. That's just my feeling.[45]

Edgar agreed with Williams concerning Woods' chance to be the first Commissioner of Education:

> I think he would have been able to get the support of the majority of the educational people. But through the process of the Legislature considering the program, he had become politically unacceptable (this is my opinion), particularly to the Senate who had to confirm him. For that reason, I think, educationally, yes, he would have been accepted. Politically, I doubt that he would have been.[46]

Another factor working against Woods getting the job of commissioner was that he was sixty-five years of age in 1949. Woods continued his opposition and fought against Senate Bill 115 until it became law.

Edgar and Woods were both thought of as good educators. As individuals, they were strikingly different. Woods was more outgoing than Edgar but had less professional training. Woods was rurally oriented while Edgar had experience in both rural and urban settings. Senator Ralph Yarborough, who worked at the Education Desk of the State Attorney General's Office from 1932–1938 and represented El Paso in a court case against the Texas Education Agency (TEA) in 1950 and 1952, compared Woods and Edgar:

> Dr. Woods ran and was elected. I am under the impression that most of the school men opposed him in that election. The official hierarchy had opposed him. He was very popular and he was very accommodating to the school superintendents. He didn't try to make waves. Dr. Woods was not himself a person who would defeat himself by irrational acts. He was slow to move, slow to act, slow to do anything. Edgar was a faster acting man, a more dynamic administrator. Woods was, you might say, of the old school. He'd remind you more of a country school superintendent. Edgar would remind you more of an urban man . . . Edgar was more of a modern administrator, more of a modern administrative type than Woods. Woods was more of a rural political type. I'd say [Edgar] would fit in with a group of city school superintendents a lot better than Dr. Woods. Texas was becoming more urban all the time. Edgar was more of a business administrative type, more than Woods who was more like a rural school superintendent.[47]

Senator Ottis Lock knew Woods and Edgar well. He was once offered the job of Deputy State Superintendent by Woods and he was on the Gilmer-Aikin Committee with Edgar. He thought highly of both men. He compared them:

> Neither one of them would be classified as glad-handed politicians. They had that in common. But as far as foresight, as far as training and experience that made foresight and vision possible, J.W. had the advantage over Dr. Woods and this is no personal criticism toward Dr. Woods.[48]

After the Gilmer-Aikin Laws were finally passed, Edgar replaced Woods as head of education in Texas. Woods had

served education in Texas for eighteen years, from 1932 to
1950. Edgar, in his turn, would serve education in Texas for an
even longer term of twenty-four years, from 1950 to 1974. Both
men served education in Texas in their own admirable way,
each way being different. The Texas Education Agency, after
the time of Woods, was in many ways different from the educational machinery that Woods was in charge of. Edgar com-
pares and contrasts the responsibilities of Woods' job of State
Superintendent of Public Instruction with his own job of State
Commissioner of Education in the following chart.

Activity	Responsibility of Superintendent	Responsibility of Commissioneer
Reelection Maintenance[1]	• Full-time	• None
Textbooks[2]	• Recommend subjects requiring textbooks.	• Develop and recommend annual Textbook Proclamation • Appoint State Textbook Committee • Hold hearings • Remove Textbooks from Committee List • Recommend adoption to State Board of Education
Executive Offices	• None	• State Board of Education • State Board for Vocational Education
Field Offices	• 24 Deputy Superintendents	• 12 Vocational Education Offices • 12 Vocational Rehabilitation Offices • 20 Regional Service Centers • 6 Deaf Day School Regions
State Financing	• Distribute Rural Aid under oversight of the Joint Legislative Committee	• Administer Foundation Program • Estimate Annual Budget • Determine Local Funds Assignment in each school district • Set qualifications for local personnel • Guarantee integrity of local attendance and personnel records
Federal Funds	• None	• Administer distribution of 250 million dollars annually monitor, evaluate, and audit local programs

Appeals[3]	• Same	• Same
Personnel (State Staff)	• Employ at his discretion	• Employ according to: – State Classification System – Federal Affirmation Action Plan
Certification	• Appoint Board of Examiners • Issue Teacher Certificates • Cancel Teacher Certificates	• Same • Same • Same • Determine Standards for Professional Certificates
Teacher Education	• Examine colleges under graduate programs leading to certificates	• Approve colleges and universities: – BA & MA degrees for State Salary Schedule – Establish standards for college undergraduate provisional certificate programs – Establish standards for graduate professional certificate programs – Monitor college programs approved for certification
Accreditation[4]	• Set requirements for high school graduation • Set and monitor standards	• Same • Same • Apply penalties under law and court rulings
Statistics and Reports	• General	• General • Gilmer-Aikin Laws and federal requirements increased the number and volume
Auditing Local School Districts	• Occasional audit for discrepancy	• Regular and systematic audits of all functions involving state or federal funds — attendance, personnel, school lunch, bus routes, integration, etc.
Census[5]	• Annual Census of Scholastic Population	• Annual Census of Scholastic Average Daily Attendance • Review annually 20,000 interdistrict pupil transfers.
General Curriculum	• Same	• Same

Special Education	• In 1945–1946 administer first state supported program — 25 districts Budget: $99,349	• Administer comprehensive program — 4 year olds through high school
		• Supervise Texas Schools for the Deaf and for the Blind;
		  – Appoint superintendents
		• Administer Regional Day Schools for Deaf
		  – Appoint State Director
		  – Appoint 6 Regional Superintendents

Vocational Technical Education	• None	• Administer High School and Junior College Programs Sponsor Vocational High ' • Sponsor Vocational High School and Adult Clubs Training of Teachers • Supervise high school programs
Adult and Veterans Education	• None	• Administer state and federally supported programs • In-Service Training of Teachers
Proprietary Schools	• None	• Develop and apply standards • License schools • Close schools if failing to meet standards
Vocational Rehabilitation	• None	• Administer state program • Determine disability of veteran
Bilingual Education	• None	• Administer state and federally supported programs • In-Service Training of Teachers
Migratory Education	• None	• Administer state and federally supported programs • In-Service Training of Teachers
Regional Education Service Centers	• None	• Approve budgets • Approve Programs • In-Service Training of Personnel • Confirm appointments of regional directors
Guidance Services	• None	• In-Service Training of Counselors and Visiting Teachers • Set qualifications of Counselors, Visiting Teachers, and Supervisors

| Integration | • Administer Delgado Decision | • Same
• Monitor all programs of local districts including extracurricular activities to determine racial balance of pupils and teachers.
• Review interdistrict pupil transfers for racial balance.
• Withhold state and federal funds and deny accreditation to districts for cause.
• Conduct workshops and other training for local personnel. |

[1]Reelection was the responsibility of each board member in his own district.
[2]The Proclamation included the calendar, all legal requirements, and subject matter descriptions of each book to be adopted.
[3]The Gilmer-Aikin Laws provided that any person not satisfied with the action of the local school board could appeal. This broadened and increased the number of appeals.
[4]Commissioner changed accreditation from approval of subjects by campus to overall system wide approval.
The Gilmer-Aikin Laws made accreditation a legal function.
[5]Transfers were not allowed if unlawful or they contributed to segregation.

From this chart of comparisons and contrasts of various responsibilities of each job, it is obvious that the new system of leadership after the Gilmer-Aikin Laws was indeed different and did represent actual change from the time of Woods. This change would become obvious through the implementation of the Gilmer-Aikin Laws which was to begin in June of 1949. Edgar would be heavily involved in the implementation of the bills during his first term in office as the first State Commissioner of Education.

CONCLUSION

Edgar's involvement and influence on the proposal and passage of the Gilmer-Aikin Bills was significant. Although he personally had no aspirations to be anything but a school superintendent, his involvement in the bills demonstrated his concern for having the best possible educational system in Texas. His actions at the time demonstrated this concern, but they also led him elsewhere: they set him up as a candidate for the office of State Commissioner. Several aspects of Edgar's role in the proposal and passage of the Gilmer-Aikin laws illuminate his skill and demonstrate his gradual movement toward the Commissionership: (1) the main thrust of Edgar's work on the bills concerned the job of State Commissioner and the process by which the selection would be made; (2) Edgar ex-

erted a great amount of influence over the members of the Gilmer-Aikin Committee; (3) Edgar's passive support of the passage of the bills by the Legislature; (4) Edgar had indirect
influence on the task of gaining support for Gilmer-Aikin from
the people of Texas; and finally, (5) Woods and the sentiment
against the organization of the Department of Public Instruction worked in Edgar's favor.

The first aspect of Edgar's role in Gilmer-Aikin which
demonstrated his gradual movement toward the Commissionership was that a good part of his work on the Gilmer-Aikin
Committee concerned the job of State Commissioner and how
that selection would be made. Edgar's work in the Texas Association of School Administrators before the organization of the
Gilmer-Aikin Committee, his work on the Gilmer-Aikin Committee, and controversy during the passage of the bills re-
volved around the job of State Commissioner. Edgar was
Chairman of the Policies Committee of the TASA, the organization that first proposed that the system of educational leadership in Texas needed to be changed. In the Gilmer-Aikin
Committee, Edgar was the Co-Chairman of the Subcommittee
on School Administration. This subcommittee proposed a reorganization of the state educational leadership that would
be based on the local school board system. During the passage
of the Gilmer-Aikin Laws the subject of the elected board and
appointed commissioner became greatly controversial. Edgar
talked of this issue:

> Following up the recommendation by the full committee of
> our reports on the elected board and appointed commissioner, this
> became the hottest issue in the Legislature. Dr. Woods and some
> of his Equalization Aid school superintendents fought it to the
> bitter end.[49]

The end result of this work during the Gilmer-Aikin process
was that, unknowingly, Edgar was working on the creation
and organization of his future job.

Another aspect of Edgar's role in Gilmer-Aikin which
demonstrated his skill was the way in which he exerted influence over the other members of the Gilmer-Aikin Committee.
This was the result of his fine work at Orange and the work he
was currently doing in Austin. He was used to coming up with
solutions to problems. Edgar was the one who went to Senator

Taylor and suggested to him that they hire Dr. Haskew since, at this time, the committee was not showing much progress. Haskew was hired at Edgar's suggestion, and he made a tremendous contribution to the whole process. Senator Taylor spoke of Haskew regarding the idea for the use of per capita based on average daily attendance:

> I think I asked Haskew, "How would you do that?" He said, "Well, if you put it on average daily attendance, if you allocated the money on average daily attendance,then if they didn't get the kids in school, they wouldn't get the money." I said, "That's what we're looking for" . . . We spent a lot of time together. He gave me a Ph.D. in public education during the eighteen months that the committee was meeting.[50]

Dr. Haskew was responsible for the Committee employing Dr. Edgar Morphitt who had worked on a similar plan in Florida. Edgar was responsible for the new salary schedule and the ten month or one hundred and eighty day school year. In addition, he influenced other members of the committee to help to create Senate Bill 117 which ensured the funding of the Foundation Program. Edgar's effectiveness in helping to direct the Gilmer-Aikin Committee is noteworthy.

A third aspect of Edgar's role in Gilmer-Aikin which demonstrated how adept he was in administration was his passive support of the bills behind the scenes. Rae Files Still wrote of Edgar:

> He was quiet, easy-going — never threw his weight around. He did not take center stage but worked effectively behind the scenes.[51]

First, Edgar sent Warren Hitt to join the TSTA to work for the legislation of the bills. Edgar, in a sense, worked through Hitt in the Legislature for the passage of the bills. They were a great team and Hitt got along with and worked well with the Legislature. Edgar made some speeches in favor of the bills, but he never got caught up in the open conflict over the bills. The way in which Edgar supported the bills but did not get involved in the heat of the debate very much exemplified his skill.

Similarly, in another aspect, Edgar worked indirectly through other citizens to get the citizens of Texas interested in the Gilmer-Aikin Bills. Again, he worked through Haskew and

Hitt. Dr. Haskew knew how to reach the people, as Edgar describes:

> The mechanisms of handling the committee . . . the idea of that was generally Dr. Haskew's idea. We had Dr. Morphitt who came in as a part time consultant from Florida and he'd had previous experience with the Foundation Programs. I think he endorsed the idea that we simply had to get the matter before the local communities. But I think the idea originally was Dr. Haskew's and the person who had to handle it was H.A. Moore who was Executive Director of the Committee.[52]

Edgar sent Mr. Hitt to TSTA not only to work with the Legislature but also to help TSTA with their campaign to support the Gilmer-Aikin Bills. Edgar also used his influence with the school people to gain their support. Whenever possible, on an individual level, he spoke to school people telling them he was in favor of the bills. Thus, Edgar gained the support of the school people and they helped build support locally for the bills. This again demonstrated Edgar's concern to have the best schools possible with the consent of the citizens of Texas.

The growing opposition in the Legislature against Woods and the Department of Public Instruction centered around the political nature of its structure and also Woods' opposition to the Gilmer-Aikin Bills. First, Woods had been elected so many times that there was a feeling that he could not be defeated no matter who ran against him. Second, his system of Deputy Superintendents was felt to be too political. Finally, there was sentiment that Woods might have been offered the job of Commissioner but this ended when he opposed the appointment of the Commissioner (Senate Bill 115). Senator James E. Taylor expresses this view:

> [Woods] testified before the [Gilmer-Aikin] Committee. Some of his people testified before the committee. He had no enthusiasm for what we were trying to do. He liked the system just like it was. He had these deputies, deputy superintendents, that were out all over the state. They spent ninety-five percent of their time being sure he got reelected. It was a good system for him and he didn't want any change in it.[53]

Miss Waurine Walker, who taught in Waco and worked for the Gilmer-Aikin Laws, expresses a similar viewpoint:

> [Woods] was satisfied with what you might call a control

through deputies. And you see he was very satisfied with this because they were all hand picked . . . It was that, that brought about the resentment to him because superintendents and teachers and colleges were all concerned about the status quo of education.[54]

Although these views show resentment toward Woods and his system of Deputies, there were other important forces which were moving toward a change in the educational system of Texas. Texas was becoming more of an urban state and there was a movement toward strong state control of education. These forces were as important, or more so, than the forces acting against Woods. In many respects, Woods was more a victim of change than anything else. Governor Preston Smith, a member of the House at the time of Gilmer-Aikin, speaks about Woods and Gilmer-Aikin:

> I voted against the [bill] that abolished the state superintendent post because I have never supported legislation that would take anything away from the people . . . I didn't think you'd want a central agency in the state telling the local school boards what they can or can't do . . . And the House, they drug their feet pretty much on the abolishment of Superintendent Woods' office. They thought that it was a deliberate effort to remove him from office, but I never really considered that.[55]

Edgar's role in helping to enact the change from the old system of political election and deputy superintendents to the new system of elected board and appointed commissioner is quite evident and perhaps demonstrates a gradual move on his part toward the Commissionership.

Edgar's skill in the many different aspects of Gilmer-Aikin is certainly admirable. His role in the proposal and passage of the bills was significant. The role he would play in the actual implementation of the Gilmer-Aikin Laws, however, would be even more meaningful. As the first Commissioner of Education in Texas, Edgar would become the heart of educational policy.

4

The Implementation of the Gilmer-Aikin Laws, 1949–1974

The implementation of the Gilmer-Aikin Laws began immediately after Governor Beauford H. Jester signed Senate Bills 115, 116, and 117 into law on May 1, 1949, and June 8, 1949. The Minimum Foundation School Program was established immediately and was to go into effect for September of 1949. The other parts of the laws would not become effective until the electorate elected a State Board and the State Board appointed a Commissioner, who would then be confirmed by the Senate. Edgar's role in the implementation of the Gilmer-Aikin Laws was vital since his tenure as First State Commissioner of Education was a major part of the implementation process. His role in the implementation of the Gilmer-Aikin Laws is covered in five sections:

   1. *Edgar During the Interim*. Edgar assumed a passive role during the interim period, from June 1949 to March 1950, when the Minimum Foundation School Program was set up. Also during this interim period Edgar was involved in the political aftermath of the federal court ruling in the *Delgado* decision.

   2. *Edgar and the State Board*. Edgar's role in the election of the First State Board of Education was significant. The First State Board's selection of Edgar for Commissioner was also significant. Edgar's relationship to the Board while he was Commissioner is vital in order to understand his role in the implementation of the Gilmer-Aikin Laws. Edgar's

philosophy of education as it applied to his work with the State Board is also important to the understanding of the way the new laws worked.

3. *Edgar's First Term as Commissioner.* Edgar's first four year term as Commissioner, from 1950 to 1953, is examined in order to perceive how he began his work as Commissioner.

4. *Edgar's Long Term Work as Commissioner.* Edgar's long term work as Commissioner is examined in terms of two programs which occupied his time on and off throughout his tenure as Commissioner. The first is the selection of textbooks and the second is the appeals process. These two examples present an illustrative profile of how Edgar worked as Commissioner.

5. *Edgar's Last Years as Commissioner.* Edgar's last years as Commissioner, from 1970–1974, are examined to further illuminate his performance and achievement in this important state educational office and to tell the story of how he retired.

These five sections, when examined, provide a fundamental understanding of the impact Edgar had on the implementation of the Gilmer-Aikin Laws. The first action toward implementation came in June 1949 when the Gilmer-Aikin Bills became law. Edgar took a passive role in this action.

THE INTERIM PERIOD, JUNE 1949–MARCH 1950

In June of 1949 Edgar was still the Superintendent of Schools in Austin. At this time he had given Warren Hitt a leave of absence to go to work with the Minimum Foundation Program Division of the State Auditor's Office. Also during this time Edgar became involved in the political aftermath of the *Delgado* decision, a decision which involved the integration of Hispanics into the Anglo schools.

Implementation Of The
Minimum Foundation Program

In June 1949, the Legislature placed the development of the Minimum Foundation Program in the hands of the State Auditor, Mr. C.H. Caveness. Mr. Caveness appointed L.P. Sturgeon as the Interim Director of the program. He also appointed others who were familiar with the problem.[1] One of the others was Hitt. Edgar gave Hitt another leave of absence from

his job as Director of Personnel and Research in the Austin
School District to become Assistant Director of the Foundation
Program under Sturgeon. Here again was another example of
how Edgar had Hitt work for him. Sturgeon says of Edgar and
Hitt:

> Mr. Edgar had become superintendent of schools in Austin
> at the time the Foundation Program was improved by the Legis-
> lature. He had no great involvement with the setting up of the
> program but he did advise with me and Warren Hitt from time to
> time as we requested his assistance. And he gave Mr. Hitt a leave
> of absence to serve as my first Assistant.[2]

Mr. Caveness employed Dr. Bascom Hayes as a Control Officer to work with Sturgeon and Hitt. Mrs. Hayes speaks of her
husband's work on setting up the Foundation Program with
Hitt:

> It was in 1949 that he [Bascom Hayes] came up and stayed
> that entire year, 1949–1950. He and L.P. Sturgeon stayed at the
> Driskill Hotel, I remember, setting up the Gilmer-Aikin Laws.
> Frank Hubert and Bill Harrison, Warren Hitt, Bascom, and
> Sturgeon, I believe, were the ones.[3]

Edgar also recalls the administrative setup during the interim:

> The State Auditor employed a school superintendent from
> Northeast Texas by the name of L.P. Sturgeon, who was an excel-
> lent choice. And, again, I gave Warren Hitt a leave of absence and
> he became Mr. Sturgeon's Assistant. They began in June as soon
> as the legislation was passed . . . to get [the program] ready to go
> into the schools in September. And they did a yeoman-type job. Of
> course they enlisted a lot of volunteers who came in and helped
> develop the preliminary policies and rules and regulations that
> needed to be established for the operation of the Foundation
> School Program the first year.[4]

The Minimum Foundation Program was developed at a
furious pace in order to get ready for the fall 1949 school year
when the plan was to actually begin. L.P. Sturgeon directed
the program with Edgar in the background. The administrators involved readied the program and put it into effect for September. This involved a tremendous amount of work and effort
in a period of less than ninety days. While all this work was
shaping up during the interim, Edgar became involved with
the repercussions of the *Delgado* decision.

Edgar, Woods, And The
Delgado Decision

Separate schools for Mexican-Americans had been common in parts of rural and urban Texas since the first part of the twentieth century. This was in part the result of separate residences and the hostile attitude of Anglos toward Mexican-Americans.[5] In 1947 Mexican-American parents in Bastrop, Caldwell, and Travis Counties filed a class action suit in Federal District Court to abolish separate schools for their children. Gus Garcia was the lawyer who handled their case. On June 15, 1948, the court declared that separate schools for Mexican-Americans was a violation of the Fourteenth Amendment. Separation of Anglo and Hispanic students was approved only for the first grade and only then after the administration of tests. September of 1949 was given as the deadline to construct or reconstruct schools which would abolish segregation.[6]

The court specifically addressed Woods in its ruling:

> The defendant, L.A. Woods, as State Superintendent of Public Instruction, is hereby permanently restrained and enjoined from in any manner, directly or indirectly,, participating in the custom, usage, or practice of segregating pupils of Mexican or other Latin American descent in separate schools or classes.[7]

Woods immediately moved to implement the injunction. In July of 1948 he issued a set of regulations stating that segregation by race or descent had never been legal in Texas and had been reaffirmed in the *Delgado* decision by a federal court. Woods sent his assistant, Mr. Trimble, to investigate the Del Rio Schools along the Texas/Mexico border. Trimble found that the Del Rio School District was in violation of *Delgado*. Consequently, Woods removed the Del Rio Schools from the accredited list of schools in February of 1948.[8] In July of 1949, however, the old State Board of Education reversed Woods' decision concerning the Del Rio Schools and put the schools back on the accredited list.[9] The Hispanic groups were disconcerted by this and they continued to seek an end to segregation of Mexican-American students in schools. When Edgar was chosen Commissioner in February of 1949, these Hispanic groups

began coming to his office in the Austin School District where
he still remained Superintendent of Schools prior to taking office as Commissioner. Edgar relates the commotion this
caused.

> I had planned to stay in Austin until I was confirmed so
> that the Austin Board could set up my successor. But what hap-
> pened was that as soon as my appointment hit the papers, people
> from all over the state began to come to the Austin office to see
> me about state business. There I was trying to operate the Austin
> Superintendency ... One of the main groups was the LULAC
> [League of United Latin American Citizens] group ... about the
> *Delgado* decision. They wanted to know what I was going to do
> with it. So finally, I just said to the Chairman of the Board, "I'm
> causing more problems in Austin than I am good" ... I resigned.[10]

When Edgar became Commissioner of Education, Gus
Garcia, the attorney who handled *Delgado*, and Dr. George
Sanchez, Professor of Sociology at The University of Texas, discussed the *Delgado* decision at Edgar's first official meeting
with the State Board of Education. The State Board entered
the findings of the court in the *Delgado* case and Woods' regulations after the decision into the minutes of a twelve page report on the segregation problem. In seeing that the court ruling and Woods' ruling were entered into the minutes of the
State Board, Edgar showed good faith on his promise to LU-
LAC that he would take the problem up with the Board. LU-
LAC wanted Woods' ruling accepted, and the Board did accept
it. Hispanic leaders, however, continued to complain about segregation.[11] Edgar received twenty-two complaints related to
segregation in nine months.

Though Hispanic leaders felt the state officials, including
Edgar, were uncooperative, they still respected Edgar.[12] Hector
Garcia, founder of the American G.I. Forum, an organization
to improve education for Hispanics and fight discrimination,
speaks favorably of Edgar.

> I would say [concerning] my feelings and my knowledge and
> my acquaintance and discussions and meetings and petitions to
> Dr. Edgar that he was a fair man. I think a man who at that time
> in Texas would be a rarity because the system, then almost com-
> pletely, and to a lesser degree now, denied us equal education fa-
> cilities under a statewide, totally dual segregation, inferior school
> system for the Mexicans ... He was a very likeable person, very

honest, straight forward . . . He was interested in education for everyone. I think if Dr. Edgar could have had his way, he would have abolished all segregation of the Mexican Americans . . . As far as we were concerned a very fair man.[13]

Edgar speaks favorably about Hector Garcia and Gus Garcia:

I knew Hector, and I knew one of his sisters, at least one of his sisters. Hector was sort of a bombastic kind of a person, but I always thought he was pretty solid. Another man, I think he's dead now, Gus Garcia from San Antonio . . . He used to visit me constantly . . . We had a pretty good relationship. I think I didn't move fast enough for him. He kind of got off me before he died, but for a while there, we worked very well together. One time I was even invited to address the LULAC convention.[14]

Both Edgar and Woods were involved with the *Delgado* case. Weinberg writes that Woods' departure from office as the result of reorganization was hastened by his effort to enforce *Delgado*.[15] No evidence exists to support this contention. E.L. Galyean, one of Woods' deputies, felt that there was no evidence to support this statement.[16] Edgar said of Weinberg's contentions:

I wasn't aware that [*Delgado*] had any influence on it.[17]

The *Delgado* case had an impact on both Woods and Edgar. With respect to Edgar, it began in the interim period and was among the first problems he had to address with the State Board of Education.

EDGAR AND THE STATE BOARD OF EDUCATION

Four aspects of Edgar's relationship with the State Board of Education are important to the understanding of how these two entities functioned together: (1) the election of the Board; (2) the Board's selection of Edgar as Commissioner; (3) Edgar's philosophy of education as it related to the Board; and (4) Edgar's work with the Board. These four perspectives contribute to an understanding of the State Board and of how Edgar's ability to work with boards peaked with his selection as Commissioner of Education.

The Election Of The First Elected
State Board Of Education, November, 1949

After passage of Senate Bill 115, some school people, as well as lay people, were concerned about who would be chosen to be on the first State Board of Education. Sturgeon writes:

> During the debate on the bill, opponents had stressed repeatedly that qualified, capable, and professional people would not be willing to give the necessary time to serve on a Board for which no remuneration was provided, that such citizens of high repute and recognized standing would not offer themselves for a political office and would not engage in a political campaign; and it was repeatedly argued that the Board would be so large and cumbersome that it could not operate effectively regardless of the quality of its membership.[18]

In October of 1949 Ottis Lock wrote a paper entitled, "The New State Board of Education, Fifty Questions and Fifty Answers," designed to help the electorate in the election of the Board.[19] The electorate had no problem in finding good people to run and in choosing them. Sturgeon writes,

> The school people of Texas were determined that there should be available high quality persons for service on the State Board; consequently, in each of the twenty-one districts, committees were selected by mutual agreement, and outstanding professional and business leaders were contacted and asked to make themselves available for election to the State Board. The response was excellent, and without exception an outstanding citizen did present himself as a candidate for the State Board of Education. With no opposition in most instances and with only token opposition in two or three districts, twenty-one outstanding Texans were elected by the vote of their fellow citizens to serve on the State Board of Education.[20]

The newly elected State Board was called to order by Secretary of State Ben Ramsey in the Senate Chamber on November 19, 1949. Edgar speaks about the quality of the Board.

> More should be said about the quality of the first elected State Board . . . They had all been picked carefully by school people to run for office. Most of them had served successfully on local school boards and understood the school operation. So they consti-

tuted a prestigious group with great public confidence.[21]

Dana Williams, who was at the time a school leader in the East Texas area, writes of the selection process in his area:

> The school administrators of Texas accepted the responsibility of identifying, contacting, and urging outstanding citizens in each of the congressional districts to offer themselves for election to the new State Board. Our first State Board was really a "blue ribbon" group, as I am sure you have already determined. I was one of the leaders in the East Texas area who convened a group of superintendents at Longview, where we decided we needed a person with class, dignity, and if possible, some school board experience. Judge Tom Ramey of Tyler was invited to a luncheon and received the word, with some shock, that he was our choice to serve on the State Board. He agreed to run and was overwhelmingly selected. He became the first Vice-Chairman of the Board.[22]

At the first meeting of the State Board of Education, Robert B. Anderson was chosen Chairman of the Board, Tom Ramey was chosen Vice-Chairman, and Mrs. Jane Wesmendorf was chosen Secretary of the board. Edgar talks about the qualifications of the board members:

> The Chairman, R.B. Anderson of Vernon, was general manager of the Waggoner Estate . . . [in] ranching, oil, and diversified business. He was very able and was held in high esteem by all elements of the public, including the legislature. Much of the initial success of that board was due to his leadership. The Vice-Chairman, Thomas B. Ramey of Tyler, headed an outstanding law firm and had devoted many years of strong leadership to Tyler schools and junior college. Mrs. Jane Wesmendorf of Richmond was Secretary. She was highly respected and was past president of the Texas Congress of Parents and Teachers. Paul Bolton was a well known journalist. He was News Director for KTBC and so on with other board members.[23]

Once the task of actually electing a State Board was completed, the Board convened its first meeting. At the meeting they began to discuss the process by which they would elect a State Commissioner of Education.

Appointment By The
First State Board Of Education

Edgar did not want to be Commissioner of Education. He simply wanted to be a school superintendent. He felt that his work on the Gilmer-Aikin Committee would automatically restrict him from being selected Commissioner. Edgar relates this situation:

> From the Austin Congressional District Ten we had elected Paul Bolton . . . He was our State Board of Education member. So Paul said to me, "The Board would like to look at your credentials." And I said, "Well, Paul, I'm really not interested." . . . I still wanted to be a school superintendent. I had never veered from that ambition. I felt like if I got away from the superintendency, even for a brief term, that I'd begin to lose my position, knowledge, and understanding of the superintendency. And that would not be the thing to do. Secondly, I had been a member of the committee. I felt like I shouldn't participate in the awards.[24]

Edgar wanted to be a superintendent even after he was elected Commissioner. Paul Mathews, a State Board member, writes this account:

> Dr. Edgar and I were very close personal friends and he confided in me on several occasions. I remember Houston I.S.D. tried to employ him at a much higher salary than our pay grade permitted. He came to Greenville and discussed the idea with me. I told him the offer sounded great, but the occupational hazard was very high.[25]

Although Edgar did not want to be Commissioner, he was very much concerned that the right kind of professional person should be chosen as Commissioner. Since the Board's search for a Commissioner was dragging on and since no one single person emerged as the "right man" for the job, Edgar finally agreed to be considered for the job. Edgar relates his feelings:

> I had a very, very strong feeling that the Board should choose the right person. In my mind that right person should be a school superintendent with good strong experience and strong ability for professional type leadership. As the days went by the Board didn't settle on anyone, no school superintendent really emerged to be drafted, so to speak. I began to get concerned because I wanted to see the plan work. I thought the key to it was

the person who was Commissioner. The Board began to talk with college administrators and also as it stayed open, more political pressure began to develop . . . Well to make a long story short, I finally said to Paul Bolton, "Okay, I'll submit my credentials." [26]

On November 29, 1950, the State Board met and formed a committee to search for a Commissioner. The committee was made up of Mr. Cecil Morgan, Mrs. Wessendorf, Mr. Dick Bivins, Mr. Emerson Stone, and Dr. W.W. Jackson.[27] The committee considered all possible candidates and narrowed the selection down to approximately ten names. Edgar was one of the ten. Paul Bolton[28] talks about Edgar and the job of Commissioner:

> I decided I wanted Fred[29] Edgar to be our first commissioner. I couldn't wield any influence from the outside, so I decided I'd better get inside. That's how I came to run for the State Board because I wanted to get Fred Edgar on it. He was a fine guy and he'd make a good administrator.[30]

The State Board interviewed Edger for the commissionership on January 28, 1949, in Waco, Texas. Edgar speaks of this interview:

> As soon as [the Board] got my application, they set a time for me to visit with them. I met with them in Waco. They had a board meeting there. I told them my philosophy . . . I said that the board was the policy maker and the commissioner should be the chief executive and the general administrator, and when the commissioner couldn't agree with the policies of the board, he should resign. The Chairman of the Board, who was Robert B. Anderson said, "Would you say that again." I repeated it. They asked a lot of questions about my philosophy, how I would organize the department. I had to answer generally because I didn't know enough about it to give them a detailed organizational plan. It was just a general discussion. I probably met with them for about an hour . . . I think the board had been solicited in my behalf . . . because Austin had given me some recognition.[31]

The Board also interviewed several other people. Mr. W.I. White, Superintendent of Schools in Dallas, had an interview with the Board. The Board also interviewed Dr. E.H. Poteet, President of the College of Arts and Industries, Kingsville, Texas, and Dr. Wilson H. Elkins, President of Texas Western College, El Paso, on January 29.[32] On February 2, 1950, the

Board met in Austin and interviewed Mr. L.P. Sturgeon.[33] Sturgeon recalls the interview:

> Several persons were interviewed, including myself. At the time of my interview, realizing I didn't possess a doctors degree, I recommended to the Board that they elect J.W. Edgar. And also recommended they set a salary of not less than seventeen thousand five hundred dollars for the position.[34]

On February 3, 1950, the Board interviewed Superintendent Nat Williams of Abilene; Mr. Bruce Shulkey, Assistant Superintendent of Schools, Fort Worth; and Dr. John A. Guinn, President of San Angelo College.[35]

After the Board's interviewing was complete, the members convened on February 4, 1950, and voted on the commissionership.

> The Board then proceeded to ballot on a prospect for Commissioner of Education and it was announced by the Chairman that Dr. J.W. Edgar had been unanimously chosen. Mr. Greenwood moved that the salary be set at seventeen thousand five hundred dollars per year. This motion was duly seconded and carried unanimously.[36]

Edgar relates the following account of the voting of the Board:

> Well, the story they tell me . . . there was one other person under consideration . . . Nat Williams who was superintendent at either Abilene or Lubbock. He was a real good man . . . the Chairman said, "All of you write down your first choice among all the people we've talked to on a piece of paper and give it to me . . ." Of the twenty-one first choices, I got twenty of them, and Nat Williams got one.[37]

The matter of Edgar's starting salary of seventeen thousand five hundred dollars per year was controversial. Edgar had made this salary a prerequisite for his being considered for the job. This salary would make the commissionership the third highest paying state position in Texas, the first and second being the presidency of The University of Texas and the Chancellorship of Texas A & M, both of which earned eighteen thousand dollars per year.[38] The Legislative Audit Committee voted four to zero in favor of the salary.[39] Some members of the Legislature felt the salary was too high. An editorial in the Corpus Christi newspaper defended Edgar's salary:

> Some members of the Legislature kicked because the new
> (and first) Commissioner of Education, J.W. Edgar of Austin, will
> draw 17,500 salary a year.
>
> The point, it seems to us, is not well taken. Dr. Edgar has
> been drawing 12,000 a year as Superintendent of the Austin city
> schools, and as Commissioner of Education he will have supervi-
> sion of millions, not thousands of students.
>
> And his salary in the new job will be the same as that paid
> the Coach of the Texas University football team for the last sev-
> eral years. If it isn't worth as much to train minds as muscles,
> then wake us up — we've been asleep.[40]

Edgar relates this story about the Board's approval of his salary:

> They also talked to Governor Shivers because he was mak-
> ing twelve thousand dollars [yearly]. And Governor Shivers said,
> "Forget it. Go on and pay what you want to." [41]

Edgar was officially appointed Commissioner on February 4, 1950, and he took office on March 8, 1950. He was forty-
five years old. Now, through the implementation of the Gilmer-Aikin Laws, Edgar could demonstrate his philosophy of
working with the State Board.

The Edgar Philosophy
And The State Board Of Education

When Edgar became Commissioner he had to develop a
good working relationship between the Commissioner and the
State Board of Education. This involved making known to the
Board his philosophy of the governance of the public schools in
Texas. Edgar writes the following concerning his philosophy of
public schools.

> The source of public school policy must derive from the peo-
> ple through the electorate. Public school policy makers should be
> lay persons chosen by the electorate specifically for that purpose.
> Lay persons or boards chosen to oversee public schools should re-
> strict their activities to policy making, general oversight, and to
> evaluation of operation and results obtained.[42]

Edgar felt the Gilmer-Aikin Laws did their best to define a unitary system which assigned responsibility to the Board, the
Commissioner, the staff, and the local school districts. But he
felt no law could cover everything. He writes:

I realized when I became Commissioner there were gaps that had to be filled by commissioner-board interactions so that the system would work smoothly. I realized that in my work as a local superintendent there had been even less laws governing superintendent-board relationships and the local system worked all right. So where the state law was silent, I followed the pattern of the local system and worked with the State Board in developing logical patterns of relationships between the board and commissioner, thus tightening and strengthening the unitary concept.[43]

The first State Board realized that as Commissioner Edgar was an administrator of the policy the Board set. Dr. Charles Mathews, Executive Director of the Texas Association of School Administrators, speaks of this:

Dr. Edgar had the philosophy that he was the chief executive officer, and he had the responsibility of recommending what he thought was best. And Robert Anderson understood administration, and that board never, to my knowledge, got over in the field of administration. They made policy. And that's the school that Edgar came from.[44]

Edgar had a philosophy about the law which applied to the State Board. The law in places gave rather specific responsibilities to the Board and specific responsibilities to Edgar. The law required that some activities of the Commissioner should have the approval of the Board before they were finalized. Dr. W.R. Goodson, Director of School Accreditation in Texas while Edgar was Commissioner, describes Edgar's general philosophy about the law.

The mediocre leaders in state departments seem to want to do nothing for education that is not required by law. Whereas J.W. Edgar wanted to do everything that was not forbidden by law. If you will analyze those two viewpoints, you will see there is a world of difference between activity of the years that J.W. was Commissioner of Education . . . and what has happened in this state at other times based on that basic philosophical viewpoint.[45]

Edgar made the Board clearly aware of this aspect of his philosophy.

In 1950 the new board appointed a Citizen's Advisory Conference to study the changes that would be brought about by the Gilmer-Aikin Laws. This group published "The Texas Way" which supported local control of education.[46] Both the

Board and Edgar were strongly in favor of local control of education. Mr. Alton O. Bowen, former Commissioner of Education from 1979 to 1981, writes:

> Dr. Edgar was a firm advocate of local control of education and all of his actions and policy recommendations reflected this belief. He believed that policies made by those closest to those being served were the best policies. He never allowed the imposition of the power of the state over local districts.[47]

As such, Edgar worked with the State Board as though he were working with a local board. He describes this:

> What I tried to do here with the Board was to remember that I was in a local school district and to fashion my relationship with the State Board in the fashion as with the local board. Many of the State Board members had been members of the local boards. They were familiar with this kind of relationship and this kind of procedure. We worked it out very well. We were able to work together very closely.[48]

Based on this idea of local control; Edgar began his work with the State Board.

One of the first problems that faced Edgar and the Board was whether or not the Board should have standing committees. Edgar analyses this dilemma:

> I had recommended to the Board that they operate as a committee as a whole, at least for a while to try it out, and appoint committees to do specific jobs, and when they got through with that job, dismiss them. Well some of the board members were agreeable, and some still thought that was the wrong thing . . . Eventually we worked it out to where there was only one standing committee. That was on the investment of the permanent school fund . . . For years we operated without standing committees. Along in the late Sixties when some of the responsibilities began to evolve, we set up standing committees.[49]

The State Board understood Edgar's philosophy of local control and his application of this philosophy to the State Board as if it was a local board; this understanding enabled Edgar and the Board to work closely and productively together.

Work With
The State Board Of Education

Edgar's long term work with the State Board of Education gave many persons, in addition to the Board members, an
opportunity to work with Edgar. Many of these people ob-
served and respected Edgar's extreme adeptness in administration, especially his skill with the Board. Edgar was re-
sourceful and creative in his work. His originality and
uncanny ability to come up with solutions to problems made
him a visionary educator. Many of Edgar's peers recall him
and his work with admiration. Following are some remem-
brances of past and present board members as well as those
who had the opportunity to work with Edgar.

Edgar began to display his administrative skills immediately. The Board hired Stella Mae Floyd as its secretary. She
also served as Edgar's secretary. She complained to Edgar
about the State Board. Mrs. Mary Thornton, Edgar's secretary
from 1968 to 1974, relates this story.

> Stella Mae was a very strong character and she was his sec-
> retary as well as secretary to the State Board of Education . . . He
> always mused over the fact that she trained the secretaries of
> members of the Board to submit their travel vouchers and do
> those kind of things the appropriate way they should be done . . .
> She taught me a lot of things about Dr. Edgar . . . One of the
> greatest stories she told me about Dr. Edgar was that she went in
> one day complaining to him that State Board members just ex-
> pected so much of her. And he just grinned and said, "Well now,
> Mrs. Floyd, they just think you're a little old lady in white tennis
> shoes." That was the end of her interview with him.[50]

Dr. Robert Mallas, a researcher who worked on an evaluation of the Gilmer-Aikin Laws for Edgar in 1954, said of Edgar's work with the Board:

> I think Dr. Edgar translated this study into the minds of the
> board so they clearly understood what fundamental changes could
> happen because of it . . . A board is only as good as its executive di-
> rector or president . . . I think the board simply waited for Edgar to
> clue them or explain to them the why of which way he wanted them
> to go. And once they got that clue they tended to move that way . . .

He's almost always right so it's good to be on his side because you're going to look good. He led. They respected him.[51]

Dr. W.W. Jackson of San Antonio, a Board member in 1958, said of Edgar's work on the Board:

He is willing to yield a point without surrendering a principle, but never hesitates to express his honest convictions. Personally, he is kind and friendly without being effusive. He gives the impression of being completely confident of his ability to handle his duties but never makes a show of either his ability or his authority.[52]

Thomas B. Ramey, who succeeded Robert Anderson as Chairman of the State Board of Education, says this about Edgar:

In J.W. Edgar, the board found the combination of talents and knowledge needed to reach their objectives . . . He has modestly but persistently built a reputation based on sound judgements, which in turn are based on the unique ability of knowing how and when to bring people together.[53]

Edgar's skill in board meetings was striking. His expertise is best explained by Mr. Paul R. Haas, a successful businessman from Corpus Christi who served on the Board from 1962 to 1972. He writes:

In a great many ways Dr. Edgar and I handled problems in a similar manner. After observing his method of accomplishing his purposes I would frequently sit back and enjoy his approach knowing what he was attempting to accomplish and how he was getting the job done. He would prepare all manner of background information on a problem and furnish it to the people involved. Then he would listen to the long and frequently tediuos discussions of the "decisions group." After a reasonable period he would make very short pointed comments which would tend to gradually shift the comments of the group in the direction he wanted in the first place. He was so innocuous in that approach that most of the time the group would feel that they had made the decision. This resulted in very good leadership when it worked, and it almost always worked for him or he would gently suggest that the final decision be deferred.

After some experience with his approach, I would enjoy trying to identify the direction he was developing and would aid him if I agreed with him. If I did not (which was seldom), I did recognize his approach and would play the same game on my side.

We respected each others comments and never found it necessary
to have a single unpleasant discussion.[54]

Edgar was patient with the Board. He always treated
every member with courtesy. Mr. Haas speaks of this trait.

He was very respectful of every individual member. Much
more so than I think I would have been. He did give detailed re-
sponses to stupid questions as well as intelligent ones, and would
take innumerable minutes, hours, and days to take care of a particularly difficult situation and try to work out a consensus if at
all possible.[55]

In addition to being patient with the Board, Edgar was sincerely interested in maintaining good relationships with Board
members. He was always very careful to remember those he
worked with. In 1956 he wrote Robert Anderson, former Chairman of the State Board of Education, about an award he (Edgar) received.

Of course, you know that I could never have been in the position to receive any kind of award if it had not been for the great
support I have had from the members of the State Board of Education . . . both past and present.
In that connection, I should like for you to know how very
much your help, encouragement, and council have meant to me
during the past six years. Above all, I deeply appreciate the gen-
uine friendship which I feel is shared between us.
Sue [Mrs. Edgar] joins me in expressing to you and Mrs.
Anderson our best wishes and very great appreciation.[56]

Edgar wrote Mr. Paul Haas a similar letter after Haas left the
State Board in 1972. Haas talks about Edgar's letter:

This letter reflects a sympathy and sincerity in his nature
that one does not find in most people. The letter is a four page
handwritten letter expressing Dr. Edgar's appreciation, in some
detail, for my work in education, particularly on the State Board.
This letter was written when I was no longer a member of the
board. The timing of the letter is important because there was no
way that I could be of any constructive help to Dr. Edgar or his career at that point. The letter reflected a characteristic of kindness
to one's fellow man that is all too seldom exhibited. Of course, I
was deeply appreciative of the letter and the flattering statements in it but was most pleased and impressed because he took
the time to write it in longhand at a date when I could be assured
of its total sincerity.

I have kept that letter for many years and intend to maintain it as an important part of my memorabilia.[57]

In this letter which Edgar wrote to Haas, Edgar said of him:

Your confidence in me has been and is of the utmost importance to me, and I hope I shall always merit it. Your perceptive influence on educational affairs as a member of the State Board of Education, as well as your acceptance by other Board members, is unique and unequaled in my experience although the influence of Bob Anderson and of Tom Ramey was comparable in many ways. You are sorely missed and I hope some member will emerge soon to assume your role (never to take your place).

I want you to know how grateful I am to you for your support of my efforts through the years, and how much Sue and I admire you and Mrs. Haas. Your continuing friendship is cherished by both of us.[58]

When Edgar left the Commissionership, some Board members expressed their thanks for his work. Paul Mathews, who had served on the State Board the entire length of Edgar's service, writes:

When Dr. E. decided it was time to retire, the Board was at a loss to contemplate the naming of his successor. No one could fill the "big shoes" left vacant — but of course no one is indispensable, but we missed him. As the board changed in personnel, we finally decided he was no longer there, and recent boards very seldom mention him. But they all respect him and admire his leadership.[59]

Vernon Baird, a member of the State Board during the latter part of Edgar's tenure, wrote Edgar the following letter after Edgar's retirement:

During a man's lifetime he meets a few people who fit into a certain niche in his mind which, for the lack of better words, might be called his "inspirational chapel."

Such has been the case with you as far as I am concerned. The opportunity of working with you since 1961 has probably been one of the paramount reasons why I have continued to stay on the State Board of Education.

The State of Texas has been blessed by having you as its Commissioner of Education for these past twenty-four years. To fill this job adequately requires a great deal more than simply being an outstanding educator. It requires an ability to maintain levelheadedness in times of stress, a dedication not only to the children but also to the public of the State, and a love for fellow man.

I want to express my appreciation to you for acquiescing to our wishes to stay on a few more years after you had decided to retire. It has helped make the transition much simpler.

Those gifted with words have expressed themselves, and many more will in months to come; so I will just say, "Thank you for the opportunity and privilege of working with you." [60]

As evidenced by the preceeding statements, Edgar's peers admired him and were inspired by him. His skill as an administrator was remarkable not only in his knowing how to carry out the work but also in his ability to be compassionate and understanding of each separate individual person he worked with. This characteristic would make his first term as Commissioner a successful one.

FIRST TERM AS COMMISSIONER

The State Board appointed Edgar First State Commissioner of Education in Texas on February 4, 1950. He took office on March 8, 1950. The majority of school people throughout Texas favorably received his appointment. These feelings are reflected in an article in the *Fort Worth Telegram* of February 5, 1950, which contains the views of several prominent school people. The first viewpoint expressed in the article is that of Miss Waurine Walker, President of the Texas State Teachers Association at the time. The article says of Miss Walker and Edgar's appointment:

> Edgar's appointment was the "best thing that happened in Texas." Miss Walker called herself "delighted" at the prospect for educational progress. [61]

The same article quotes Miss Jewel Askew of Houston, President of the Texas Association for Childhood Education, as saying about the appointment of Edgar:

> We are indeed very fortunate at Dr. Edgar's appointment. He is one of our outstanding educators. If he can do for our State Department what he has done for the Austin school system, we will be very fortunate indeed. [62]

The article goes on to quote Miss Gladys Simons of Fort Worth, President of the State Elementary Principal and Supervisors

Association. The article quotes her feelings about Edgar's appointment.

> A very fine selection. He has done some very outstanding work over the state and he did some progressive work at Austin with which we were all very delighted.[63]

The article also quotes the sentiments of other people who were interviewed for the commissionership. Mr. B.C. Shulkey of Fort Worth is quoted as saying:

> He [Edgar] has the confidence and respect of the school people of Texas. [He is] a very capable individual, a successful administrator and one who knows instructional programs . . . He should be able to administer the affairs of the state school system ably and efficiently.[64]

Edgar accepted his appointment with calm reserve. In another newspaper article in the *Fort Worth Telegram*, Sam Kinch writes of Edgar's reaction when the press began calling him "Dr. Edgar":

> He explained that he got the Doctor of Education Degree pretty late in life (and had to listen to his three children ask Mrs. Edgar if he had failed and still had to go to school). He also was deflated when the middle daughter, Sally, 10, told a friend that he wasn't the kind of doctor who does anybody any good.[65]

Edgar began his first term in office on a positive note with the overwhelming approval of educators, legislators, and lay people. These persons put their hopes for educational reform in Edgar and backed him wholeheartedly with their confidence. Edgar's first term as Commissioner encompassed three significant aspects: (1) his reorganization of the Department of Education into the Texas Education Agency; (2) the initial dilemmas he faced as Commissioner; and (3) his relationship with Warren Hitt.

Organization Of The Texas Education Agency, 1950–1951

The reorganization of the Department of Education into the Texas Education Agency was the first task that faced Edgar.[66] He accomplished this task in a relatively short period of time. Edgar retained most of Woods' staff for his own. Edgar talks about this:

The staff was pretty well in place from the Department of
Education . . . Dr. Woods' staff. There were only three members of
that staff that I did not retain. All the rest of them, I had some
way to give them assurances in the very beginning that their jobs
would continue. As long as they were able to perform them, there
would be no changes.[67]

First, Edgar realized that he needed a Deputy Commissioner to run and operate the Agency. For this job, he chose
Warren Hitt. Second, he created an Assistant Commissioner
for Administration to operate the Foundation School Program.
Edgar placed L.P. Sturgeon in the job. Third, Edgar created an
Assistant Commissioner for Vocational Education, and he
chose M.A. Browning for the job. Fourth, he created an Assistant Commissioner for Instruction. Edgar filled this job himself
for a while until he gave it to Lee J. Wilborn. He also created a
position for a Business Manager; T.J. O'Connor filled this position.[68] Edgar submitted these job requests to the State Board.
The Board, in turn, submitted them to the Legislative Audit
Committee which had to approve their salaries. Edgar talks
about the committee:

> Well I wanted L.P. Sturgeon to be Assistant Commissioner
> for Administration. He was already in place on the Foundation
> School Program. He was an excellent man. He wanted twelve
> thousand dollars if he was going to stay . . . the most we could get
> for him was eleven thousand . . . I wanted to pay the Deputy ten
> thousand . . . and the Legislative Committee approved ten thou-
> sand. Then the Legislative Audit Committee tightened up on us
> . . . They said, "Can you postpone that Assistant Commissioner of
> Instruction and give us a chance to get a hold of this thing?" I
> said, "Okay, I'll do that myself."[69]

Before Edgar appointed T.J. O'Conner Business Manager, he
brought in William A. Harrison, from the staff of the Audit
Committee, as acting business manager. Edgar felt this would
give him a good relationship with the Audit Committee. Finally, Edgar chose Frank Hubert, the former band director of
Lutcher Stark's band who Edgar had worked with in Orange,
as Director of Professional Standards.

With the creation and legislative approval of these new
personnel positions, Edgar's reorganization was complete. The
creation of these new positions in the Texas Education Agency

enabled the Agency to be a functioning, productive entity. Edgar had carefully thought out and meticulously planned these positions so that this excellent group of administrators could now get the new machinery of the TEA in motion.

Early Problems As Commissioner

Probably the most important early problem Edgar faced in his implementation of the Gilmer-Aikin Laws was to develop public confidence in the Texas Education Agency as a professional leader in the field. In order to do this Edgar had to: (1) establish the integrity of the administration of the Minimum Foundation School Program; (2) analyze all existing rules and regulations which in any way applied to education to ensure that these rules were within the law and that they adhered to Edgar's philosophy of local control of schools; (3) establish good working relationships with professional education organizations; and (4) personalize his leadership of the TEA.

The Establishment of Confidence in the Minimum Foundation School Program. The Minimum Foundation School Program cost one hundred and eighty million dollars the first year. Of this, forty-five million was to be furnished by the local districts. The rest came from state funds. Since such a great amount of money for the Foundation Program was to be derived from local funds, Edgar wanted to be sure the program was run correctly. He states:

> So with that much money involved and the new formulas going into effect, it just became necessary that we take the proper actions to be sure that this was an honest, correct, accurate administration of the program. The program provided for classroom teachers and special personnel like counselors and supervisors and administrators and so forth. And allocations to the school district were based on Average Daily Attendance in the school districts. The Average Daily Attendance would earn so many classroom teachers. So many classroom teachers would earn so many counselors and supervisors or special personnel or administrators — principals or superintendents. So the key to the administration of this entire program was the accuracy of the Average Daily Attendance figures in each local school district.[70]

To keep an exacting record of Average Daily Attendance, Edgar set up an Audit Division under John Clemens. The Audit Division employed Certified Public Accountants and regular auditors, not school people. The CPAs and auditors were trained to go into the schools to examine the records. Edgar discusses the role of these auditors:

> Of course after an Average Daily Attendance figure had been placed in the records there was no way to check whether it was honest or not. So we trained these auditors to go into the classrooms and find out — to take the teacher's register, to look at that day's entry in the register to see how many were present, and then to count the kids in the room, and if there was a discrepancy, to find out why.[71]

Strong reaction existed to this practice at first. When the auditors found a discrepancy, Edgar would call in the superintendent from the district in which the discrepancy was found and challenge his certificate. Edgar relates one example of a cancellation:

> I cancelled one superintendent at a small school in East Texas. He came to me and asked me for a job. He said, "I want to go out and spread the gospel. Nobody can tell them any better than I can because I've been through the mill on it." I, of course, didn't hire him. Word got around pretty quick.[72]

Edgar found special problems regarding Average Daily Attendance in the Black schools. He explained what action he took:

> One of the unfortunate parts of it [Foundation Program] that went on with this was in the Black schools. Honestly, some of them didn't think they were cheating. They had been told by their school superintendents to maintain a certain attendance or they'd probably lose their jobs. I had a number of Black principals and Black teachers to talk with. I took a little bit of a different view of them because I realized — I did cancel some of them — but I realized that they were not the real culprits.[73]

Edgar also had the auditors check the personnel records of the teachers who were employed in each district because the teacher salary schedule was based on the kinds of degrees and certification that each teacher held. The auditors often found discrepancies, and when they did, the TEA would deduct money from that district's state share. The schools very quickly became more careful in their personnel accounting.

In addition to the problem of Average Daily Attendance,

the auditors encountered another problem which could potentially have a negative affect on the integrity of the Foundation Program. This problem had to do with phony mileage routes of the school buses. The schools were paid for the number of miles their buses had to travel. The auditors found that some of the routes that drivers actually followed did not match up with the routes that were officially approved. Also, Woods had allowed children attending Catholic schools and other private schools to ride the state buses. Edgar had to stop this practice right away. He recalls an incident related to this problem:

> I remember I got a letter from a woman in Victoria who was a Catholic and big ranch owner and so forth. She said to me, "We were all in favor of you being Commissioner because we knew of your work here in Victoria. But now I'm disappointed in you because you have taken our children off the buses." I had to write her that as much as I regretted it, it was just a constitutional requirement — something I was just bound to do.[74]

Through the use of auditors Edgar accomplished the first phase of building public confidence in the Texas Education Agency — the integrity of the Minimum Foundation School Program.

Molding the TEA towards Local Control. Another of the early tasks Edgar faced as Commissioner was the task of molding the Texas Education Agency toward his philosophy of local control of schools. Frank Hubert speaks of Edgar's philosophy of local control of schools:

> Edgar's dominant theme during, and that of the State Board, from his inauguration ceremony through every other formal and informal act was to emphasize local initiative and local control on the part of school districts. This was a heavy principle, policy principle which he enumerated with the State Board and felt quite strongly about it. He geared up his staff in that mode of thinking.[75]

Edgar felt strongly about local control of schools. He wanted the local community and the local school board to control the schools. Edgar wanted to ensure that the state and federal governments did not interfere with that local control. Edgar discusses this fact:

> I think one of the reasons that I was chosen as Commissioner was because I had some experience in administering local

school systems that had federal money among other kinds of money . . . I think I was well known because of my policy of an absolute stand on the philosophy of local control of public schools . . . But we had to be sure that one regulation didn't have some things in it that would [enable us] to take over the control of the school board, the local school . . . We had to review all the policies and rules and regulations first to be sure they were in accordance with the law and second, that we didn't add things that would tend to weaken the local administration of the school system. It was a constant matter that you had to give attention to. I think we established early that we were not going to go beyond the law ever in trying to take over the operation of the schools.[76]

Several aspects of the Foundation Program had certain centralizing tendencies which had to be guarded against. The first centralizing tendency was that the auditing of local school records could have spread into restriction on the local school boards. Edgar describes this problem:

Well, there again was the opportunity, had we not been very careful, to take on more authority than we actually had. We had to set standards for the special personnel, visiting teachers, supervisors, counselors, vocational teachers, special education teachers. Above their just basic teaching certificates, we had to determine what other qualifications they should have. These were allocations that did not count against the Average Daily Attendance, and therefore were called "bonus units." The classroom teacher units — all those that were derived from the Average Daily Attendance, were called "basic units." So here again we had to be very careful that we didn't set maximum standards rather than minimum standards, but leave the school boards freedom to go above the standard that we set.[77]

The second centralizing tendency which the TEA possessed involved the yearly determination of how much money in local school funds would be appropriated from each school district for their support of the Foundation Program. The appropriation was based on Average Daily Attendance, so again, the auditors had to take painstaking steps to assure the accuracy of these records and the fairness of the program.

The Establishment of Good Relations with Professional Education Organizations. Another important early task which Edgar faced that helped him establish the TEA as a professional leader was the establishment of working relationships with the professional education organizations. He wanted to give support to some of the new emerging groups. One such group was a group that had supported Woods which was called the "Rural School Administrators." The name of this organization was changed to the "Small School Association." Edgar says of this organization:

> I felt like that, having been in a small school, that we ought to pay [them] particular attention — to make a long story short, we set up in our staff a person who worked with the small schools . . . We went out and got what we thought was the best small school superintendent in the State . . . Charles Bitters. He acted as kind of a staff member for the organized small schools, their board of directors acted as sort of a staff. We had annual meetings, and one thing or another, just gave it special attention.[78]

At about the same time that the Small School Association was seeking attention, the urban school districts and the suburban city school districts were also seeking the same sort of attention. Consequently, Edgar established an Assistant Commissioner for Urban Education.

Edgar was also anxious to work with the already established professional organizations. These relationships, too, would establish the TEA as a professional leader. Edgar wanted to work with the Texas State Teachers Association (TSTA). L.P. Sturgeon, therefore, left the Agency and went to work for the TSTA. Sturgeon eventually became Executive Director of the TSTA. Dr. M.L. Brockette, former State Commissioner of Education, describes the impact of Sturgeon's move:

> Dr. Edgar and Mr. Sturgeon and Senator Aikin could usually have a three way conference on the telephone. They didn't have to hold any kind of formalized meetings. They knew each other so well they could talk about legislative matters and they could come to a consensus. And it was that sort of consensus that, you know, looking in retrospect, I think was valuable. Now that might be a critical area for somebody.[79]

The Personalization of Edgar's Leadership. Edgar believed that the personalization of his leadership of the TEA was crucial to the establishment of confidence in the Agency. As such, Edgar believed he could accomplish this by visiting the schools in all two hundred and fifty-four counties in Texas during his first year. He was not able to accomplish this goal, but he worked hard at it and did come close. Frank Hubert describes Edgar's attempt to visit all of the counties that first year:

> Hard worker himself. Drove himself. In fact one of his early physical setbacks was toward the end of his first year as Commissioner. Edgar felt upon becoming Commissioner that the school people of this state had the right to know the Commissioner, to hear him, to see him, to visualize him, to engage in conversation with him. I think he made every effort to accept every speaking engagement which came his way. Whether from Amarillo to Brownsville, or from El Paso to Texarkana, he would go and respond and be there and meet with the school people and interpret the program and be a missionary for them. And after about a year of that he was hospitalized with exhaustion. But it simply indicated that there's a man who felt he had to give himself to the task and he did in an admirable fashion.[80]

L.P. Sturgeon relates a story about an exhaustive trip he made with Edgar that first year which demonstrates Edgar's unbelievable dedication.

> Let me give you one example of a day in Mr. Edgar's life and in mine which indicates his willingness to give of himself. One afternoon he called me and stated the next morning he wanted me to pick him up at four o'clock a.m. and that we were going to Leon County to spend a day in the schools of that county. At that time the Texas Education Agency had one smooth mouthed Chevrolet several years old without air conditioning or radio which we had inherited from the old Department of Education. I drove the car to Mr. Edgar's house and picked him up at four o'clock a.m. and we met Jack Bryant, member of the House, in Buffalo, Texas, about seven o'clock a.m. and had breakfast with him. We then spent the entire day and visited every school in Leon County. This was in late May. The weather was extremely hot, was dry, and there was no air conditioning anywhere. You may be assured that by the time we had visited all these schools, we were completely exhausted. However, Mr. Edgar then agreed to speak to the Lion's Club in Normangee, Texas. And we visited that school last that day. The meeting started late since most of the members were farmers who got in from their work at eight o'clock or nine o'clock. And the speech which Mr. Edgar made was concluded about eleven o'clock p.m. We then had more than a three hour drive to Austin. At about two-thirty that morning we tumbled into bed. This was a J.W. Edgar day.[81]

These speaking trips which Edgar made were a great personal

sacrifice on his part to the school people of Texas because he did not like to make speeches. Alton O. Bowen, former Commissioner of Education, writes:

> He was unpretentious and unassuming and a damn poor speech maker. He disliked making speeches and accepted as few speaking engagements as possible.[82]

On April 18, 1951, Edgar suffered a heart attack in Burnet, Texas, while making a speech. He relates what happened:

> I happened to be up in Burnet making a talk. There was a group up there that invited me up there to make a talk. My family who lived in Burnet at the time . . . my brother and sister, and my brother's family . . . were at the program. We walked out of the auditorium and were standing there talking, and all of a sudden I had it. My brother and his wife drove me back to Austin . . . I was out of the office for about six weeks. I was in the hospital about four weeks. But I had Warren Hitt there, he covered for me very nicely. The doctor just told me, "Now you can forget abut this and go on and live your life normally, or you can make yourself a heart cripple for the rest of your life" . . . So I said, "Okay, I'm going to forget it." And I did. So I went on. I guess I was grounded in Austin for a period of three or four months. After that I resumed my normal travel activity.[83]

Edgar's establishment of the integrity of the Foundation School Program, his meticulous analyzation of rules and regulations, his relationships with professional organizations, and his personalization of his leadership contributed to his establishment of the TEA as an undisputed first-ranked professional leader in the field of education. Another important aspect of this leadership was the related task of establishing successful relations with the State Legislature. For this task, Edgar employed Warren Hitt.

Edgar And J. Warren Hitt

From the time of Hitt's first arrival in Austin, he and Edgar worked productively together. Edgar had given Hitt two leaves of absence, once to work with the TSTA during the Gilmer-Aikin hearings, and once to work with L.P. Sturgeon to set up the Minimum Foundation Program. Edgar speaks about hiring Hitt at the Texas Education Agency:

> All the time I was there I had good relationships . . . the

whole Agency had good relationships with the Legislature . . .
But I never was comfortable with the Legislature. I just never did
enjoy appearing before the committees. As much as possible I let
Warren Hitt do the legislative liaison work. And he was very good
at it, and adapted to it. As I say, I got along fine with the Legislature. But one thing Senator Aikin said to me early [on] was,
"Now, don't you come over here every day. You stay out of the
way because every time you come, somebody is going to ask a favor of you." I took that advice and [went there] when it was proper
for me to be there. The leg work was all done by Warren Hitt.[84]

The fact that Edgar had Hitt to do his leg work with the Legislature may account, in part, for Edgar's long tenure in office. Mr.
Raymon Bynum, current State Commissioner of Education, talks
about the job of Commissioner and the Legislature:

> I am more knowledgeable in public school finances and more
> knowledgeable in the political process [than Edgar was] . . . I would
> not say that Dr. Edgar was not knowledgeable, but he had a long-
> time Deputy, Warren Hitt. And Warren handled the Legislature
> just almost entirely in all of his career. Whereas when I was Asso-
> ciate Commissioner, I was assigned that. And when I was Deputy I
> was assigned that. And I still do it as Commissioner . . . In the leg-
> islative process or the political process, educators who get overly in-
> volved in that have a burnout factor. Either they burn out them-
> selves and get tired of the process or their face becomes too familiar
> and they burnout on the Legislature. And I think anyone who deals
> on that, including myself, has to be very aware of that. I say three
> sessions [Legislative sessions] is the limit, personally, of a great
> deal of involvement by normal situations.[85]

Hitt was a true diplomat when it came to working with
the Legislature, and he enjoyed his work. He did not burn out
after three terms, and he protected Edgar from the burnout.
Hitt was an extremely hard worker. Mrs. Hitt talks of her husband's work:

> He was a workaholic, there's no doubt about that. I told him
> he would die at the office and that's exactly what he did . . . They
> filled his place with four Deputy Commissioners . . . I always felt
> that Warren did more than his share . . . He'd start home in the
> afternoon and he'd be thinking about something that was going
> on and he'd get lost coming home . . . And a lot of times we'd go
> places and we'd be sitting in his car and nothing said, and Warren
> would say, "I know how to figure that out, I know how to follow

that up." And I'd say, "What are you talking about?" And as I
said, [the job] was first, last, and always.[86]

Hitt had chances to leave the Agency but he liked his job
and he liked working with Edgar. Mrs. Hitt talks about this:

> Well they were both dedicated to education, for one thing.
> They had inquisitive minds, they thought a lot alike, just an awful
> lot alike. Personality wise they were kind of alike that way too.
> They didn't, either one, seek fame or fortune. They were just happy
> to go along and do their jobs . . . He (Hitt) was perfectly happy with
> what he was doing. He had free reign to do what he pleased with Dr.
> Edgar's blessing. And there was no conflicts at all.[87]

Not only did Hitt like his job, but the fact that he and Edgar
worked so well together and were such a great team undoubtedly contributed a large part to the success of the Agency. Mrs.
Carolyn Ruhman, Hitt's secretary and the current secretary of
the State Board, confirms this.

> They were a great team. Mr. Edgar, of course, carried out
> the policies as adopted by the Board. He made the decisions. Mr.
> Hitt carried out Dr. Edgar's decision; he worked closer with the
> staff. Mr. Edgar did too, but Mr. Hitt, well there were a lot of
> times I would hear him say to a group of people he would have in
> here — ten or twelve people — , he'd say "You all stay right here.
> I've got to go talk to the boss." He would go in Mr. Edgar's office
> and he would come back and they would go from there. They were
> good friends besides a great working team. They had a great deal
> of respect for each other.[88]

Hitt usually worked alone with the Legislature, but during the budget process, both Edgar and Hitt worked together.
Mr. Vernon McGee, who worked for the Legislative Budget Director, describes how Hitt and Edgar worked during the budget
process.

> There were three phases to the budget process. One [was]
> after we had copies of the budget and my staff was preparing for
> [the] hearing, sometimes you'd hit policy questions. Now gener-
> ally, we'd try to see the Commissioner — we'd try to see Dr. Edgar
> on the policy issues. Very often we would call in Warren Hitt, if
> Warren was not otherwise tied up. Where there was a detail
> where something didn't add or where the justification we thought
> conflicted and we wanted clarification, we went to Warren. Some-
> times Warren sent us to some divisions for clarification. But once

the analysis of the examiners had been completed, we were ready
for the hearing. These hearings were conducted jointly with the
Governor's budget office . . . And here Dr. Edgar generally was
the leadoff witness explaining the overall objectives and the main
things he was trying to accomplish in the next biennium. There
he was supported by his immediate staff, people like Warren Hitt
. . . On details I worked with Warren Hitt who was an excellent
man. I don't remember Warren ever missing a point. You could
depend on whatever he said.[89]

Hitt clearly contributed in great measure to the overall
success and prestige of the Texas Education Agency. His dip-
lomatic expertise in working with the Legislature ensured that
the TEA would have a good working relationship with the Legislature, a relationship which was vital to the success of the
Agency's programs. Hitt and Edgar were a dynamic team from
1950, when they both became a part of the TEA until 1970,
when Hitt died. An account of Hitt's death appeared in *Texas
School Business:*

Hitt was conducting a meeting at the Texas Education
Agency on Monday, January 5, when he was stricken at his desk
and rushed to the hospital where he died. He had not been ill and
had recently had a physical and was pronounced in good health.
He had the week before, been on a trip visiting schools in the Gulf
area. There is no other way to say it but that Warren Hitt gave
his life to Education.[90]

Hitt's contribution to the success of Edgar's administration of
the TEA is significant and cannot be underestimated. His contribution was a constant help which Edgar could depend on
when facing the ongoing problems of the commissionership.

ONGOING PROBLEMS AS COMMISSIONER, 1950–1970

Throughout Edgar's tenure as Commissioner, ongoing
problems existed which occupied much of his time. Some of
these problems were integration, teacher certification, school
accreditation, vocational education and rehabilitation, and
special education. Textbook adoption and the appeals process
are two of the more interesting programs which occupied Edgar's time.

The Textbook Adoption Process

Edgar devoted a good portion of his time and attention to the subject of textbook adoption. The Gilmer-Aikin Laws had considerably changed the process by which textbooks were adopted. Before Gilmer-Aikin, the responsibility for review and adoption of a book was placed in the hands of the State Board of Education. The board would select a multiple list of five books for the high school grades and a basic book for the elementary grades. A Textbook Advisory Committee, of which Edgar was a member, recommended books to the Board. Edgar discusses his membership on the Textbook Advisory Committee and the changes brought about by the Gilmer-Aikin Laws:

> When I was on the Committee, the Board [old State Board] had required that the committee submit four books for each subject that was to be adopted. Then the Board would take one of the four, or they could go outside of the committee recommendation if they wanted to adopt whatever book they cared to adopt. But the Gilmer-Aikin Laws changed that and provided that there should be a State Textbook Committee of fifteen members. That committee was to decide which books were to go on the list. There were to be five books in each category, including the elementary grades ... if five books were available, but there couldn't be more than five and there couldn't be less than two. There always had to be a multiple choice. But the majority vote of the State Textbook Committee was the only way for a book to get on the adopted list. I [as Commissioner] appointed the committee. The State Board confirmed my appointments.[91]

The list of potential books for adoption originated from a majority vote of the State Textbook Committee which Edgar appointed. He describes the makeup of the Committee:

> They had to be composed of active school teachers or administrators. We always put a majority of teachers on there, and then we'd put maybe some supervisors or superintendents on too.[92]

After the State Textbook Committee had carefully chosen a suitable list of books to be recommended for adoption, their report would go to the Commissioner. The Commissioner would then review the list. He could take a book off of the list, but he could not reduce the list to fewer than two books. Edgar describes an incident when he took a book off the list.

There were very few instances when I took a book off. But I would do so. I remember probably the very first adoption after I went into office . . . I had published some criteria which I was going to use in reviewing the book. I had given a set of criteria to the publishers. One statement I had made in there was that one book that was approximately the same content as the others offered, and was considerably higher in price — that that would be one reason for taking that book off — if we could get approximately the same material at a cheaper cost. When the first adoption came along, I've forgotten what book it was, but there was one book that was way out of line in price. I decided I had to take it off. But I called the publisher and gave him a chance to be heard on it. And I hung him after I gave him the hearing — I took the book off. I think that many of the publishers felt that probably I wouldn't exercise the privilege — that I really didn't have the nerve to do it. But I established, I think, the fact with the publishers that I would take a book off if I had to. But I didn't take many off during that twenty-four years.[93]

Dr. Lorrin Kennamer, Dean of The University of Texas College of Education, relates a similar experience:

He [Edgar] retained me as a consultant one year when they were involved in textbook selection for a series, an elementary series, in Geography. And he asked me to take the five series that were chosen by the Textbook Committee and to see if those series met the charge which was that they had to be Geography series not Social Studies series. That was a very interesting occasion — that was all done where I was quietly asked to do this. No one knew I was doing it for the Commissioner. And so I set some criteria as to what I would say is a Social Studies series versus a Geography series. That was one way I approached it. The second way I approached it was how the books were advertised in journals across the nation. Thirdly was, of course, an examination of the books to see just how they were. And so my report to him was such that [there were] three companies [which] I recommended negative on as not meeting the charge the Commissioner [had given] to all publishers to submit Geography series. And one of the companies, I believe it was McMillan at first. Ginn was another. And interestingly, the McMillian series, my major professor at the University of Tennessee was the main geographer on it. However, those had been prepared as a Social Studies series. And they'd advertised nationally that way. And when they came to Texas, they'd replaced one page and that front page said it's a Geography series. So when they found out that they had been removed from the list, they demanded a hearing. And so there I was at the hearing with stenotypist and all — and they with their representatives. We had at it with the Commissioner watching. And finally it came down to, I just pulled out from my briefcase, the book that was accepted in Georgia [as a social studies book] and the book in Texas. And I said, "The only difference in these two books — you call this one Social Studies and this one you call Geography — is one page. And if you can find any other difference, why then I withdraw my report." Of course I'd gone through it carefully. Well, they huffed and puffed, attacked me, and this and that. Of course the Commissioner was listening to all this very quietly, but he was getting redder in the face. And finally he told them in no uncertain terms that he was definitely keeping them off the list — that he was going to consider whether or not they should be allowed to submit textbooks in any field in the State of Texas anymore because of this approach that they had used. Well, they quickly folded up their briefcases and left. Word got out pretty quickly — so Ginn chose not to have a hearing.[94]

After the Commissioner reviewed the report of the State Textbook Committee and made the changes he felt were necessary, he submitted his report to the State Board. The State Board, in turn, could remove books from the list, but it could not reduce the list to fewer than two books. Edgar summarizes the entire process:

> Then the Commissioner's report with the books that were left on the list, would go to the State Board of Education. They, in turn, could take a book off the list, but neither could they reduce the list to fewer than two books. Well, of course, with that kind of set up, we had to develop a calendar for the adoption of textbooks. The law required that the first step would be the issuance of an annual proclamation by the State Board of Education, listing the books that would be considered for adoption — describing their specifications as much as the Board desired to do so. This was then distributed to all the publishers and the others interested. The publishers then, would select the ones they wanted to submit for the annual — this happened every year — for the annual adoption. We set a calendar for the Board to adopt the proclamation in March of each year. The proclamation had to be prepared, so our staff had to make recommendations to me as to what books should be readopted. So if we were going to readopt, we didn't submit in the proclamation, we would just extend the contract with the publisher. For those subjects for which there was to be new books to be adopted — the adoption was staggered — the contracts were

staggered so that not all contracts expired the same year — so we
had a balanced adoption each year. Anyway, the staff studied the
books from their curriculum aspects, and recommended to me the
books that should be placed in the call of the proclamation for new
adoptions. I, in turn, would develop with the Textbook Director,
the proclamation, including a list of books to be called for. We
would submit this to the State Board of Education, and they
would either change it or accept it, and adopt it in their March
meeting each year. Then in May — the May meeting — I would
submit names of persons to be appointed to the Textbook Committee. They would either accept it or reject it; if they did reject it,
I would have to recommend another person to take the place of
the one who had been rejected. The Board could not add names,
could not select names of their own. So then the Textbook Committee would go to work. There were deadlines for the publishers
to submit their books and materials. It would be distributed to
Textbook Committee members. Then there was a scheduled hearing for publishers to go before the individual members of the committee. We had to be very careful about this because the publishers would resort to any tactic to get their books identified to
members of the committee. So we had to be very strict about the
times they could interview the committee members. Otherwise,
the members of the Committee never would have had a chance to
teach school. They would've been with publishers all day long —
all night long. Then the Committee would make its study and report to me in October, I guess — they would have their final meeting, and they would study the books that were, had been approved
by the Textbook Committee, and we'd decide if we were going to
take any off or not. Our report would go to the Board. They would
meet each November to make the adoptions. Then the adoption
list, being up to five in each subject, would be submitted to the local school boards. We required them to establish a local committee with the Superintendent as Chairman. The local committee
would make recommendations to the local school board, and the
local board would choose one of the five — maybe they'd choose
more than one — that they wanted to use in their local school system. They would report their choices to us. We'd order the books,
and they would be available the next September the following
year.[95]

Because of the nature of the process for textbook adoption,
Edgar had to stay involved with some aspect of the process at all
times. As time passed, interest in textbooks grew. Some citizens
began to protest about some of the books. The Legislature, there-

fore, appointed a temporary committee to investigate the textbook problem. All over the state, the committee held hearings
which Edgar attended. This temporary committee made its report to the Legislature, and the Legislature did not recommend
that any changes be made in the process. Edgar, however, did
make some changes which he developed along with the State
Textbook Committee. Edgar describes this:

> I talked with the President of the State Board then. He was
> Thomas B. Ramey of Tyler. A very astute person, a lawyer, inter-
> ested in education. He'd been sort of the father of school improve-
> ment in Tyler . . . We decided it was time to include in the adop-
> tion process opportunity for the public to be heard. So we adopted,
> and recommended to the Board, a process for the public to be
> heard.[96]

All that could be done under the law was to hear those that
protested a book. The law clearly stated that only publishers
could speak for a textbook. Edgar describes the procedure
which the State Textbook Committee developed:

> We'd set up these rules where these protestors had to file a
> bill of particulars in which they wrote out their objections to each
> book — detailed page numbers and everything. We would take
> these "bills of particulars," we called them, and submit copies of
> them to the publishers that were involved. The publishers would
> then file their bill of particulars which we would send back to the
> protestor, so that before the hearing, the protestors and the pub-
> lishers had a written bill of particulars before them to consider.
> The first hearing would be before the Textbook Committee.[97]

The new hearing process was incorporated as a part of the
already established textbook adoption process. These hearings
allowed the administrators making decisions on the books to
hear the protestors. This process involved three sets of hearings: one with the Textbook Committee; one with the Commissioner; and one with the State Board. Edgar felt the influences
of the hearings were minimal at the State Textbook Committee level because the Textbook Committee's voting was already
pretty much predetermined by local textbook committee
groups. Edgar conducted the hearing of the Commissioner
himself because he felt textbooks were important and so he
wanted to be personally involved. After the Commissioner's
hearing, the State Board would review Edgar's list and conduct

their own hearings. Again, the Board could remove a book, but could not put an already removed book back on the list.

The groups of protestors who objected to certain books, wanted to be able to examine all the books which the Board finally recommended for adoption. Oftentimes, the only way these groups had access to the books was through buying them. This was more often than not a problem, so Edgar began putting a complete set of the books that were being offered for adoption in each of the twenty Education Service Centers around the state. These sets were made available to anyone who wanted to look at them.

The Gablers were one of the most well known of the textbook protest groups. Edgar describes them:

> They [the Gablers] perfected their operation. It's a real professional type operation now. They started out as just amateurs. Mrs. Gabler was the main protestor and she was very careful to follow every rule that we had. Of course she'd give me hell if I allowed someone else not to follow the rules. She knew her lesson pretty well from her point of view, and she could defend her point of view very well with the publishers and anybody else that disagreed with her. I always found her pretty reasonable and we got along fine.[98]

Edgar worked with the ongoing process of textbook adoption throughout his entire tenure as Commissioner. His interest in textbook adoption remained constant. Edgar was considering a plan to have the state make a general list of approved books for each school district. Each school district would then be given a certain amount of money with which to purchase the books of their choice. Though this plan could perhaps be developed into a good one, no such plan has yet been adopted. In addition to working with the textbook adoption process, the appeals process also occupied Edgar throughout his tenure as Commissioner.

The Appeals Process

The Gilmer-Aikin Laws provided that any person dissatisfied with a local school action had the right to appeal the action to the Commissioner of Education. The Commissioner's decision could then be appealed to the State Board of Education, after which a remedy could then be sought in the courts.

Edgar was personally involved in the appeals from local citizens, teachers, administrators, and boards. Dr. Thomas E. Anderson has made a complete study of the appeals process.[99] Edgar describes what he did at the beginning of his term to prepare for the appeals process.

> One of the first things we had to do was set up the procedure to govern the appeals. The Board had several lawyers in it, and of course they knew the due process procedures. They gave very careful attention to helping develop these procedures. We finally did develop them, and codify them and publish them so that all parties who might come along later would have advance notice of what the [procedure was like].[100]

Anderson classified the appeals Edgar heard into the following six categories:

> 1. Dismissals/Termination of Professional Personnel
> 2. Status of Professional Employees
> 3. District Territory Matters
> 4. Student Matters
> 5. District Operation Matters
> 6. Professional Practice Actions by the Texas Education Agency.[101]

Edgar carefully analyzed the appeals process and established some ground rules for himself. He talks of these ground rules:

> I knew that I was not a judge. This was not a court room procedure. I didn't want to take on the appearance of trying to make it one. I tried to remind everybody that it was an administrative proceeding although we would try to follow the reasonable rules of the evidence as far as we could . . . Many times we allowed heresay evidence and so on. Anything that I felt like I could get to the heart of the problem [with], I didn't rule out . . . Anyway, I also decided I had to be very careful not to substitute my judgement for the local school board, or whoever it was that had the initial authority.[102]

One of Edgar's primary criteria for judgement of these appeals was that he wanted to be sure that he did not interfere with the local school boards. This was in keeping with his philosophy of local control. Anderson writes about this in concluding his study.

> Historically, the concept of "local control" has been a basic

premise for public education in Texas. By law, boards have the authority to manage and govern the affairs of the district. Conceptually, the membership of boards is representative of the majority of the population of the political subdivision. Boards have the authority to render decisions that imply the collective judgement of those represented. The appeals process, although consistent with the concept of the state's ultimate responsibility for education, is somewhat inconsistent with the concept of "local control" that is generally espoused by the Legislature, State Board of Education, county and local school district personnel, and the general public. Based on this predicate, one might expect the Commissioner's decisions to sustain appellees in the vast majority of decisions. One-third of the actions appealed were overruled by the Commissioner. This percentage of holdings for appellants is sufficiently significant to conclude that the appeals process is not a futile gesture for appellants and that the Commissioner does not serve as a "rubber stamp" for local board actions. The appeals process is therefore an alternative from which parties may expect a fresh resolution to disputes.

Over the twenty-five years studied, the device has shown a striking migration toward the legal system and away from the system for wise-persons' administration of the public school system. In earlier years, appeals smacked impressively of pleas in equity, and informality characterized the processes used in the device. True, the Commissioner's decisions have always cited "the law," but in the first five years or so, it appears often as if the Commissioner was searching out the wise administrative, good-of-the-order, resolution of contentions and interpreting "the law" as justifying that resolution. Under the increasing impact of legalism, the device has become more and more structured, more and more equipped with legal protocols and rules, and increasingly beholden to the statutory law, rather than the common law.[103]

Anderson's conclusions verify what Edgar said concerning the informal way in which he chose to conduct the hearings, but his conclusions also verify that the appeals process was a reasonable and fair alternative for the resolution of disputes.

Edgar heard hundreds of appeals while he was Commissioner. One case which was especially difficult for him involved his hometown of Briggs and the annexation of one school district to another school district without a vote. Edgar speaks about the dilemma of Briggs.

One of these that finally came home to me was my home town of Briggs. Of course it got progressively smaller over the

years. We had tried to help them keep their high school as long as
they could. My staff used to say, "Well, we've got small schools,
then we have Briggs." I really bent over backwards to help them.
Finally they just got so weak and so small that the county board
annexed them to Burnet. Well, they came down on appeal. I had
the hearing, and had to rule against Briggs finally and uphold
the Burnet County Board because it was clearly within the law.[104]

This Briggs appeal, though the county board's action was
clearly justified, demonstrates how Edgar took the time to personally preside over every appeal, no matter how small or how
opened and closed the case was.

Edgar was proud of his rate of being upheld by the State
Board. He was overruled by the Board only three times in
twenty-four years. He recalls all three cases. One case was that
of a Black principal from Dallas who had been fired. Edgar recalls:

> The school had fired this principal. I don't remember the rea-
> sons. But they seemed to me to be very superficial reasons. So I felt
> the principal [should be upheld]. But the Board didn't agree with
> me. They overruled me and upheld the local school board action.[105]

The second case, from Kerrville High School, involved a
young teacher who was growing a beard. Edgar relates the
story.

> There was a young man [a teacher] over there who was
> growing a beard. They had fired him. But they had warned him
> several times by giving him sufficient time to change,and he re-
> fused to change. I heard the case. I was in sympathy with the
> teacher, but I felt under the law that they had given him warning
> and so forth, and were enforcing the law uniformly with other fac-
> ulty members, that I had to uphold the Board. But when this ap-
> peal got to the Board, they sort of exploded. They thought it was
> ridiculous that the school board would fire the teacher. They were
> an elected body, and they could look at these matters with a little
> broader authority than I could. So they overruled me on that. But
> it went on to a district court, and the district upheld me. But I al-
> ways felt badly about that ruling because I was in sympathy with
> the young man.[106]

The third case involved a group of citizens in the western
part of Houston which had decided to separate from the Houston School District and form their own district. Edgar discusses
this case:

[It was] called the Westheimer Independent School District. They had a lot of political power in their leadership . . . and money. They had pursuaded the county — on that kind of situation you had to go to the county board first — the county board had approved the separation. Of course the Houston School District didn't want it at all. They were struggling there to keep a balance between their Whites and Blacks and so on. They were very much opposed to it. I heard the case. I recognized the political implications that it had. By that time I was under injunction from the Federal Court not to participate in any changes of boundaries that would perpetuate segregation. This clearly was for that purpose so I turned them down, and they went to the Board. Now this was one of the very few times that I felt the Board had yielded to political pressure . . . The political leaders had gone around to every member of the Board at their homes and solicited . . . and played up to them the fact that this was a federal court interference and so forth. The Board overruled me pretty solidly on that. I think the vote was fifteen to seven . . . But again, that went on to the Federal District Court, and the court sustained me on it because the Federal Court didn't have any option on it because it was so clearly a segregation matter.[107]

Anderson wrote of this 1972 decision by Edgar:

This decision reaffirmed that boundary changes contrary to a district's court ordered desegregation plan . . . would be denied. It also indicated that improved educational opportunity as a reason for requesting a boundary change would be difficult to substantiate.[108]

Many people admired Edgar's fairness in handling the appeals process. His legal counsel, Mr. Chester Ollison talks of Edgar's handling of the appeals cases:

He was a man that knew how to listen to the people that were appealing to his office. And he would hear them out no matter how long it took. If it ran into midnight, okay, he'd stay there. If it was necessary to go beyond, he'd postpone it to go to their place or if they were able to stay over another day, he would [continue the hearing]. Once he got through and had his few questions asked, he'd render that decision almost the same day.[109]

Ollison worked with Edgar as his legal counsel from 1952 to 1974. He describes how Edgar conducted himself in the appeals hearings and how people reacted to Edgar:

I remember people used to come in his office irate, mad, they didn't expect any help here. They didn't get any at the local board hearing. Oh, they'd come just red hot. He'd sit there and listen to them. And listen and listen. And say, "Go ahead. Is there something else you want to say?" . . . He'd say, "This is my decision." They'd come up [and say], "Dr. Edgar, even though the decision was adverse, you know this is the first time in these problems we've been having with our local school district that we've been able to get anybody to listen to us. And we surely do appreciate it. We may not be fully satisfied with your response, but we just appreciate it" . . . It was that way the whole twenty years.[110]

As the Texas Education Agency grew larger, the number of appeals increased. Edgar's last years as Commissioner saw the number of appeals grow so large that hearing officers had to be hired to handle the load.

LAST YEARS AS COMMISSIONER, 1970–1974

Edgar worked as hard his last four years in office as he had the first twenty years. In 1970 Warren Hitt died. Dr. Brockette took Hitt's place. There are two aspects to Edgar's last years as Commissioner: (1) how Edgar conducted himself in his office on a daily basis as Commissioner; and (2) Edgar's retirement in 1974.

At Work As Commissioner: A Profile

Mrs. Mary Thornton was Edgar's secretary during the latter part of his tenure, from 1968 until he retired in 1974. She worked with Edgar on a day-to-day basis around the office when he was not traveling. The following is a profile of Edgar the way that Mrs. Thornton saw him. Here she described Edgar's reputation of being a perfectionist.

I heard a lot of stories [that] he was a very demanding person. One of the secretaries asked me one day after I'd been working for him for a couple of weeks how I did perfect letters. I said, "Well, I don't." She said, "You have to. If you work for Dr. Edgar you have to make perfect letters." I said, "Well, I don't. I just make perfect corrections" . . . he would practically grade the carbon copies of the letters I would type for him . . . He would make check marks and x's and write little notes in the margins about the letter and have me re-do the letter. And one of the secretaries remarked that that was a fallback from his superintendency

days. He was the kind of person that commanded a lot of respect.[111]

In addition to liking his letters as close to perfect as possible,
Mrs. Thornton also relates how neat and well organized Edgar
was.

> His office was a huge barn-like room. His desk was a large
> desk[112] with real big drawers. He was very organized. There was
> not one thing on his desk. Every drawer had a definite purpose.
> Incoming correspondence went in one drawer. Outgoing corre-
> spondence he would dictate from [in another drawer] . . . He
> would dictate twenty or thirty letters at a time. All the corre-
> spondence he was answering would go into the drawer. It was my
> responsibility to keep all this straight. Of course it made it very
> easy for me that he was so well organized. Then there was a
> drawer with matters that were pending. He was very methodical
> about [his work] . . . He wanted every piece of correspondence an-
> swered. He was always accessible by phone. There were very few
> times that he ever refused to take a phone call. His phone number
> was listed in the telephone directory purposely because he always
> wanted to be accessible to the public. He felt that he worked for
> the public as a public servant.[113]

Edgar wanted the public to feel that he was accessible. He
tried to personalize his leadership as much as possible, and he
had a compelling sense of human nature. In the following passage, Mrs. Thornton relates a story which demonstrates this.

> Most of the time he was there when I got there at 8:00. We
> used to joke about the fact that he never left his office. He would
> occasionally get up and walk through the building. He might go
> up on another floor and talk to someone. He had a better under-
> standing of human nature than anybody I've ever worked for.
> [For example], we had a senator come in our office one morning. I
> prefer not to name his name . . . This gentleman stopped at the re-
> ception desk out front in front of our office. And the first thing I
> heard him say was, "Well that's a fine way to treat a State Sena-
> tor." He was very indignant. He came steamrolling across our of-
> fice and was headed for Dr. Edgar's door. And I got up from my
> desk to receive him. And he started toward Dr. Edgar's door and
> he just walked past me. And when he got the first step in the door
> he started yelling. And Dr. Edgar was sitting at his desk with his
> hands clasped, leaning forward looking at the gentleman. And
> the gentleman yelled at him all the way across the room. And
> when he got even with Dr. Edgar's desk, near a chair, Dr. Edgar

said to him, "I'm sorry, Senator, I didn't understand a word you said." And the gentleman sat down, put his hand on his head and began to speak in a very calm and collected manner.[114]

After the senator calmed down, he had Edgar's complete attention. Edgar was a good listener and would hear people out with his complete attention. Mrs. Thornton describes Edgar's desk in this connection, then goes on to talk about a typical day.

But that was the thing about not having anything on his desk. It was a psychological advantage that he knew he had. He wanted anyone that stepped into his office to know that they had his complete attention. A lot of times he'd let someone talk for five minutes without interrupting them. He'd let them tell their story then he'd ask them questions. He'd give them his opinion . . . A lot of times I wouldn't hear anything from him until nine o'clock . . . He would take calls, be composing letters or whatever. We had an intercom system and he would call me on the intercom and ask me to step in for a few minutes. He might dictate a memo or something. He would give me priorities as far as his correspondence was concerned . . . Most of the time he wanted his correspondence out the same day he dictated it . . . A lot of times I never knew what he did for lunch. His afternoons were pretty much the same.[115]

From this profile, one can see that Edgar was a hard worker. He was always at work before eight o'clock in the morning and oftentimes did not leave his office for lunch. His working habits were deliberately neat and meticulously organized. In dealing with people he was always calm and he gave his full attention to the matters at hand. Edgar began to think about retirement in the fall of 1972.

Retirement From The
Commissionership

In the fall of 1972 Edgar felt that he should think about retirement. He was sixty-eight years old. The Texas Education Agency needed a major reorganization. Every so often, when the Agency needed it, Edgar would do some reorganizing. He felt it was time again to reorganize, but he did not want to undertake this task. Edgar explains why:

I was getting tired, frankly. I knew that the Agency needed a drastic overhaul in reorganization. I didn't want to do it if an-

other Commissioner was coming in because I wanted him to have
the privilege and the responsibility of setting the organization as
he saw fit.[116]

After thinking about retirement, Edgar went to the President of the State Board to discuss it. Edgar describes what
transpired:

> He was not very cooperative with me, you might say. In the
> election of 1972, three more congressional districts had been
> added. So this required, in the election of 1972, that all Board
> members run even though their terms hadn't expired yet. It was
> a new Board as far as the law was concerned, twenty-four mem-
> bers instead of twenty-one. Every member had to run and then
> the twenty-four members would draw for terms. The term was six
> years. To make them come out right, they would draw for six,
> four, or two year terms in January when they first met in 1973.
> So the members that had been on the Board, some of them decided
> not to run for reelection. So we had in January of 1973 a new
> Board coming in with any number of new people who had not
> been on the Board before. We also had the Legislature coming
> into town. Finally some of the Board members met with me and
> they just said to me, "Now, look, we can't afford to be appointing
> a new State Commissioner of Education right at the time we have
> to organize a new Board and at the time the Legislature is there.
> So we want to reappoint you for another term beginning June 1,
> 1973 . . . a four-year term." [117]

Edgar agreed to stay at least one more year. During that year
he helped reorganize the Board and got the new machinery
working properly. In the November 1973 Board meeting, Edgar requested that he be allowed to retire on June 1, 1974. The
Board accepted his request and he retired June 30, 1974. The
Board appointed Dr. M.L. Brockett, the Deputy Commissioner,
to replace Edgar. Edgar discusses Brockett's appointment.

> Of course they started looking for a replacement, and grad-
> ually Dr. M.L. Brockett's name began to hold to the top. He was
> my Deputy Commissioner. He had taken Warren Hitt's place in
> 1970. So they appointed Dr. Brockett as the next Commissioner
> . . . the Chairman of the Finding Committee, the Search Commit-
> tee, I guess you call it — talked to me about it. We talked over pos-
> sibilities of some people. I never did try to influence the Board in
> any way about it.[118]

L.P. Sturgeon wrote an editorial in *Texas Outlook* when

Edgar announced his retirement. Following is part of what he wrote.

> The long-term Commissioner has the particular ability to delegate responsibility and to get the most from the able staff he has assembled. And yet he always has kept in touch with every phase of the operation of this most important department of state government.
>
> J.W. Edgar is a man of the people. He has never lost the common touch. He has been required to make thousands of decisions, and his fairness has been demonstrated in the acceptance of these decisions by those affected.
>
> We believe J.W. Edgar will be identified in the future as one of Texas' legendary heroes because of his great contribution to the education of Texas youth. Teachers of Texas as well as lay citizens do well to honor him as he concludes his great career.[119]

Edgar's friends and admirers held a large retirement party for him in Austin; more than one thousand people attended. Dana Williams, the long-time Superintendent of Schools in Corpus Christi, was chairman of a committee which was charged with the task of buying Edgar a gift. Williams talks about what they bought and gave Edgar:

> I was chairman of the committee that raised the money to buy him a gift when he retired. Well I wrote the superintendents and we got a committee together. I can't remember how I got appointed chairman of the committee. But he had some parties in Austin. After he retired we told him we wanted to buy him a gift. And he said he didn't want a gift. He didn't deserve it. It wasn't right. We paid no attention to him. Finally we raised the money. We gave the Edgars an Oldsmobile Ninety Eight. He told me he didn't want it. So we drove it down there one morning to the house. L.P. Sturgeon was there . . . Joe Parker, who's with the Education Service Center, went down and picked out the car. He took Sue with him . . . So she did pick out the color. So we drove the car down and I was there. We told them we wanted to come down and have a cup of coffee with them one morning about ten o'clock. So we were sitting back there in his den where he talks to you, and after awhile the doorbell sounded. It was all the news media and the people all gathered out in the yard. So we told him we wanted him to come out and get some pictures of this. So we brought him out and he said, "What's this all about?" We said, "Well, we've got a little presentation for you. You just have to wait here a minute — maybe a truck will come along and bring

it." About two or three minutes later here came Joe Parker driving up in the blue Oldsmobile . . . I gave the keys to Sue. We told him it was our desire that he be allowed to ride in the car. He may still have it . . . We also gave him — I had about eight thousand dollars in cash left — so we gave him [the] cash.[120]

Edgar left the Commissionership after twenty-four years of service to Texas education. He has stayed out of education since that time.

CONCLUSION

Edgar's role in the implementation of the Gilmer-Aikin Laws was more significant than his role in the proposal and passage of the laws because he was one of the main instruments of implementation. By serving as Commissioner, together with the State Board of Education, Edgar assumed control of the implementation of the Gilmer-Aikin Laws. Three overall factors of this control were important throughout Edgar's involvement in the implementation process: (1) his choice of people to work with him; (2) his philosophy of local control of schools; and (3) his ability to work with the State Board of Education. At least six more specific aspects further illuminate the importance of his role in the implementation of the laws: (1) his decision to be considered for the job of Commissioner; (2) his support of the *Delgado* decision, which demonstrated his support against the segregation of Mexican-Americans in schools; (3) his commitment to the job of Commissioner once he made his name available to the Board for consideration, and his ability to influence the Board; (4) his rapid organization of the Texas Education Agency; (5) his ability to stick with programs and monitor them throughout his tenure of office; and (6) his personal skill as Commissioner in delegating authority.

The first of the overall factors which was important to Edgar's control of the implementation process was his excellent choice of people to work with him when he set up the TEA. A striking example of his excellent choice was Warren Hitt. Not only did Hitt work with Edgar before the TEA was set up (first with the TSTA, then with Sturgeon and the Minimum Foundation School Program) but he continued to serve him for twenty years after the establishment of the TEA, from 1950 until his death in 1970. Hitt exemplifies Edgar's wise choice of people to work for him. Dr. W.R. Goodson comments on Edgar's knack for choosing the right people for the right jobs:

> He had the great ability to select people, give them a responsibility, and work with them in accomplishing this.[121]

In addition, the people who did work for Edgar wanted to do the best job they possibly could for him. M.L. Brockette speaks about this:

> People who worked with him [Edgar] and for him, I think always had such a really high regard [for Edgar] that they wouldn't want to in any way disappoint him.[122]

The second overall factor which was significant in Edgar's control of the implementation process was Edgar's firm belief in the philosophy of local control of schools. Many persons, from legislators to lay people, held this view all over Texas. Edgar's philosophy of local control guided his actions throughout his tenure as Commissioner. Edgar remarks:

> It [local control] had to be that kind of an arrangement in Texas because everybody believed in it, the legislature and everybody else.[123]j

The third overall factor which was vital to Edgar's control of the implementation process was his ability to work the State Board of Education. Alton O. Bowen, former State Commissioner of Education, writes this about Edgar's work with the State Board:

> Dr. Edgar made it a point to get to know personally the superintendents in the school districts in which his State Board members resided because he knew that his State Board would ask his local superintendents for their advice and council on issues that he brought to the board for action. Especially those items that imparted local control of education.[124]

In addition to constant, overall factors which contributed to Edgar's control of the Gilmer-Aikin Laws, more specific aspects of his control are also apparent.

Of these specific aspects which contributed to Edgar's control, the first was Edgar's decision to be considered for the commissionership. Initially, Edgar did not want to be considered for the job, but when it became apparent that some persons from a background unacceptable to Edgar would be considered, he decided to submit his credentials to the State Board. This decision meant that Edgar chose to be in control of the implementation process.

The second specific aspect which aided Edgar in his control of the Gilmer-Aikin Laws was his early support of the *Delgado* decision. Woods had enforced it; Edgar took over where Woods left off. By supporting and enforcing the *Delgado* decision early on, Edgar showed that he would take control of these laws in so far as segregation went. He demonstrated that he was charged with carrying out the law and that through his control he would do everything in his power to abolish segregation. Anderson writes about Edgar's enforcement of the *Delgado* decision:

> Five decisions have been rendered on appeals of board of trustee policies or actions that allegedly resulted in segregation within a district. All five of these decisions were between 1953–1955 and all five concerned the alleged segregation of Mexican-American pupils ... at the time they were reached the rulings were of "landmark" importance. The letter of the decisions sensitized school officials to class action fallacies in traditional school practices, in all likelihood, and certainly the spirit of the decisions gave warning that Mexican-Americans are full-fledged Texas citizens not to be sentenced to separate school treatment.[125]

These five "landmark" decisions were demonstrative of Edgar's support of integration. As Hector Garcia had said, the resistance to integration was systemic in nature and not with Edgar.

The third specific aspect which demonstrated Edgar's control of the implementation of the Gilmer-Aikin Laws had two parts. First was Edgar's commitment to getting the commissionership once he made his name available for consideration. He took the task seriously and answered as best he could all the questions the Board put to him in his interview with its members. Mrs. Paul Bolton's description of what Edgar was doing while the Board was making its final deliberation proves this.

> He sat right here in this living room and walked the floor, carried on and everything, waiting to find out how the Board [came out].[126]

The second part is that when Edgar actually became Commis-

sioner, it immediately became apparent that he could lead the
Board. His expertise in leading the board was so "innocuous,"
as Paul Haas said, that Edgar could lead the Board without the
Board even realizing it was being led. Alton O. Bowen discusses how much respect Edgar commanded:

> Mr. Charles Hart, who was a member of the Bryan School
> Board when I was Superintendent, ran and was elected to the
> State Board of Education from Congressional District Six. When
> Mr. Hart came to me for advise the first time I said, "Charles, if
> you want to be right most of the time on policy issues that come
> before the Board, just vote yes on Dr. Edgar's recommendations."
> That is how much respect I had for J.W. Edgar's judgement and
> integrity.[127]

The fourth specific aspect of Edgar's control was his rapid
reorganization of the Department of Education into the Texas
Education Agency. Dr. Larry Haskew comments on Edgar's organizing the Agency:

> He just had uncanny judgement it turned out later in whom
> he selected in the first place — uncanny judgement in organizing
> the Agency . . . He searched around for the top people to head
> every division. And again it was uncanny, really, as to how he so
> expertly set up that Agency. And set up the men.[128]

Edgar accomplished his organization of the TEA by bringing in
several key people at the top whom he could completely trust
and always depend on. Woods' staff, for the most part, stayed
in tact, and Woods himself stayed on as an advisor. This reorganization was fast and smooth which made the transition of
authority calm and strong. All of this can be accredited to Edgar's superb administrative abilities.

The fifth specific aspect which demonstrated Edgar's control of the implementation of the Gilmer-Aikin Laws was his
ability to stick with programs and monitor them throughout
his tenure in office. With the textbook adoption process, he not
only stayed with it and upgraded it, but he also recommended
an alternative process when he retired. Edgar also devoted
close attention to the appeals process and was personally involved in it throughout his tenure. Anderson concludes in his
study of the appeals process:

> Finally, the investigator is convinced that utilization of the
> devices [appeals process], in spite of many potentially unpopular

and sticky decisions which resulted from its use, has not lowered the prestige of the Commissioner's office, nor has it resulted in carping criticisms of the occupant of that office. Two individuals have served as Commissioner during the period of study, one from 1951 [1950] to 1974 and the other from 1974 to present. The study of the device and its results had only served to increase this investigator's respect for the far-reaching wisdom and fairness of those two individuals.[129]

In addition to the textbook adoption process and the appeals process, Edgar also stayed involved with other programs such as Special Education. Mrs. Dora Huston, long time supporter of Special Education in Texas, comments:

> From the time he [her son] was seven years old until he died [in 1981] I spent a lifetime working in the field, volunteer as well as professionally. Many of the projects I developed were picked up nationally. Way back in the early stages of this thing, there had to be key people . . . And Dr. Edgar was one of them. All through the years I always discussed with J.W. the problem of the handicapped and specifically my son . . . He knew a real need . . . From the minute he became Commissioner . . . He was always somebody I could go and talk to . . . He'd give me good advice . . . He was very much interested in seeing this come to pass. He wanted all children to be helped. You cannot believe . . . when I tell you that retarded people . . . nobody believed they could be helped . . . These children were like you hid them away.[130]

Edgar did help these retarded children by constantly supporting Special Education.

The sixth specific aspect which demonstrated Edgar's control was his personal skill in administering the office of Commissioner. Dr. Larry Haskew comments on Edgar's guidance of the Texas Education Agency.

> He was just a highly superior analyst of situations — "Does this mean anything?" or "Is it of any importance?" — always absolutely neutral toward what answers [one might give] . . . He has been so broad in his conception of what that agency was for that he could always make preference of that. He thought that Agency ought to be a leadership agency not an enforcement agency.[131]

Edgar wanted the TEA to be an educational leader, and through his personal skill in the field of administration he reached his goal.

The three significant overall factors (Edgar's choice of people; his philosophy of local control; and his expertise in working with the State Board) in Edgar's control of the implementation of the Gilmer-Aikin Laws, assured Edgar's strong leadership of the TEA. The six more specific aspects (Edgar's agreeing to be considered for the commissionership; his support of *Delgado*; his commitment to the commissionership and his ability to lead the board; his organization of the TEA; his ability to stay with programs; and his personal skill in administration) demonstrate the importance of Edgar's role in the Gilmer-Aikin Laws. The combination of all these factors illuminates Edgar's remarkable skill as a leader and show that he not only served long, but he served well.

5

Educator For Texas

Edgar's long career spanned the years from 1923 to 1974. Throughout these fifty-one years he worked in the field of education, first as a teacher, then as an administrator. Edgar rose from rural school teacher to First State Commissioner of Education in Texas. He became a part of Tyack's "invisible college" of informed elites, a network of men who were in the forefront of the campaign in Texas to equalize the funding of public education through the Gilmer-Aikin Laws.[1] Edgar was one of the leaders of the "invisible college" and he was sincerely dedicated to the improvement of education in Texas, spending the entirety of his career in Texas. Edgar was a member of various professional education groups which were also dedicated to education and he used these groups to extend his network. Edgar worked toward his advanced degrees while he held full time jobs in the field of education, taking a number of years to earn them.[2] As Commissioner of Education he served education in Texas for twenty-four years. Edgar's peers had a high degree of respect for him, and he could have served as Commissioner longer, if he'd wished.

This concluding chapter is divided into four sections. The first section is a summary of Edgar's career as presented in this research. This first section summarizes the rural and urban phases of Edgar's work in addition to his tenure as Commissioner. The second section is an analysis of what kind of a man Edgar is, including his positive and negative traits as seen from the perspective of those who associated with him. The third section is a discussion of Edgar's contributions to education. It analyzes: (1) his role in Gilmer-Aikin; (2) his innovations as an educator; and (3) his integrity as a leader, and his integrity in his use of the law.

SUMMARY

In the course of this research, the investigator has attempted to analyze the step by step progression of Edgar's career, from his days as a rural school teacher to his last years as Commissioner of Education. This encompasses Edgar's time spent in Lake Victor as a teacher; Bethel as a teacher; Lake Victor again as a teacher and principal; Heidenheimer and Mirando City as a superintendent; Victoria as an assistant superintendent; Orange and Austin as a superintendent; and the State of Texas as Commissioner. Through the gradual progression from one job to the next, Edgar evolved into a first-rate educator and administrator. His excellence was largely derived from experience.

The Rural Phase

Edgar began his experience in education as a teacher of fifth, sixth, and seventh grade in a three-teacher school in Lake Victor during the fall of 1923 after one year of college. In the fall of 1924 Edgar taught the last four grades in a two-teacher school in Bethel which was five miles from Lake Victor and eight miles from Burnet. After teaching one year in Bethel, Edgar returned to Lake Victor as teacher, high school coach, and principal. He remained as principal in Lake Victor for three years from 1925–1927. During the 1927–1928 school year, Edgar married and finished school at Howard Payne. From 1928–1929 Edgar became Superintendent of Schools in Heidenheimer. Here the school district which Edgar supervised comprised two schools (one White and one Black) and five teachers (one Black and four White), Edgar and his wife, Sue, being included as two of the White teachers. From 1929–1936 Edgar was superintendent and Tax Accessor Collector for the Mirando City School District, in which twelve teachers taught approximately three hundred students, one third of which were Mexican-American. The Mirando City District had one Black school with about eight children in it. The above mentioned jobs comprised the rural phase of Edgar's career.

This rural phase of Edgar's early career can, in many respects, be defined as Edgar's "training ground," especially the years from Lake Victor to Heidenheimer. As each year progressed Edgar was adding to his knowledge of education on all levels, from pupils to administrators. In Lake Victor Edgar was especially interested in helping the students develop academic interests of all kinds through the Interscholastic League competitions. He worked at developing a technique for individualizing instruction on a one-to-one basis. As such, Edgar worked closely with pupils and parents on a one-to-one basis. In as small a community as Edgar often lived in while he held these rural jobs, he worked and lived closely in the communities as an important citizen. Consequently, he developed good relations with individual members of the community as well as with pupils and parents. In addition, Edgar became very aware of the importance of school boards, starting with his getting fired by the Lake Victor School Board. Though the school board's action may not have been proper, it made Edgar aware of school boards, the power they could wield, and the importance of getting along with them. During this time Edgar was able to make mistakes, learn from them, and at the same time not harm his career.

Edgar's superintendency at Mirando City was unique and warrants special mention because not only was the superintendency unique since Edgar also served as Tax Accessor Collector, but he served there for seven years, from 1929–1936. Edgar led an independent school district which was financed by the Magnolia Petroleum Company, while all around him were school districts controlled by the Webb County Superintendent. These were early depression years. Of these years, Tyack writes:

> During the early Depression, fiscal support of schools, parks, public health, and libraries, dropped while public demand for social services increased. Perhaps even more frightening than the actual extent of retrenchment for school people was uncertainty about what the future would bring. Educators felt beleaguered by tax cutters and abandoned by former allies.[3]

The presence of the Magnolia Oil Company in Mirando City insured that the Mirando City School District would not shrink during Edgar's tenure. He had adequate funds and support to run the school system; thus, the depression did not have the same impact on Edgar as it did the other school superintendents.

The experience Edgar gained in dealing with rural school people and rural school politics during his early career was undoubtedly a big plus when he was being considered for the commissionership. Not only was he skilled in the practice of small school politics, but since he worked and lived closely with these people, he was well liked and well accepted. Ottis Lock, who was on the Gilmer-Aikin Committee, speaks about the rural school people's acceptance of Edgar.

> Those of us, unofficially, who were on the [Gilmer-Aikin] Committee, we knew that the Board would likely be receptive to recommendations from the [Gilmer-Aikin] Committee. And so we, on an unofficial basis, started searching the State for the man who would breathe life into these then dormant bills . . . We wanted an educator who would be respected by both the rural and city administrators . . . He [Edgar] was considered by the rural superintendents as being a friend, one of them, and understanding of their problems.[4]

The rural school people's acceptance and support of Edgar was a testimonial of his good work in their schools.

Edgar's time spent in Victoria deserves special mention also because, like Mirando City, his situation here was unique. This was a transitional phase for Edgar, between rural and urban settings. Edgar left his job as Superintendent of Schools in the small district of Mirando City to become Assistant Superintendent of Instruction and Personnel in the large district of Victoria. Edgar felt it was simply time to leave Mirando City, he wanted experience in an urban setting, and he felt like the "curriculum bug" had bitten him. Victoria was a district with two thousand students and a junior college. Edgar had the opportunity to work with teachers on planning curriculum and developing strategies for individualizing instruction. He quickly learned that he did not know as much about curriculum as he thought he did and that curriculum was not his field in education. Edgar describes this:

I don't count my years in Victoria in comparison with my other experience as being full, although I did become better acquainted, of course, with the teaching program and instruction program . . . I found out later that I didn't know as much about curriculum as I thought I did . . . I really learned what was my major field of interest — it confirmed the fact that I wanted to be a school superintendent, not a curriculum expert.[5]

While Edger did not become a curriculum expert in Victoria, he did learn to operate in an urban setting. This readied Edgar for the urban phase of his career which comprised his superintendencies in Orange and in Austin.

The Urban Phase

Edgar's tenure as Superintendent of Schools in Orange, from 1939–1947, was the most important job he held in terms of his being chosen State Commissioner of Education. Edgar became well known throughout the state and nation because of his progressive work in Orange. Orange gave Edgar the opportunity to supervise a school district during a period of tremendous growth, from a pre-defense community to a defense and then war community. The school age population in Orange grew from two thousand in 1940 to seven thousand in 1945. During this time Edgar became well-versed in dealing with the federal government through his work with the Lanham Act. Edgar not only used the Lanham Act once it was implemented, but he supported and helped gain support for its passage. Edgar worked with such organizations as the Works Progress Administration (WPA) and Public Works Administration (PWA) through which the Lanham Act was administered. L.P. Sturgeon describes Edgar's work at Orange:

He was a relatively young man, quiet, intelligent, fully aware of the needs of his school district, and willing to take any necessary steps to secure assistance. We were successful in getting legislation enacted. And that legislation is still in effect and operating today.[6]

Through the federal legislative devices available to him, Edgar made his schools in Orange exceptional, and other superintendents used his school as a "model" for their own. Edgar's work in Orange gave him recognition on the state and national level and also gave him solid experience with a large, growing community which depended on the federal government for its support.

Edgar's reputation in Orange secured him the job of Superintendent of Schools in Austin. Many people considered Austin the top superintendency in the state due to its location at the State Capital. The war program was winding down in Orange and Edgar actively sought the superintendency in Austin. Once he got the superintendency, Edgar immediately began making progressive renovations in the Austin School District. Before Edgar arrived in Austin, a planning engineer had located sites for fifteen new schools in Austin. Edgar had the task of constructing new schools, which he accomplished with the help of the teachers who decided what purpose the inside of the schools should serve, and the help of an architect, who would then design the buildings according to the teachers' wishes. Edgar renovated the system of hiring teachers by getting the principals actively involved in the hiring process. Edgar began to organize administratively by having regular meetings with the principals (Black and White together) and faculty representatives. Edgar raised the teacher's pay and organized a ten-month school year for the addition of "curriculum days." In short, Edgar got the school district going. A sign of Edgar's support in this work was when the Austin School Board and Mayor Tom Miller called a bond election on the same day. The city's proposals were defeated and the school proposals were overwhelmingly supported. Again, Edgar had gained the support of community, school people, and school board.

Edgar's support in Austin was indicative of the successful programs which he implemented. Edgar felt that in Austin, more than any other place, he had been forced to come up with solutions to totally new problems, such as his solution to the dilemma of what to do concerning high school sororities and fraternities. Austin also gave Edgar the opportunity to really sharpen his skills in working with school boards. The Austin Board had had the reputation of interfering in the superintendent's job. Edgar proved to be a strong leader, however, and the Austin Board had no need to interfere in his administration. This support was a valuable aspect of Edgar's Austin job, but perhaps the most valuable aspect of his work in Austin was that it gave Edgar self-confidence. He felt that after his experiences in reworking the Austin School District, he could handle anything. Edgar had accomplished a lot in a short period of time.

Edgar's work both in Orange and in Austin prepared him for the job of State Commissioner. In Orange Edgar gained a reputation on the state and national levels for his "model" schools. In Austin he was close to the State Legislature, the Governor, and other influential people. Key people were aware of Edgar and his work. They knew his name even before the search for a State Commissioner began in earnest.

The Commissionership

After Edgar's series of jobs from Lake Victor to Austin, he assumed the awesome role of First State Commissioner of Education in Texas. This job had been a long while in the making. Throughout Edgar's tenure in Austin he had worked on the Gilmer-Aikin Committee. Even before that Edgar had worked with the Texas Association of School Administrators (TASA) on their Committee on Educational Policies, of which he was Chairman, and had developed the report, "Legislative Policies for 1947," which Hollis Moore took to Representative Gilmer. This report was the impetus for the creation of the Gilmer-Aikin Committee. Once Lieutenant Governor Shivers appointed Edgar to the Gilmer-Aikin Committee, Edgar served as Co-Chairman of the Subcommittee on School Administration which proposed a complete reorganization of the methods for selecting the State Board of Education and the State Superintendent of Public Instruction. The work of this subcommittee resulted in Senate Bill 115 which created the job of State Commissioner of Education. This same bill also provided for the election of a twenty-one member State Board of Education, one member from each of the congressional districts in the state. Edgar, along with several other persons, helped to influence the choice of candidates for this first State Board. Dr. Larry Haskew, who was a consultant to the Gilmer-Aikin Committee, speaks about the selection of the candidates.

> Dr. Edgar and a few others, we had sort of a secret contrivance that made sure that in every one of these twenty-one districts where they were going to elect a board member, that at least one super candidate was conjoled into running.[7]

Edgar's work on the Gilmer-Aikin Committee led to the development of a new machinery for the administration of education in Texas, a machinery which Edgar would lead since he was one of the few persons who had the educational credentials to assume the job.

When Edgar did actually take office as State Commissioner on March 8, 1950, he became an active instrument in the implementation of the Gilmer-Aikin Laws which brought untold progress to Texas education. Edgar was appointed by the State Board of Education and approved by the Senate for seven consecutive four-year terms. The following account by Dr. Dana Williams illustrates how secure Edgar was as Commissioner.

> He called me one day and said, "When are you going to be in town?" . . . So I found some reason to go to Austin . . . I went into his office and he said, "Do you know of any reason as to why I shouldn't continue as Commissioner of Education? . . . Has anybody talked to you about it?" I said, "No, I don't know of anybody talking about it. Why do you ask me?" . . . He said, "Well, the State Board of Education for years at this particular monthly meeting . . . has voted to send my contract back for confirmation." He said they didn't do it . . . I said, "Why don't you leave that to me?" I came back to Corpus Christi and went to see Paul Haas. Paul was on the Administrative Committee [of the State Board] . . . I told Paul that and he said, "Gosh, we forgot. That will be done the next time we meet." The matter of his serving was so automatic that there was no movement . . . They didn't bother to do it. He was so sensitive about it. He wouldn't say, "Hey, you forgot to look at my contract." [8]

During Edgar's Commissionership he had his hands in every aspect of education. He dealt with integration, teacher certification, school accreditation, vocational education and rehabilitation, to name just a few programs. He also developed programs for special education for the mentally retarded, for the handicapped, for veterans, for adults. Edgar's accomplishments are innumerable. He personally oversaw all appeals cases and closely worked with the textbook adoption process. During the latter part of his Commissionership Edgar began to get federally oriented again, as the federal government began to take an active role in education. From Edgar's first day as

Commissioner until his last, he was a devoted worker to the cause of the betterment of Texas education.

Throughout his tenure as Commissioner, almost every person who came in contact with Edgar, being friend or foe, admired him as an administrator and respected him as an individual. His long and excellent service as Commissioner will likely never be equaled. Mr. Alton O. Bowen, former Commissioner of Education in Texas, writes of Edgar:

> He was not only the first Commissioner of Education Texas ever had but he was also the best. No other person has ever or will ever serve as long and as well as he did. There have been three commissioners since Dr. Edgar, two of these were trained under him. Dr. Brockette was a good commissioner, but neither he, nor I, or the present one [Raymon L. Bynum], ever reached the standard of service set by Dr. J.W. Edgar, and I seriously doubt that anyone ever will.[9]

EDGAR, THE MAN

What kind of man is J.W. Edgar? What made him so unique and so successful? The investigator will attempt to answer these two questions in terms of Edgar's positive and negative traits as seen from the point of view of people who knew and worked with Edgar. Almost all of the persons who came in contact with Edgar, whether they were on his side or not, held him in high regard. One must not forget, however, that Edgar is a man and does have weaknesses. This research would be incomplete without examining some of the few criticisms about Edgar.

Criticisms

During the early part of Edgar's career as a superintendent, several people thought Edgar was a little too harsh as far as his teachers were concerned. Mrs. E.J. Lunz, whose husband was on the Mirando City School Board, wrote the investigator that her husband told her that some teachers involved with Edgar in Mirando City felt he was difficult to talk to and that he expected too much of them. Many people who the investigator interviewed said that a person was naturally inclined to work above their level as a matter of course when working with Edgar. As such, this criticism can be seen as having some positive value. Mrs. Lunz felt that neither her husband or Edgar were good at small talk since they were both heavily involved in their own work.[10]

Dr. M.G. Bowden also felt that Edgar was a little harsh on teachers. Dr. Bowden tells the following story about when he was a teacher while Edgar was at Victoria.

> He was the kind of a person who always was very dignified. For example, I remember showing up one day in short sleeves . . . He said if I had thought the meeting was important, I would have worn a tie. It was hotter than you know what in Texas in the summer. I was amused by it. It didn't offend me. I was not terribly happy because I thought it was too hot. We didn't have air conditioning in those days.[11]

Mrs. Mary Smithheisler, Edgar's secretary in Orange and in Austin, brings out another weakness of Edgar. This has to do with his temper. She recalls that he had a bad temper and threw things when he was angry, but he only did this when he was alone. She recalls a story about Edgar getting so mad after some people had left his office that he took a book and threw it.[12] This story illustrates how Edgar did try to control his temper in front of other people. By the time Edgar got to Austin, it seems he may have had his temper completely under control. Mrs. O.D. Weeks, one of the Austin School Board members, states of Edgar's manner:

> He would talk very slowly and calmly and never get excited. I never heard him raise his voice — no matter how disgusted he got at somebody. He'd just let them rave and rant, then he'd come off with a humorous comment.[13]

Miss Waurine Walker, Director of Teacher Certification at the Texas Education Agency, said of Edgar's temper:

> I don't think I ever saw him lose his temper. You could tell there were times he was getting a little on edge, but I never did see him actually lose his temper and storm out at people.[14]

Edgar learned to control his temper, and in fact, developed a reputation for being quite calm. The results of holding everything in over the years may have resulted in Edgar's operation for a double aneurysm in his abdomen in 1981. Though it may have not been good for his abdomen, Edgar's reputation of being a relaxed, controlled listener was no doubt due to his calm countenance.

Dr. M.L. Brockette, former State Commissioner of Education and Edgar's successor, felt Edgar had an austere countenance.[15] This may have been partially due to Edgar's leadership role as Commissioner.

As Commissioner, Edgar received some criticism for perhaps being too lax. Dr. Robert Mallas states:

> I doubt seriously that he could ever really fire a person, short of moral turpitude or perhaps dishonesty. I'm not certain he could ever fire a person because they were incompetent . . . He is such a nice tolerant person that he would overlook it.[16]

Edgar did not fire people, but he did discipline workers when it was called for. Dr. W.R. Goodson, former Director of School Accreditation for Edgar, states of Edgar and his staff:

> During the time I was Director of the Division of School Accreditation, we had many school boards to appear in an appeal [as a result of] a report that had been written by staff members. In many instances the phraseology of the report might be weak, and at times, questionable. But never did I see Dr. Edgar embarrass a staff member in public, even though he might not sustain all that had been said. But after the visitors had gone and only the staff was left, then he would take the opportunity to say to the staff member, "I didn't really understand what this is all about, and I would like to know what in the hell you meant by that paragraph." [17]

Dr. James Jeffery, Director of Internal Management under Warren Hitt, relates this account of Edgar's disciplining an employee.

> I was involved with a disciplinary problem with an employee . . . I'm sure you've heard the term, "He slices off your head and you don't know what's going on until you turn around." That's the way the interview went. He [Edgar] was the most skilled man I've ever seen.[18]

Though Edgar did not fire people, his skill in the sensitive area of discipline is unquestionable.

Mrs. Warren Hitt had only one complaint about Edgar:

> If I had any complaint at all against him [it was that] he did not work hard enough salary wise for people in the Agency, in-

cluding himself.[19]

Mrs. Hitt felt that Edgar, her husband, and many other Agency members worked extremely hard, doing more than their share, without compensation for the work. She felt that once Edgar retired the salaries in the TEA staff increased greatly.

These criticisms give a little more humanness to Edgar as a man. They are, however, minor in comparison with his overall excellence. Edgar's positive traits far outweigh his negative ones.

Positive Attributes

Every person the author interviewed was asked the same two questions: What kind of a man is Edgar? What made him so unique and so successful? Several answers continually repeated themselves: (1) Edgar had an excellent and dry sense of humor; (2) he was shy and quiet; (3) he was a hard worker; (4) he was extremely intelligent and was an excellent administrator; (5) he had the ability to choose the right people to work for him; (6) he was a visionary in terms of education. The overwhelmingly positive response which the investigator got to these questions is indicative of Edgar's excellence in the field of education.

In addition to these six general qualities which continually surfaced, other specific attributes deserve individual mention which portray Edgar in a special way.

Mrs. Sally Edgar Ward, Edgar's middle daughter, recalls a story about her father when she got her first job and was leaving home. Sally got a job in the Spring Branch School District in Houston, Texas, and was all packed and ready to leave home. Edgar gave her a box with her birth certificate, teacher certificate, and car insurance papers. After getting in her car and driving a few blocks away from home, Sally turned around and went back to the garage to get some coke bottles to exchange to buy a soda. Edgar came to the garage and said, "It's time for you to buy your own coke bottles." This, she thought, was his way of saying, "You're on your own." [20]

As a superintendent and also as Commissioner, Edgar had special concern for teachers and students. Ottis Lock, when discussing Edgar's selection as Commissioner, speaks of the type of superintendent Edgar was:

Superintendents usually fall into two categories, and we wanted this new commissioner to epitomize one of the two . . . [The first type], he considers everything of being equal standing: his bus program is created to haul children; his cafeteria program is created to feed children; his building program is created to seat children; his maintenance program is created to replace broken window panes. That's one superintendent . . . Now the right kind of superintendent, some of us feel like, [feels] that what transpires between the teacher and the pupil in the classroom . . . is what having school is all about. And everything else is auxilary . . . He [Edgar] put his emphasis on the academic program.[21]

Edgar's continual efforts to raise the quality of the educational programs in Texas as superintendent and as Commissioner are a testimonial to his belief in the importance of the interaction between student and teacher in the classroom. Edgar never lost sight of this important goal, and this was one of the reasons for his success.

Dr. Larry Haskew discusses another reason for Edgar's success. Here he talks about Edgar's use of leadership rather than governorship:

The thing I admire about him the most is his practice has always been that leadership is much better than governorship. So almost every fateful decision that was made there, the policy really was: "Let's demonstrate, persuade, show, and people will come around." Rather than say, "Here are fifteen things you've got to do." Approach the school district with the idea that, "We're here to help you." [22]

One of Edgar's goals when he became Commissioner was to make the Texas Education Agency a leadership agency. He accomplished this goal and in doing this brought integrity to the Agency.

One of Edgar's great personal accomplishments which contributed in great measure to his success was his skill with words and writing. Dr. Frank Hubert discusses this trait.

One of Edgar's great strengths was in the field of policy development. He is a very astute policy analyst . . . He is very careful and measured with the written word. He has a great flair for policy writing and development itself . . . He had unusually fine communication skills . . . particularly in writing. J.W. wasn't a spellbinder orator, but didn't need to be . . . He had messages that were succinct, clear, free of ambiguity . . . Another factor which contributed to his success was his mastery of the English language. This was a contagious thing especially from the man at the top. When it became known throughout the organization that here's a man who's concerned about words and what they mean and what they say, that had a contagious effect throughout the organization . . . He shied away from the verbose. If a word was unnecessary, he simply would not use it.[23]

Dr. Herbert La Grone, former Director of Teacher Education at the Texas Education Agency, captures best the essence of what kind of a man Edgar is and why he was so unique and so successful:

Dr. Edgar exemplifies the perfect integration of all the fine attributes you can give to a person. He was trying to impress no one. He is totally committed to the betterment of mankind. He is constructively progressive [and] actually believes that things can always be improved and consequently is willing to work toward that end. He has the capacity to make one better than one would be. Then he also has the capacity to see where each person can contribute to the betterment of the enterprise. He is able to give them the freedom and the encouragement to move beyond the restriction of self. I think it is the integration of all these attributes into one being that's important. He is so unassuming, so open . . . I found in working with him that I was going well beyond my own level because he just made it possible.[24]

In addition to having a perfect combination of the above attributes, La Grone also discusses how Edgar's values and education helped his success.

This is what Dr. Edgar was so strong on. He had a deep set of values of dignity and worth, and he had a love of mankind. He had a patience, a tolerance. He sought to help rather than hinder. Dr. Edgar's a free man. He's had education and consequently he's become free. And freedom from self, from pressure, freedom from ignorance, are priceless.[25]

La Grone also believes Edgar's simplicity contributed to his success.

Dr. Edgar was a very simple person . . . He exemplifies how complex simplicity is. I believe if you put it all together, and put it into proper perspective, it's really pretty simple. And it backs down to really the values . . . He was able to see through the well of deceit and cheating. He was perfectly free.[26]

La Grone felt that the key to understanding Edgar and his success was in knowing the values which Edgar lived by. In examining Edgar's many contributions to education, his most important contribution, in the opinion of the author, involves his values.

CONTRIBUTIONS TO EDUCATION

Edgar contributed to Texas education in several ways. First, he made a great overall contribution because of his work with the Gilmer-Aikin Laws, the laws which constituted a major educational reform in Texas. Second, Edgar made specific contributions to education in the form of innovative school programs. Third, the most important contributions Edgar made to education were his personal integrity and his integrity in the use of the law.

Edgar And Gilmer-Aikin

The Gilmer-Aikin Laws constituted a major reform for Texas education, a reform which was much needed and which was very well received. Edgar's part in the proposal, passage, and implementation of the Gilmer-Aikin Laws represented a significant contribution to education. First, Edgar was Chairman of the Committee on Educational Policies of the Texas Association of School Administrators, which first proposed the need for educational reform in Texas. Second, Edgar served on the Gilmer-Aikin Subcommittee on School Administration which worked on the section of the Gilmer-Aikin Laws (Senate Bill 115) that changed the entire administrative machinery of education in Texas from the "three-headed monster" that it was to a unitary system of administration. This cohesiveness was necessary to Texas education and was a major reason for the success of the TEA. Third, while remaining in the background, Edgar quietly gathered support for the passage of the Gilmer-Aikin Bills. He did this through the well developed network of school people to which he belonged and helped develop. He was one of the leaders of the network. Fourth, Edgar became the primary instrument for the implementation of the Gilmer-Aikin Laws by being selected the first State Commissioner of Education. His position meant that he was the primary implementor of the laws by the nature of his job. Edgar had a direct role in the creation of the laws and in their implementation. This entire process was a considerable contribution to education as were some of his programs.

Innovative Programs

Many of the persons which the author interviewed described Edgar as an innovative and visionary educator. He did seem to have the extraordinary ability to see what the future needs of schools would be and set up programs for those needs. Edgar did this throughout his whole career.

In Orange, Edgar established schools which would be used as "models" in the future. He developed "summer school recreation programs; kindergarten; school nurses; libraries in all schools; dietitians; and well organized maintenance programs." [27] In addition, Edgar established nurseries in Orange for preschool children which were forerunners of the day care and child development centers in existence today. Also in Orange, classes existed for retarded children. Trained physical education teachers, teachers aids, visual education, art and music teachers on all levels, head teachers, and night classes for adults were programs which Edgar also developed in Orange which became models for our schools today. Edgar's contributions to education in Orange were lasting ones.

Edgar's time spent as Superintendent of Schools in Austin also proved to be an innovative time for education. Edgar would send his staff out to meetings and conferences so they could gain knowledge of new programs. Dr. Lee Wilborn, Director of Instruction for Edgar at Austin, describes Edgar's activities:

> We knew that he was a strong believer in special services, carrying on a solid foundation curriculum, but still offering many special services in the schools. He gave us every opportunity to go and visit and study and evaluate other programs that seemed to be innovative ... We visited programs all over this nation that were innovative where they were doing things that appeared to be unique in a way or highly developmental in the area of instruction. We visited the famous Winnetka Schools. We visited a program over in Louisiana that had a strong implementation for vocational education ... We would come back here and apply whatever seemed to be practical or appropriate for our own programs.[28]

In Austin, Edgar extended the teaching year from nine to ten months, and added what he called "curriculum days" (days for conferences and administration) to the ten-month calendar. An important innovation in connection with the ten-month school year was raising the minimum teachers salary to twenty-four hundred dollars per year. This major contribution of a pay schedule was later added to the Minimum Foundation Program through the Gilmer-Aikin Committee. As such, this proved to be an important, lasting contribution to the improvement of Texas education.

As Commissioner, Edgar worked on innumerable innovative programs from special education to programs for veterans. Dr. Lee J. Wilborn discusses one unique program during Edgar's tenure as Commissioner.

> We had a strong shortage of teachers. We made contact with the Ford Foundation . . . They gave us a grant at one time. We operated a program of teacher education by television. We had a weekly program of television coming through twenty-six stations when we were attempting to recruit liberal arts graduates, who had not qualified for certification, in their original baccalaureate program. And through the program we offered by television we could give them a provisional certificate to teach. And we filled many positions with some highly competent people.[29]

For Edgar's many innovations in education he was recognized by awards, life memberships, and other honors.[30]

Edgar, The Law, And Integrity

The most important contributions Edgar made to education were his personal integrity and his integrity in the use of the law. Though Edgar strictly followed the letter of the law, he did absolutely anything that was not specifically forbidden by law. Dr. Charles Mathews, Superintendent of Schools in Longview, Texas, comments on this.

> I always thought that Dr. Edgar had the philosophy that anything that was good for the schools, he would involve the Agency [in] if there was not a statement to prohibit [it]. Since that time so many of the policies are that "We'll not do it unless it is authorized by law." Edgar always said, "If its good for the schools, and there is no law against it, we're going to do it." [31]

Of Edgar and the law, Dr. Wilborn states:

We made no step in any direction that would in any way border on violating the law. We knew that we were within the law on everything we did. As history will tell you there never was an item ever brought up in his [Edgar's] department of any question of wrongdoing. To me that is a pretty strong reflection of his character and his personality.[32]

Edgar did have an honest character and much personal integrity.

Edgar's single most important contribution to education is his personal integrity. He was an honest man. He brought integrity to education in Texas by the example of his own person. Dr. Robert Mallas discusses Edgar's stature.

Texas is the only state I've known that had during a particular period of its history, a De Witt Greer, highways; an Edgar, education; a Winters, welfare; a Homer Garrison, public safety. To put it in the words of a president of the United States . . . he said, "Texas has incredibly tall timber" . . . All of those men turned down the opportunity to move to the national level.[33]

Edgar was certainly capable of moving to the national level, but he chose to remain in his home state.

Dr. Charles F. Mathews relates a story of Edgar's integrity, and how Edgar felt that Mathews was wrong in traveling on his [Matthews] school money and asking Edgar for a job.

His last year in Austin, I talked to him about the possibility of being a high school principal. Just an interview. First time I ever met him . . . I was principal in Midland High School and I was in Austin attending a state convention. And he let me know that he didn't think that I was as professional as I should be, down attending a convention, talking to him about a job.[34]

Dr. Herbert La Grone relates a story about some cowboy boots which illustrates Edgar's honesty.

A group visited a College at Wichita Falls to review their Master's Degree Program. The city of Wichita Falls gave them boots. They all came home proud of their new boots. He [Edgar] told them they'd have to send them back. [He said], "It just was a dangerous precedent. It blocked what you could do in the future *because there was a chance for complaint."* [35]

Dr. Brockette also relates how Edgar's integrity dominated his actions.

I came to know him [Edgar] as an exceedingly honest individual. Sue Edgar has remarked to me a time or two, "Pop never even would let us use one of those little yellow pencils from the Agency he would bring home." He felt so responsible about that sort of thing that when I cleaned out his desk I found gold pencils and stuff like that . . . you know, fountain pens that had been given to him and had his name on them, and so forth, that he'd left behind. Which is a simple example, but it nonetheless brings out the fact that he was honest with himself and honest with the codes he lived under.[36]

Edgar's personal integrity as the state leader of Texas education for twenty-four years made the Texas Education Agency a fine leader, a credible one, an honest one, and one that all could trust in and place their future hopes for education. Edgar's personal integrity serves as an example for all persons to follow and is the finest contribution to education that one individual can make. James Winfred Edgar is perhaps the finest and most significant educator Texas has seen. He is: Educator for Texas.

APPENDICES

APPENDIX A

Burnet High School Commencement Program, May 24, 1921

Commencement Exercises
Burnet High School
School Auditorium, Tuesday Evening, May 24, 1921

Program

Prelude—"Under Sealed Orders".....................Olive D. McLean,
Leta Howell, Helen Kinkead and Graduates.

Piano Solo—"Il Rusignuolo".......................Miss Nell Holland

Invocation.....................................Prof. W. E. Fry

Address—President's Proclamation...............Winfred Edgar

Chorus—"Voices of the Woods"....................Sappho Club

Salutatory—The Class Yell......................Vance A. Percy

Class Poem—The High School O'er the Way":—
   1. The Verdant Freshman..............Ada Jackson
   2. The Crushed Soph...................Alta Jackson
   3. His Junior Year....................Estelle Piper
   4. The Wisdom of the Seniors.......Clara Shirley
   5. The School of Experience...........Vyva Hahn

Class Song—The Call to Action...................Class of 1921

Oration—Old Rose and Gray......................Thomas Ferguson

Class History—"Many Are Called : Few Are Chosen"....Vyva Hahn

Essay—The Rose.................................Ima Schilling

Song—"Roses, We Love You".....................The Pleiades Club

Prophecy—"Things Are Not What They Seem"..........Estelle Piper

Giftatory—The Class Scrap-bag..................Helen Duggan

Class Will—"We Give and Bequeath"..............John Sheridan

Valedictory—"Sunrise not Sunset"...............Thad Glimp

Presentation of Diplomas........................Supt. E. W. Baker

Song—America...................................School Children

---

BACCALAUREATE SERVICE SUNDAY 11 A. M., MAY 22.
Address by Dr. W. J. Battle of Texas University
SCHOOL AUDITORIUM

APPENDIX B

LIST OF PROFESSIONAL GROUPS
TO WHICH EDGAR BELONGED

Texas State Teachers Association

1. Committee on Teacher Retirement, Member, 1935–37. Prepared report that led to passage of Teacher Retirement Law, 1937.
2. State-Federal Relations Committee, Chairman, 1945–47
3. Executive Committee, Member, 1946–48
4. Legislative Committee, Member, 1947–49

Texas Association of School Administrators

1. Vice President, 1940–42
2. President, 1942–44
3. Educational Policies Committee, Chairman, 1946–47. Prepared report which led Representative Claud Gilmer to introduce in the legislature a resolution calling for the Gilmer-Aikin Committee.

Editorial Board — School Executive Magazine, Member, 1947–52

1. Met periodically with Editor and staff to advise on editorial policy. Published in New York City National Circulation.

Boy Scouts of America

1. National Committee on Scouting in Schools, Member, 1948–54. Met annually with Boy Scout Executives to advise on School-Scouting relationships.

State Board of Education

1. State Textbook Advisory Committee, Chairman, 1947–48. Recommended four textbooks in each subject for State Board of Education Adoption.

Gilmer-Aikin Committee, 1947–49

1. Subcommittee on Administration, Co-Chairman. Developed recommendations to Committee on State School Administrative Structure.

Teacher Retirement System of Texas

1. Board of Trustees,Member, 1948–50.

American Association of School Administrators

1. Yearbook Commission, Member, 1950. Wrote and produced, "Public Relations for American Schools"; published, 1950.
2. Committee for the Advancement of School Administration, Member, 1957–62. This committee originated and developed

programs for improving school administration to be sponsored by the American Association of School Administrators.

3. The Educational Policies Commission, Member, 1963–66 (AASA-NEA Sponsored). Developed and produced statements of policy on various issues. Examples: "Universal Opportunity for Education Beyond the High School" (1964); "Educational Responsibilities of the Federal Government" (1974); "American Education and the Search for Equal Opportunity" (1965); "The Unique Role of the Superintendent of Schools" (1965); "Education and the Spirit of Science" (1966).

Ford Foundation

1. Fund for the Advancement of Education Consultant (part-time), 1959–61. Worked with Fund's Great Cities School Project. Consulted in Chicago, Philadelphia, Detroit, Cleveland, Pittsburg, etc. on improving intercity schools.

Kellogg Foundation

1. Advisory Committee on Education, Member, 1961–64. Advised on policies if Foundation should follow in funding educational grants.

President Johnson

1. President's Task Force on Education, Member, 1966. Developed a report (classified) to President Johnson on current educational problems.

U.S. Commissioner of Education

1. Advisory Committee on Vocational Education, Member, late 1960's and early 1970's.

The University Interscholastic League

1. Literary and athletic programs of the League were very attractive to me in my early teaching years as an excellent means of enriching instruction and school life for boys and girls. It was a substantive factor in influencing me to continue school work as a career.

APPENDIX C

MEMBERS OF THE GILMER-AIKIN COMMITTEE

Senator James E. Taylor, Chairman
Kerens, Texas

Mr. H. W. Stilwell, Vice-Chairman
Superintendent of Schools
Texarkana, Texas

Senator A.M. Aikin, Jr.
Paris, Texas

Mr. C.B. Downing
Superintendent of Schools
Iraan, Texas

Mr. J.W. Edgar
Superintendent of Schools
Austin, Texas

Mr. Claud Gilmer
Rock Springs, Texas

Mr. Ottis E. Lock
Lufkin, Texas

Dr. H.A. Moore (Formerly
Superintendent of Schools
Kerrville, Texas)

Mr. Wright Morrow
1307 Commerce Building
Houston, Texas

Mr. J.C. Peyton
Peyton Packing Company
El Paso, Texas

Dr. B.F. Pittenger
822 East 37th
Austin, Texas

Miss Nan Proctor
Victoria, Texas

Mrs. J.G. Smith
2308 Campbell Street
Commerce, Texas

Mrs. Rae Files Still
Waxahachie, Texas

Senator Gus Strauss
Hallettsville, Texas

Mr. R.L. Thomas
Dallas National Bank
Dallas, Texas

Mr. Peyton L. Townsend
1400 Main
Dallas, Texas

Dr. R.J. Turrentine
1021 Oakland
Denton, Texas

* * * * *

Dr. L.D. Haskew
Technical Consultant
The University of Texas
Austin, Texas

Dr. Pat H. Norwood
Executive Agent
Capitol Station
Austin, Texas

Miss Betty Dunlavey, Secretary
Capitol Station
Austin, Texas

APPENDIX D

List of Texas Education Agency Personnel after Edgar took over as
Commissioner, 1949–50

TEXAS EDUCATION AGENCY

STATE BOARD OF EDUCATION
State Board for Vocational Education

Leon Coker, Naples .... First District
A.D. Moore, Beaumont............................... Second District
Thomas B. Ramey, Tyler .... Third District
Paul Mathews, Greenville........................... Fourth District
J.F. Kimball, Dallas.................................... Fifth District
Jack R. Hawkins, Groesbeck .... Sixth District
Emerson Stone, Jacksonville .... Seventh District
Jack Binion, Houston .... Eighth District

Mrs. Joe A. Wessendorff, Richmond .... Ninth District
Paul Bolton, Austin .... Tenth District
Leslie Huff, Waco................................. Eleventh District
Cecil A. Morgan, Fort Worth .... Twelfth Districe
R.B. Anderson, Vernon (chairman).............. Thirteenth District
Neal B. Marriott, Corpus Christi................ Fourteenth District
Paul B. Greenwood, Harlingen.................... Fifteenth District
Herman Rosch, El Paso.......................... Sixteenth District
E.J. Woodward, Sweetwater................... Seventeenth District
A.R. Bivins, Amarillo.......................... Eighteenth District
E.H. Boulter, Lubbock .... Nineteenth District
W.W. Jackson, San Antonio..................... Twentieth District
Penrose B. Metcalfe, San Angelo .... Twenty-first District

J.W. EDGAR, Commissioner of Education
Executive Secretary of the State Board of Education

OFFICE OF PUBLIC SCHOOL ADMINISTRATION AND FINANCE

L.P. Sturgeon .... Associate Commissioner of Education
Director, Division of Finance
H.A. Glass.. Director, Division of Textbooks and Instructional Materials
Bascom B. Hayes...... Director, Division of Administrative Services

OFFICE OF AGENCY ADMINISTRATION

J. Warren Hitt.................. Deputy Commissioner of Education
T.J. O'Connor .... Business Office
Guy C. West.................. School Census, Statistics and Reports
Vane C. Burnett........................ School Bonds, Investments
John C. Clemens .... Field Audit Service

OFFICE OF INSTRUCTIONAL MATERIALS

Lee J. Wilborn.............. Assistant Commissioner for Instruction,
Director of Curriculum Development
Frank W.E. Hubert.............. Director of Professional Standards
H.E. Robinson... Director of Special Education for Exceptional Children

OFFICE OF VOCATIONAL SERVICES

M.A. Browning....... Acting Assistant Commissioner for Vocational Services
Robert A. Manire....... State Supervisor for Vocational Agriculture
Ruth C. Huey......... State Supervisor for Homemaking Education
Plasco G. Moore .... Acting State Supervisor for Distributive Education
W.R. Cate ...... State Supervisor for Trade and Industrial Education
J.J. Brown............... State Supervisor for Vocational Education
B.C. Davis................ State Supervisor for Veterans Education

APPENDIX E

STATE OF TEXAS
CHIEF STATE SCHOOL OFFICERS

B.M. Baker	1884–1887
O.H. Cooper	1887–1890
H.C. Pritchett	1890–1891
J.M. Carlisle	1891–1899
J.S. Kendall	1899–1901
Alfred Lefevre	1901–1905
R.B. Cousins	1905–1910
F.M. Bralley	1910–1913
W.M. Doughty	1913–1919
Annie Webb Blanton	1919–1923
S.M.N. Marrs	1923–1932
C.N. Shaver	1932
L.W. Rogers	1932–1933
L.A. Woods	1933–1950
J.W. Edgar	1950–1974
M.L. Brockette	1974–1979
Alton O. Bowen	1979–1981
Raymon Bynum	1981–

APPENDIX F

Edgar's Awards for Distinguished Service to Education, Life Memberships, and Honors

AWARDS FOR DISTINGUISHED SERVICE TO EDUCATION

1. Texas State Teachers Association: 1955
2. A. Harris & Co. Texas Award: 1956
3. Texas Vocational Agriculture Teachers Association: 1958 & 1970
4. Boy Scouts of America Silver Beaver Award: 1959
5. National Mover and Shaper of Education, Citation by *Saturday Review Magazine*: 1960
6. Vocational Industrial Clubs of Texas: 1960
7. Boy Scouts of America: 1960
8. Texas Association of Secondary Principals: 1962 & 1969
9. Vocational Homemaking Teachers of Texas: 1963 & 1965
10. Freedoms Foundation at Valley Forge American Educators Medal: 1963
11. *Texas School Business Magazine*, Texas Educator of the Decade: 1954–1964
12. Texas Association of Distributive Education Clubs: 1965
13. Texas Association of Future Farmers of America, Honorary State Farmer Award: 1966 & 1974
14. Texas Association of School Boards: 1969

15. Visiting Teachers Association of Texas: 1969
16. Civil Air Patrol Areospace Education Leadership Award (Presented by Texas Areospace Education Council): 1969
17. Blackshear Elementary School (Austin) Parent Teachers Association: 1970
18. Golden Deeds in Education Award, Texas A&M University Conference: 1970
19. Texas Personnel and Guidance Association: 1972
20. Texas Congress of Parents and Teachers: 1973
21. Texas Educational Secretaries Association: 1973
22. University Interscholastic League of Texas: 1973
23. Texas Association of Teacher Educators Ben E. Coady Award: 1973
24. Texas Classroom Teachers Association: 1974
25. Carl Bredt Award — U.T. College of Education Outstanding Alumnus: 1974
26. Texas Industry Council for Career Education: 1974
27. Texas Commission on Fire Protection, Personnel Standards, and Education: 1974
28. National School Public Relations Association: 1974
29. Southwest Educational Development Laboratory: 1974
30. Texas Council for Exceptional Children: 1974
31. Texas Association for Retarded Children: 1974
32. Mechanical Contractors Association of Texas: 1974
33. U.S. Department of Health, Education, & Welfare, Region VI, Office of Education Award: 1974

LIFE MEMBERSHIPS

1. Texas Congress of Parents and Teachers. Presented by Orange Schools Parent Teacher Council: 1944
2. National Education Association. Presented by Orange School Teachers Council: 1947
3. National Congress of Parents and Teachers. Presented by Texas Congress of Parents and Teachers: 1950
4. Texas Association of Future Homemakers of America: 1951
5. Texas Association of New Farmers of America: 1961
6. Texas Association of New Homemakers of America: 1963
7. Texas Association of Young Homemakers of America: 1966
8. Texas Association of Young Farmers of America: 1966
9. National Council of Chief State School Officers: 1974
10. Texas Association of School Administrators: 1975

HONORS

1. Austin College Doctor of Laws Degree: 1958
2. Southwestern University Doctor of Literature Degree: 1967
3. The Chamizal Settlement Medallion from U.S. President Lyndon B. Johnson and Mexico President Gustavo Diaz Ordaz: 1967
4. Paris, Texas, Junior College Medallion: 1972

APPENDIX G

IDENTIFICATION OF PERSONS
WHO WROTE LETTERS AND WERE INTERVIEWED

Senator A.M. Aikin. Senator in the Texas Senate who sponsored the Gilmer-Aikin Bills. (Interviewed July 23, September 19, and November 4, 1975.)

Robert V. Anderson. Chairman of the First Elected State Board of Education. (Letter of July 30, 1956.)

Mr. Vernon Baird. Member of State Board of Education when Edgar retired from the commissionership. (Letter, July 1, 1974.)

Mrs. Pauline Berry. Wife of Dr. Edgar's brother. Currently runs his funeral home. (Interviewed July 16, 1983, Burnet, Texas.)

Dr. Alton O. Bowen. Assistant Commissioner for Education Service Center for the T.E.A., 1971. Deputy Commissioner of T.E.A., 1975. Commissioner of T.E.A., 1979–1981. Currently Vice President of Citizens Banks, Bryan, Texas (Letter, September 2, 1983.)

Dr. M.G. Bowden. Was a student in the primary grades when Dr. Edgar was at Lake Victor. He was a principal in Victoria when Dr. Edgar was there. During Dr. Edgar's tenure in Austin, he was principal at Woodridge school and then later at Casis school. He taught at Trinity College in San Antonio. Currently retired. (Interviewed July 13, 1983, Austin, Texas.)

Mr. Paul Bolton. News Director KTBC, Channel 7, 1944. Elected to Austin School Board and served while Dr. Edgar was Superintendent in Austin. Elected to the first State Board of Education, 1949. Currently retired. (Interviewed July 25, 1983, Austin, Texas.)

Dr. M.L. Brockette. Superintendent at Orange, Texas, 1967. Made Assistant Commissioner for the Regional Service Center in 1967. Made Deputy Commissioner of Education in 1970. Made State Commissioner of Education in 1974. (Interviewed August 4, 1983, Austin, Texas.)

Mr. Raymon Bynum. Started teaching the year Dr. Edgar became Commissioner. Assistant Superintendent of Richmond in charge of finance, administration, and growth. Current State Commissioner of Education. (Interviewed August 23, 1983, Austin, Texas.)

Mr. C.O. Chandler. Principal in Orange while Dr. Edgar was there. Assistant Superintendent at Orange, Texas. Superintendent at Orange. (Letter, August 2, 1983.)

Dr. Clyde Colvert. Ran the Junior College Program at The University of Texas at Austin from 1944 to 1970. (Interviewed August 26, 1983, Austin, Texas.)

Mr. S.P. Cowan. Taught and coached by Dr. Edgar at Lake Victor. Superintendent at Brownsfield. (Interviewed July 9, 1983, Seguin, Texas.)

Governor Price Daniel. Former Governor of Texas. Texas Attorney General at the time of the passage of Gilmer-Aikin. (Interviewed November 17, 1977.0

Dr. J.W. Edgar. First State Commissioner of Education in Texas. (Interviewed April 6, 7, 9, 11, 12, 13, 15, 16, 17, 18, 19, 1983, Austin, Texas.)

Mrs. Sue Edgar. Wife of Dr. J.W. Edgar. (Interviewed July 6, 1983, Austin, Texas.)

Judge Thomas C. Ferguson. Went to high school with Dr. Edgar. Currently semi-retired. (Interviewed July 17, 1983, Burnet, Texas.)

Mr. J.E. "Jack" Fulbright. Worked as a Principal and Coach at Mirando City, Texas, while J.W. Edgar was Superintendent. (Letter, June 2,, 1983.)

Mr. E.L. Galyean. Was acting Executive Secretary of the Texas State

Teachers Association in 1974. Was Associate Executive Secretary of the T.S.T.A. Was a Deputy Superintendent for the Fort Worth and Denton districts under Dr. L.A. Woods. (Interviewed August 11, 1983, Austin, Texas.)

Dr. Hector Garcia, M.D. Founder of American G. I. Forum. (Interviewed November 17, 1983, Corpus Christi, Texas.)

Dr. E. Marie Gilbert. Ran only business college owned and operated by a Black person. Taught at Keeling Junior High School while Dr. Edgar was superintendent. Worked with NAACP and is a life member. Currently active in Austin affairs. (Interviewed August 6, 1983, Austin, Texas.)

Representative Claud Gilmer. Representative in the Texas House of Representatives who sponsored the Gilmer-Aikin Bills (Interviewed April 6, 1968, and November 15, 1976.)

Dr. W.R. Goodson. Superintendent of Copperas Cove. Taught at Southwest Texas State Teachers College, San Marcos. Director of School Accreditation in T.E.A. 15 years. (Interviewed September 19, 1983, Austin, Texas.)

Mr. Paul R. Haas. Member of State Board of Education, 1962–1972. (Interviewed November 18, 1983, Corpus Christi, Texas. Letter, October 13, 1983.)

Dr. Lawrence D. Haskew. Principal in Georgia. Worked on a reform of the the Georgia schools. Came to The University of Texas in 1947. Was consultant to the Gilmer-Aikin Committee. Still at The University of Texas at Austin. (Interviewed August 17, 1983, Austin, Texas.)

Mrs. Bascom Hayes. Wife of Dr. Bascom Hayes (deceased), Assistant Commissioner of Administrative Services, T.E.A., 1954–57. (Interviewed August 15, 1983, Austin, Texas.)

Mrs. J. Warren Hitt. Wife of J. Warren Hitt (deceased), Deputy of Personnel and Research in Austin while Dr. Edgar was Superintendent. Deputy Commissioner of Education under Dr. Edgar. Interviewed August 15, 1983, Austin, Texas.)

Dr. Frank W.E. Hubert. Taught at Orange while Dr. Edgar was Superintendent at Orange. Director of the Bureau of Professional Standards, 1950–54. Orange Superintendent of Schools, 1954–59. Dean of College of Education at Texas A&M, 1969–79. Chancellor of Texas A&M, 1979–82. Currently retired. (Interviewed August 2, 1983, College Station, Texas.)

Mr. P.E. Hutchinson. Worked with the Legislative Accounts Office, 1944. Helped set up Minimum Foundation Program. Director of Finance at T.E.A., 1950–74. Currently worked with teacher retirement fund. (Interviewed August 10, 1983, Austin, Texas.)

Mrs. Dora Huston. First husband, Mr. John P. Manning worked for T.E.A. and for Dr. Edgar. Mrs. Huston a pioneer for Special Education. Worked for Vocational Rehabilitation. (Interviewed September 16, 1983, Austin, Texas.)

Dr. James Jeffrey. Worked for T.E.A. from 1960 to 1967. Currently Director of Noninstructional Affairs for Austin Independent School District. (Interviewed August 3, 1983, Austin, Texas.)

Dr. Lorrin Kennamer. Consultant on Textbook Committee for Dr. Edgar. Currently Dean of the College of Education at The University of Texas at Austin. (Interviewed August, 24, 1983.)

Mrs. Betty King. Worked for Senator Claud Gilmer. Secretary of Gilmer-Aikin Committee. Was Secretary for L.P. Sturgeon. Currently Secretary of the Texas Senate. (Interviewed August 8, 1983, Austin, Texas.)

Mr. Willie I. Kocurek. Austin Board of Education, 1947–50. Currently practicing lawyer. (Interviewed July 27, 1983, Austin, Texas.)

Dr. Herbert La Grone. Principal of University Junior High in Austin. Director of Teacher Education at T.E.A., 1954. Currently professor at T.C.U. (Interviewed August 1983, Fort Worth, Texas.)

Senator Ottis Lock. Served in Texas House of Representatives from 1939–49. Texas Senate from 1949 until 1959. On Gilmer-Aikin Committee. Currently retired. (Interviewed September 17, 1983, Burnet, Texas.)

Mrs. Peg Lunz. Her husband, Mr. E.J. Lunz, was on the Mirando City School Board while Dr. Edgar was Superintendent. (Letter, August 1, 1983.)

Dr. Robert Mallas. Evaluated the Gilmer-Aikin Bill in 1954. Evaluated the Vocational Rehabilitation Program in 1960. Worked on Special Education in 1967. Currently a businessman in Austin. (Interviewed September 9, 1983, Austin, Texas.)

Mr. Pete Marcheck. Attended Howard Payne when Dr. Edgar attended. Taught and coached at Mirando City when Dr. Edgar was Superintendent. (Letter, August 9, 1983.)

Mr. J.A. Marshall. Knew Dr. Edgar when he was at Heidenheimer, Texas. Director of Vocational Agriculture in T.E.A. (Interviewed July 20, 1983, Austin, Texas.)

Dr. Charles F. Mathews. Superintendent of Plainview, Texas. President of Texas Association of School Administrators (T.A.S.A.), 1961. Currently Executive Director of T.A.S.A. (Interviewed August 11, 1983, Austin, Texas.)

Mr. Paul Mathews. Member of State Board of Education, 1949–1983. (Letter, August 1, 1983.)

Mr. Vernon McGee. Worked for the Legislative Budget Director. Currently retired. (Interviewed September 9, 1983, Austin, Texas.)

Mr. Chester Ollison. Legal Council for T.E.A., 1952–1976. (Interviewed August 9, 1983, Austin, Texas.)

Mr. Friendly R. Rice. Principal in Austin, Blackshear, while Dr. Edgar was Superintendent. (Interviewed July 29, 1983, Austin, Texas.)

Mrs. Bettina Charles Rosett. Attended school in Mirando City when Dr. Edgar was Superintendent. (Letter, August 1, 1983.)

Mrs. Carolyn Ruhman. Secretary for Warren Hitt, 1965–70. Became Secretary of the State Board of Education, 1971 (Interviewed August 16, 1983.)

Governor Allan Shivers. Lt. Governor of Texas during Gilmer-Aikin legislation. Governor in July 1949. Currently works at InterFirst Bank, Austin. (Interviewed September 9, 1983, Austin, Texas.)

Governor Preston Smith. Former Governor of Texas. Member of the Texas House of Representatives at the time of the Gilmer-Aikin Laws. (Interviewed July 31, 1975.)

Mrs. Mary Louise Smithheissler. Secretary for Dr. Edgar in Orange. Secretary for Dr. Edgar in Austin. Currently a housewife. (Interviewed September 17, 1983, Burnet, Texas.)

Mrs. Rae Files Still. Member of Texas House. Wrote thesis on Gilmer-Aikin Bills. Member, Gilmer-Aikin Committee. (Letter, August 15, 1983.)

Dr. John Stockton. Created economic index for the Minimum Foundation Program. Currently retired. (Interviewed August 5, 1983, Austin, Texas.)

Mr. L.P. Sturgeon. Superintendent in New Boston. Interim State Commissioner. Executive Secretary of T.S.T.A. Currently retired. (Interviewed August, 1983, New Boston, Texas. Letter, August 26, 1983.)

Senator James E. Taylor. Chairman of the Gilmer-Aikin Committee. Texas State Senator. (Interviewed July 30, 1983, Austin, Texas.)

Mrs. Mary Thornton. Secretary for Dr. Edgar, 1968–79. Currently a housewife. (Interviewed September 14, 1983, Austin, Texas.)

Miss Waurine Walker. Worked on Gilmer-Aikin. Director of Teacher Certification for T.E.A. (Interviewed August 16, 1983, Austin, Texas.)

Mrs. Sally Edgar Ward. Daughter of Dr. J.W. Edgar. (Interviewed September 9, 1983.)

Mrs. O.D. Weeks. Member of Austin School Board. Publicity Director of T.E.A. 18 years, 1953–71. (Interviewed August 6, 1983, Austin, Texas.)

Dr. Lee J. Wilborn. Principal of Allen Junior High while Dr. Edgar was Superintendent at Austin. Assistant Commissioner for Instruction at T.E.A., 1950–1977. (Interviewed October 7, 1983, Austin, Texas.)

Dr. Dana Williams. Superintendent of Schools in Corpus Christi, 1962–1981. Currently Executive Vice President Coastal Bend Community Foundation. (Interviewed November 17, 1983, Corpus Christi, Texas. Letter, October 17, 1983.)

Ms. Mary Frances Winston. Elementary school teacher in Austin when Dr. Edgar was Superintendent. (Telephone interview, July 27, 1983, Austin, Texas.)

Senator Ralph Yarborough. U.S. Senator from Texas from 1958–1971. El Paso court case (was lawyer for El Paso School District) against T.E.A. (Interviewed October 13, 1983, Austin, Texas.)

ENDNOTES

CHAPTER 1.   YOUTH TO VICTORIA: THE RURAL PHASE

1. J.W. Edgar, "The Edgar Transcripts" [A 325 page transcript of nine taped interviews with Dr. Edgar by Stephen C. Anderson (hereafter referred to as SCA) in April, 1983, in Austin, Texas, on file in the University of Texas Oral History Education Collection (hereafter referred to as UTOHEC)], April 6, 1983, pp. 1–2.

2. *Ibid.*, p. 17.

3. *Ibid.*, p. 17.

4. *Ibid.*, p. 16.

5. *Ibid.*, p. 18.

6. *Ibid.*, p. 17.

7. *Ibid.*, p. 6.

8. *Ibid.*, p. 7.

9. *Ibid.*, p. 8.

10. *Ibid.*, p. 7.

11. *Ibid.*, p. 8.

12. J.W. Edgar, "The Edgar Transcripts," April 9, 1983, p. 51.

13. The others were Neil Holland and Thomas Ferguson.

14. See Appendix A.

15. Judge Thomas Ferguson, taped interview by SCA on July 16, 1983, in Burnet, Texas. Side B. UTOHEC.

16. J.W. Edgar, "The Edgar Transcripts," April 7, 1983, pp. 22–24.

17. J.W. Edgar, "The Edgar Transcripts," April 9, 1983, p. 18.

18. *Ibid.*, p. 20.

19. *Ibid.*, p. 19.

20. *Ibid.*, p. 14.

21. S.P. Cowan, taped interview by SCA on July 9, 1983, in Seguin, Texas. UTOHEC.

22. Dr. M.G. Bowden, taped interview by SCA on July 13, 1983, in Austin, Texas. UTOHEC.

23. J.W. Edgar, "The Edgar Transcripts," April 7, 1983, p. 32.

24. Mrs. J.W. Edgar, taped interview by SCA on July 6, 1983, in Austin, Texas. UTOHEC.

25. J.W. Edgar, "The Edgar Transcripts," April 7, 1983, pp. 36–37.

26. *Ibid.*, p. 39.

27. *Ibid.*, p. 41.

28. Peter Marcheck, letter to SCA on August 9, 1983, from Pawnee, Texas. UTOHEC.

29. J.W. Edgar, "The Edgar Transcripts." April 7, 1983, p. 42.

30. *Ibid.*, p. 43.

31. *Ibid.*, p. 45.

32. *Ibid.*, p. 45.

33. *Ibid.*, p. 49.

34. Mr. J.A. Marshall, taped interview by SCA on July 20, 1983, in Austin, Texas. UTOHEC.

35. J.W. Edgar, "The Edgar Transcripts," April 9, 1983, p. 61.

36. Mrs. E.J. Lunz, letter to SCA on April 16, 1983, from Hebbronville, Texas. UTOHEC.

37. J.W. Edgar, "The Edgar Transcripts," April 9, 1983, p. 57.

38. Mrs. Bettina Charles Rosett, letter to SCA on August 1, 1983, from San Antonio, Texas. UTOHEC.

39. J.W. Edgar, "The Edgar Transcripts," April 9, 1983, pp. 59–60.

40. J.E. Fulbright, letter to SCA in August, 1983, from Hebbronville, Texas. UTOHEC.

41. J.W. Edgar, "The Edgar Transcripts," April 9, 1983, p. 65.

42. *Ibid.*, pp. 66–67.

43. J.W. Edgar's Master's Thesis is entitled, "A Study of the Elements and Sources of Public School News."

44. For a complete list of Edgar's memberships see Appendix B.

45. J.W. Edgar, "The Edgar Transcripts," April 9, 1983, pp. 69–70.

46. *Ibid.*, p. 65.

47. Mrs. Bettina Charles Rosett, letter to SCA on August 1, 1983, from San Antonio, Texas. UTOHEC.

48. Dr. M.G. Bowden, taped interview by SCA on July 13, 1983, Austin, Texas. UTOHEC.

49. J.W. Edgar, "The Edgar Transcripts," April 7, 1983, p. 75a.

50. J.W. Edgar, "The Edgar Transcripts," April 9, 1983, p. 72.

51. J.W. Edgar, "The Edgar Transcripts," April 7, 1983, pp. 48–49.

52. J.W. Edgar, "The Edgar Transcripts," April 9, 1983, p. 82.

53. Mrs. Bettina Charles Rosett, letter to SCA on August 1, 1983, from San Antonio, Texas. UTOHEC.

54. Peter Marcheck, letter to SCA on August 9, 1983, from Pawnee, Texas. UTOHEC.

55. Mrs. Pauline Berry, taped interview by SCA on July 16, 1983, Burnet, Texas. Side B. UTOHEC.

CHAPTER 2.   ORANGE AND AUSTIN: THE URBAN PHASE, 1939–1949

1. J.W. Edgar, "The Edgar Transcripts" [A 325 page transcript of nine taped interviews with Dr. Edgar by Stephen C. Anderson (hereafter referred to as SCA) in April, 1983, in Austin, Texas, on file in the University of Texas Oral History Education Collection (hereafter referred to as UTOHEC)], April 11, 1983, p. 87.

2. *Ibid.*, p. 99.

3. Dr. Frank Hubert, taped interview by SCA on August 2, 1983, in College Station, Texas, UTOHEC.

4. J.W. Edgar, "The Edgar Transcripts," April 11, 1983, p. 90.'

5. Dr. Frank Hubert, taped interview by SCA on August 2, 1983, in College Station, Texas. UTOHEC.

6. J.W. Edgar, "The Edgar Transcripts," April 11, 1983, p. 92.

7. *Ibid.*, p. 93.

8. *Ibid.*, p. 93.

9. *Ibid.*, p. 103.

10. *Ibid.*, p. 107.

11. For a complete description of the Lanham Act see J.W. Edgar, *A Study of Federal Assistance to Schools Under the Lanham Act*, Ph.D. Dissertation, University of Texas at Austin, 1947.

12. Agnes E. Meyer, *Journey Through Chaos*, (New York: Harcourt, Brace, and Co., 1943), p. 166.

13. *Ibid.*, pp. 163–164.

14. C.O. Chandler, letter to SCA on August 2, 1983, from Lufkin, Texas. UTOHEC.

15. J.W. Edgar, "The Edgar Transcripts," April 12, 1983, p. 111.

16. *Ibid.*, p. 115.

17. *Ibid.*, p. 115.

18. *Ibid.*, p. 117.

19. *Ibid.*, p. 118.

20. N.S. Holland, *A Brief History: First Quarter Century of the Texas Association of School Administrators*, (Henrietta, Texas: A.J. Nystrom and Co., 1953), p. 82.

21. J.W. Edgar, "The Edgar Transcripts," April 12, 1983, p. 121.

22. N.S. Holland, *A Brief History: First Quarter Century of the Texas Association of School Administrators*, (Henrietta, Texas: A.J. Nystrom and Co., 1953), p. 83.

23. *Ibid.*, pp. 90–91.

24. C.O. Chandler, letter to SCA on August 2, 1983, from Lufkin, Texas. UTOHEC.

25. Mrs. Mary Louise Smithheisler, taped interview by SCA on September 17, 1983, in Burnet, Texas. UTOHEC.

26. There is a letter written by Edgar to Mrs. O.D. Weeks in response to a telephone call from Mr. R.W. Byram, President of the Austin School Board on file UTOHEC.

27. Mrs. O.D. Weeks, taped interview by SCA on August 6, 1983, in Austin, Texas. UTOHEC.

28. This is one of the most complete resumes the author had ever seen. See UTOHEC for the credentials in their entirety.

29. Mrs. O.D. Weeks, taped interview by SCA on August 6, 1983, in Austin, Texas. UTOHEC.

30. Willie Kocurek, taped interview by SCA on July 27, 1983, in Austin, Texas. UTOHEC.

31. Paul Bolton, taped interview by SCA on July 27, 1983, in Austin, Texas. UTOHEC.

32. J.W. Edgar, "The Edgar Transcripts," April 13, 1983, p. 133.

33. *Ibid.*, p. 139–140.

34. *Ibid.*, p. 142.

35. *Ibid.*, p. 145.

36. *Ibid.*, p. 146.

37. Dr. Lee J. Wilborn, taped interview by SCA on October 7, 1983, in Austin, Texas. UTOHEC.

38. J.W. Edgar, "The Edgar Transcripts," April 13, 1983, p. 147.

39. Dr. M.G. Bowden, taped interview by SCA on July 13, 1983, in Austin, Texas. UTOHEC.

40. J.W. Edgar, "The Edgar Transcripts," April 13, 1983, pp. 150–151.

41. *Ibid.*, p. 165.

42. On file at UTOHEC.

43. J.W. Edgar, "The Edgar Transcripts," April 13, 1983, p. 157.

44. Dr. James Jeffrey, taped interview by SCA on August 3, 1983, in Austin, Texas. This account not on tape.

45. J.W. Edgar, "The Edgar Transcripts," April 13, 1983, p. 152.

46. Friendly R. Rice, taped interview by SCA on July 29, 1983, in Austin, Texas. UTOHEC.

47. Mrs. Mary Frances Winston, telephone interview by SCA on July 27, 1983, in Austin, Texas. UTOHEC.

48. Dr. E. Marie Gilbert, taped interview by SCA on August 6, 1983, in Austin, Texas. UTOHEC.

49. Dr. M.G. Bowden, taped interview by SCA on July 13, 1983, in Austin, Texas. UTOHEC.

50. "J. Warren Hitt: He Gave His Life," *Texas School Business*, February 1970, Vol. XVI, No. 5, pp. 20–21.

51. Mrs. Warren Hitt, taped interview by SCA on August 15, 1983, in Austin, Texas. UTOHEC.

52. J.W. Edgar, "The Edgar Transcripts," April 13, 1983, p. 162.

53. *Ibid.*, pp. 98–99.

54. Mrs. O.D. Weeks, taped interview by SCA on August 26, 1983, in Austin, Texas. UTOHEC.

55. Dr. Clyde C. Colvert, taped interview by SCA on August 26, 1983, in Austin, Texas. UTOHEC.

56. J.W. Edgar, "The Edgar Transcripts," April 13, 1983, p. 167.

CHAPTER 3. THE PROPOSAL AND PASSAGE OF THE GILMER-AIKIN LAWS

1. Rae Files Still, *The Gilmer-Aikin Bills*, (Austin: The Steck Company, 1952), p. 13.

2. Claud H. Gilmer, transcript of taped interview on April 6, 1968, by Dr. Fred Gavitt in Rocksprings, Texas. North Texas State University Oral History Collection. pp. 40–41.

3. Rae Files Still, *The Gilmer-Aikin Bills,* (Austin: The Steck Company, 1952), p. 14.

4. J.W. Edgar, "The Edgar Transcripts" [a 325 page transcript of nine taped interviews with Dr. Edgar by Stephen C. Anderson (hereafter referred to as SCA) in April, 1983, in Austin, Texas, on file in the University of Texas Oral History Education Collection (hereafter referred to as UTOHEC)], April 15, 1983, p. 173.

5. N.S. Holland, *A Brief History: First Quarter Century of the Texas Association of School Administrators*, (Henrietta, Texas: A.J. Nystrom and Co., 1953), p. 108. The committee consisted of: Chairman: J.W. Edgar; M.P. Baker; S.M. Brown; H.L. Foster; Murry Fly, Fred Kaderli; Hollis A. Moore; Edward T. Robbins; Charles M. Rogers; and R.L. Williams.

6. *Ibid.*, pp. 108–109.

7. J.W. Edgar, "The Edgar Transcripts," April 15, 1983, pp. 173, 175.

8. See Hollis Andrew Moore, "Equalization of Educational Opportunity and the Distribution of State School Funds in Texas," Ph.D. dissertation, The University of Texas at Austin, 1947.

9. J.W. Edgar, "The Edgar Transcripts," April 15, 1983, p. 173.

10. Claud H. Gilmer, transcript of taped interview by Corrinne E. Crow on November 15, 1976. Archives/Oral History, East Texas State University, Commerce, Texas. pp. 3–4.

11. J.W. Edgar, *The Edgar Transcripts*, April 15, 1983, p. 174.

12. A.M. Aikin, Jr., transcript of taped interview by Corrinne E. Crow on July 23, 1975, Archives/Oral History, East Texas State University, Commerce, Texas. p. 24.

13. For a complete list of the members of the committee and who appointed them, see Rae Files Still, *The Gilmer-Aikin Bills*, (Austin: The Steck Company, 1953), pp. 17–19. Also see Appendix C for a list of the members.

14. Claud H. Gilmer, transcript of taped interview by Corrinne Crow on November 15, 1976, Archives/Oral History, East Texas State University, Commerce, Texas, p. 7.

15. Governor Allan Shivers, taped interview by SCA on September 9, 1983, in Austin, Texas. UTOHEC.

16. Senator James E. Taylor, taped interview on July 30, 1983, by SCA in Austin, Texas. UTOHEC.

17. Betty King, taped interview on August 8, 1983, by SCA in Austin, Texas, from the index.

18. J.W. Edgar, "The Edgar Transcripts," April 15, 1983, pp. 180A–187.

19. Dr. Lawrence D. Haskew, taped interview by SCA on August 17, 1983, in Austin, Texas. UTOHEC.

20. J.W. Edgar, "The Edgar Transcripts," April 15, 1983, pp. 177–178.

21. E.D. Yoes, Jr., "Texas," in *Education in the United States*, edited by Jim B. Pearson and Edgar Fuller, (Washington, D.C.: National Education Association of the U.S., 1969), pp. 1203–1204.

22. P.E. Hutchinson, taped interview on August 10, 1983, by SCA, in Austin, Texas. UTOHEC.

23. J.W. Edgar, "The Edgar Transcripts," April 15, 1983, p. 179.

24. *Ibid.*, p. 180.

25. Senator Ottis Lock, taped interview by SCA on September 17, 1983, in Burnet, Texas, not on tape, but from index.

26. Dr. John Stockton, taped interview on August 5, 1983, by SCA, in Austin, Texas. UTOHEC.

27. J.W. Edgar, "The Edgar Transcripts," April 15, 1983, p. 181.

28. For a complete view of the results of Edgar's subcommittee see The Gilmer-Aikin Committee, "State Management of Education in Texas — Proposals of Subcommittee No. 1 and the Advisory Committee on State Management." July 30, 1948, 22 pages. UTOHEC.

29. The report is "To Have What We Must . . . A Digest of Proposals to Improve Public Education in Texas," Submitted to the People of Texas by the Gilmer-Aikin Committee on Education, September 1948, 43 pages.

30. For a complete account of the passage of the Gilmer-Aikin Bills, see Rae Files Still, *The Gilmer-Aikin Bills,* (Austin: The Steck Company, 1953).

31. Rae Files Still, *The Gilmer-Aikin Bills,* (Austin: The Steck Company, 1953), pp. 44–45.

32. J.W. Edgar, "The Edgar Transcripts," April 15, 1983, p. 171.

33. Miss Waurine Walker, taped interview by SCA on August 16, 1983, in Austin, Texas. UTOHEC.

34. Mr. L.P. Sturgeon, transcript from taped interview by Corrinne E. Crow on January 15, 1976. Archives/Oral History, East Texas State University, Commerce, Texas, pp. 22, 24.

35. J.W. Edgar, "The Edgar Transcripts," April 15, 1983, pp. 183–184.

36. *Ibid.,* p. 184.

37. For this provision, see Rae Files Still, *The Gilmer-Aikin Bills*, (Austin: The Steck Company, 1953), p. 146.

38. J.W. Edgar, transcript of taped interview by Corrinne E. Crow on May 28, 1975. Archives/Oral History, East Texas State University, Commerce, Texas. p. 21.

39. For the text of the complete bills, see "Minimum Foundation Laws (Gilmer-Aikin Laws), Senate Bills 115, 116, 117." Distributed by the Texas State Teacher Association. 32 pages.

40. E.D. Yoes, Jr., "Texas" in *Education in the United States*, edited by Jim B. Pearson and Edgar Fuller, (Washington D.C.: National Education Association of the U.S., 1969), p. 1207.

41. Mr. E.L. Galyean, taped interview by SCA on August 11, 1983, in Austin, Texas. UTOHEC.

42. J.W. Edgar, "The Edgar Transcripts," April 15, 1983, p. 178.

43. Dr. Dana Williams, taped interview by SCA on November 17, 1983, in Corpus Christi, Texas. UTOHEC.

44. Mr. L.P. Sturgeon, transcript of taped interview by Corrinne E. Crow on January 15, 1976. Archives/Oral History, East Texas State University, Commerce, Texas, pp. 18–19, 21.

45. Dr. Dana Williams, taped interview by SCA on November 17, 1983, in Corpus Christi, Texas. UTOHEC.

46. J.W. Edgar, transcript of taped interview by Corrinne E. Crow on May 28, 1975, Archives/Oral History, East Texas State University, Commerce, Texas, p. 10.

47. Senator Ralph Yarborough, taped interview by SCA on October 13, 1983, in Austin, Texas. UTOHEC.

48. Ottis Lock, taped interview on September 17, 1983, by SCA in Burnet, Texas. UTOHEC.

49. J.W. Edgar, "The Edgar Transcripts," April 15, 1983, pp. 182–183.

50. Senator James E. Taylor, transcript of taped interview by Corrine E. Crow on March 17, 1976, Archives/Oral History, East Texas State University, Commerce, Texas, p. 49.

51. Rae Files Still, letter to SCA in August, 1983, from Waxahachie, Texas. UTOHEC.

52. J.W. Edgar, transcript of taped interview by Corrinne E. Crow on May 28, 1975, Archives/Oral History, East Texas State University, Commerce, Texas, p. 27.

53. Senator James E. Taylor, transcript of taped interview by Corrinne E. Crow on March 17, 1976, Archives/Oral History, East Texas State University, Commerce, Texas, p. 35.

54. Miss Waurine Walker, taped interview by SCA on August 16, 1983, in Austin, Texas, UTOHEC.

55. Governor Preston Smith, transcript of taped interview by Corrinne E. Crow on July 31, 1975, Archives/Oral History, East Texas State University, Commerce, Texas, pp. 28–30.

CHAPTER 4. THE IMPLEMENTATION OF THE GILMER-AIKIN LAWS, 1949–1974

1. Caveness employed: J. Warren Hitt, Assistant Director; L.H. Griffin, Transportation Officer; Bascom Hayes, Control Officer; P.E. Hutchinson, Program Review Officer; Dr. W.R. Shipping, local Finance Officer; and Frank Hubert, Administrative Assistant. The name given this temporary division of the Auditor's Office was the Foundation School Program Act Division. For an excellent account of the entire interim period, see Mr. L.P. Sturgeon, "An Interim Period in Texas Public School History (June 9, 1949–April 1, 1950), unfinished dissertation. Available in the University of Texas Oral History Education Center (hereafter referred to as UTOHEC), Austin, Texas.

2. Mr. L.P. Sturgeon, taped interview in response to a letter from Stephen C. Anderson (hereafter referred to as SCA), August, 1983, from New Boston, Texas. UTOHEC.

3. Mrs. Bascom Hayes, taped interview by SCA on August 3, 1983, in Austin, Texas. UTOHEC.

4. J.W. Edgar, "The Edgar Transcripts" [A 325 page transcript of nine taped interviews with Dr. Edgar by SCA in April, 1983, in Austin, Texas, on file in the UTOHEC], April 15, 1983, pp. 191–192.

5. Paul Schuster Taylor, *An American-Mexican Frontier, Nueces County, Texas,* (Chapel Hill: The University of North Carolina Press, 1934), pp. 214, 225–226.

6. Meyer Weinberg, *A Chance to Learn: The History of Race and*

Education in the United States, (Cambridge and New York: Cambridge University Press, 1977), p. 168.

7. Delgado vs Bastrop Independent School District (1948), *No. 388,* Civil., District Court of the United States, Western District of Texas in minutes of the State Board of Education, April 14, 1949, p. 7.

8. Meyer Weinberg, *A Chance to Learn: The History of Race and Education in the United States,* (Cambridge and New York: Cambridge University Press, 1977), p. 168.

9. *Ibid.,* p. 168.

10. J.W. Edgar, "The Edgar Transcripts," April 15, 1983, p. 201.

11. Letter from Dr. Hector Garcia, M.D., to the Commissioner of Education, J.W. Edgar, and the State Board of Education, April 13, 1950, on file with Dr. H. Garcia in Corpus Christi, Texas, in Jorge C. Rangel and Carlos M. Alcala, "De Jure Segregation of Chicanos in Texas Schools," Harvard Civil Rights-Civil Liberties Review, 7, (March, 1972), p. 337.

12. *Ibid.,* pp. 339–340.

13. Dr. Hector Garcia, M.D., taped interview by SCA on November 17, 1983, in Corpus Christi, Texas. UTOHEC.

14. J.W. Edgar, "The Edgar Transcripts," April 16, 1983, p. 224.

15. Meyer Weinberg, *A Chance to Learn: A History of Race and Education in the United States,* (Cambridge and New York: Cambridge University Press, 1977), p. 168.

16. Mr. E.L. Galyean, taped interview by SCA on August 11, 1983, in Austin, Texas. UTOHEC.

17. J.W. Edgar, "The Edgar Transcripts," April 15, 1983, p. 189.

18. L.P. Sturgeon, "An Interim Period in Texas Public School History," unfinished dissertation, pp. 176–177. UTOHEC.

19. Ottis E. Lock, "The New State Board of Education, Fifty Questions and Fifty Answers," Lufkin, Texas, October, 1949, 18 pages. UTOHEC.

20. L.P. Sturgeon, "An Interim Period in Texas Public School History," unfinished dissertation, p. 177. UTOHEC.

21. J.W. Edgar, "The Edgar Transcripts," April 15, 1983, p. 192a.

22. Dr. Dana Williams, letter to SCA on October 17, 1983, from Corpus Christi, Texas. UTOHEC.

23. J.W. Edgar, "The Edgar Transcripts," April 15, 1983, p. 192a.

24. *Ibid.,* p. 193.

25. Paul Mathews, letter to SCA in August, 1983, from Greenville, Texas. UTOHEC.

26. J.W. Edgar, "The Edgar Transcripts," April 15, 1983, p. 194.

27. Minutes of the State Board of Education, January 2, 1950, Vol. 1, p. 44.

28. When I wrote Mr. Bolton a letter thanking him for the interview, I misspelled his name. He wrote me a letter which said: "Stephen — My political friends always said — say what you want about me, but get my name right. See above [correct name printed on letter], P.B."

29. Mr. Bolton called Edgar "Fred." His family always called him

"Pop." Edgar said of his name. "As I remember the circumstances, they wanted to name me James, but they didn't want to call me by the name of James because they would call me Jim. That's what they called my father. My mother didn't like the name Jim. So they didn't give me a second name for several years. As I recall, my mother asked me to select it. I selected Winfred. I don't know why. I've always regretted it . . . I just never liked the name. I started going by J.W. I couldn't put Jr. because there was not a Jr. My father went by the initials J.W. Since I wasn't a junior, I couldn't add Jr. to it. See "The Edgar Transcripts," p. 83.

30. Mr. Paul Bolton, taped interview by SCA on July 25, 1983, in Austin, Texas. UTOHEC.

31. J.W. Edgar, "The Edgar Transcripts," April 15, 1983, pp. 195–196.

32. Minutes of State Board of Education, Vol. 1, p. 48.

33. *Ibid.*, p. 49.

34. Mr. L.P. Sturgeon, taped interview in response to a letter from SCA, August, 1983, from New Boston, Texas. UTOHEC.

35. Minutes of the State Board of Education, Vol. 1, p. 49.

36. *Ibid.*, p. 69

37. J.W. Edgar, "The Edgar Transcripts," April 15, 1983, p. 197.

38. Sam Kinch, "J.W. Edgar Appointed at 17,500 Yearly Pay," *Fort Worth Telegram*, February 5, 1950.

39. *Ibid.*

40. Editorial, "Education Commissioner Should Be Worth as Much as Grid Coach," *Corpus Christi Caller*, Corpus Christi, Texas, Thursday Morning, February 9, 1950.

41. J.W. Edgar, "The Edgar Transcripts," April 15, 1983, p. 199.

42. Statement by J.W. Edgar, June, 1983. UTOHEC.

43. *Ibid.*

44. Dr. Charles Mathews, taped interview by SCA on August 11, 1983, in Austin, Texas. UTOHEC.

45. Dr. W.R. Goodson, taped interview by SCA on September 19, 1983, in Austin, Texas. UTOHEC.

46. "The Texas Way, A Guide for Measuring Programs in the Big Idea of Gilmer-Aikin Legislation," by the 1950 Citizens Advisory Conference on Education, October 9, 1950, Austin, Texas, p. 13.

47. Mr. Alton O. Bowen, letter to SCA on September 2, 1983, from Bryan, Texas. UTOHEC

48. J.W. Edgar, "The Edgar Transcripts," April 16, 1983, p. 220.

49. *Ibid.*, p. 220.

50. Mrs. Mary Thornton, taped interview by SCA on September 14, 1983, in Austin, Texas. UTOHEC.

51. Dr. Robert Mallas, taped interview by SCA on September 9, 1983, in Austin, Texas UTOHEC.

52. "Mr. Public Education: Dr. Edgar Quietly Leads Texas School System," *San Antonio News*, November 20, 1958, p. 1.

53. *Ibid.*, p. 1.

54. Mr. Paul R. Haas, letter to SCA on October 13, 1983, from Corpus Christi, Texas. UTOHEC.

55. Mr. Paul R. Haas, taped interview by SCA on November 18, 1983, in Corpus Christi, Texas. UTOHEC.

56. J.W. Edgar, letter to Robert B. Anderson on August 29, 1956, from Austin, Texas. UTOHEC.

57. Paul R. Haas, letter to SCA on October 25, 1983, from Corpus Christi, Texas. UTOHEC.

58. J.W. Edgar, letter to Paul R. Haas on June 7, 1973, from Austin, Texas. UTOHEC.

59. Mr. Paul Mathews, letter to SCA in August, 1983, from Greenville, Texas. UTOHEC.

60. Mr. Vernon Baird, letter to J.W. Edgar on July 1, 1974, from Fort Worth, Texas. UTOHEC.

61. "Educators Hail Appointment of Dr. Edgar," *Fort Worth Telegram*, February 5, 1950.

62. *Ibid.*

63. *Ibid.*

64. *Ibid.*

65. Sam Kinch, "Local School Control Believed in by Edgar," *Fort Worth Telegram*, February 5, 1980.

66. For an explanation of the reorganization see Texas Education Agency, "Thirty-sixth Biennial Report 1948–49, 1949–50, Bulletin 511," Austin, Texas, 55 pages.

67. J.W. Edgar, "The Edgar Transcripts," April 16, 1983, p. 207.

68. For a complete list of the top Texas Education Agency Personnel for 1949–51, see Appendix D.

69. J.W. Edgar, "The Edgar Transcripts," April 16, 1983, p. 204.

70. *Ibid.*, p. 208.

71. *Ibid.*, p. 210.

72. *Ibid.*, p. 211.

73. *Ibid.*, p. 212.

74. *Ibid.*, p. 215.

75. Dr. Frank Hubert, taped interview SCA on August 2, 1983, in College Station, Texas. UTOHEC.

76. J.W. Edgar, "The Edgar Transcripts," April 16, 1983, pp. 216, 218–219.

77. *Ibid.*, pp. 217–218.

78. *Ibid.*, pp. 221–222.

79. Dr. J.L. Brockette, taped interview by SCA on August 4, 1983, in Austin, Texas. UTOHEC.

80. Dr. Frank Hubert, taped interview by SCA on August 2, 1983, in College Station, Texas. UTOHEC.

81. Mr. L.P. Sturgeon, taped interview in response to a letter from SCA in August, 1983, from New Boston, Texas. UTOHEC.

82. Mr. Alton O. Bowen, letter to SCA on September 2, 1983, from Bryan, Texas. UTOHEC.

83. J.W. Edgar, "The Edgar Transcripts," April 19, 1983, pp. 321–322.

84. *Ibid,* p. 206.

85. Mr. Raymon Bynum, taped interview by SCA on August 23, 1983. UTOHEC.

86. Mrs. (Warren) Hitt, taped interview by SCA on August 15, 1983, in Austin, Texas. UTOHEC.

87.*Ibid.*

88. Mrs. Carolyn Ruhman, taped interview by SCA on August 16, 1983. UTOHEC.

89. Mr. Vernon McGee, taped interview by SCA on September 9, 1983, in Austin, Texas. UTOHEC.

90. "J. Warren Hitt — He Gave His Life," *Texas School Business,* February 19, 1970, Vol. XVI, No. 5, p. 20.

91. J.W. Edgar, "The Edgar Transcripts," April 16, 1983, p. 253.

92. *Ibid.,* p. 253.

93. *Ibid.,* p. 261–262.

94. Dr. Lorrin Kennamer, taped interview by SCA on August 24, 1983, in Austin, Texas, UTOHEC.

95. J.W. Edgar, "The Edgar Transcripts," April 16, 1983, pp. 254–256.

96. *Ibid.,* pp. 257–258.

97. *Ibid.,* p. 259.

98. *Ibid.,* pp. 258–259.

99. For a thorough coverage of appeals from 1950 to 1976, see Thomas Emerson Anderson, "Appeals to the State Commissioner of Education: A Study of Administrative Adjudication," unpublished dissertation, University of Texas at Austin, 1977.

100. J.W. Edgar, "The Edgar Transcripts," April 16, 1983, p. 239.

101. Dr. Thomas E. Anderson, "Appeals to the Commissioner of Education: A Study of Administrative Adjudication," unpublished dissertation, University of Texas at Austin, 1977, pp. 69–70.

102. J.W. Edgar, "The Edgar Transcripts," April 16, 1983, pp. 240–241.

103. Dr. Thomas E. Anderson, "Appeals to the Commissioner of Education: A Study of Administrative Adjudication," unpublished dissertation, University of Texas at Austin, 1977, pp. 97–98, 208.

104. J.W. Edgar, "The Edgar Transcripts," April 16, 1983, p. 244.

105. *Ibid.,* p. 245.

106. *Ibid.,* pp. 246–247.

107. *Ibid.*

108. Thomas Emerson Anderson, "Appeals to the State Commissioner of Education: A Study of Administrative Adjudication," unpublished dissertation, 1977, p. 177.

109. Mr. Chester Ollison, taped interview by SCA on August 9, 1983. UTOHEC.

110. *Ibid.*

111. Mrs. Mary Thornton, taped interview by SCA on September 14, 1983. UTOHEC.

112. This desk was made for Edgar at Fox Tech Vocational Educational High School in San Antonio. It is still in his old office at TEA.

113. Mrs. Mary Thornton, taped interview by SCA on September 14, 1983. UTOHEC.

114. *Ibid.*

115. *Ibid.*

116. J.W. Edgar, "The Edgar Transcripts," April 19, 1983, p. 314.

117. *Ibid.* pp. 314–315.

118. *Ibid.* pp. 316–317.

119. Mr. L.P. Sturgeon, "J.W. Edgar's Contributions Will Be Remembered," *Texas Outlook*, January, 1974.

120. Dr. Dana Williams, taped interview by SCA on November 17, 1983, in Corpus Christi, Texas. UTOHEC.

121. Dr. W.R. Goodson, taped interview by SCA on September 19, 1983. UTOHEC.

122. Dr. M.L. Brockette, taped interview by SCA on August 4, 1983. UTOHEC.

123. J.W. Edgar, "The Edgar Transcripts," April 16, 1983, p. 216.

124. Alton O. Bowen, letter to SCA on September 2, 1983, from Bryan, Texas. UTOHEC.

125. Thomas E. Anderson, "Appeals to the State Commissioner of Education: A Study of Administrative Adjudication," unpublished dissertation, University of Texas at Austin, 1977, pp. 199–200.

126. Mr. Paul Bolton, taped interview by SCA with Mrs. Paul Bolton on July 25, 1983, in Austin, Texas. UTOHEC.

127. Alton O. Bowen, letter to SCA on September 2, 1983, from Bryan, Texas. UTOHEC.

128. Dr. Larry Haskew, taped interview by SCA on August 17, 1983. UTOHEC.

129. Thomas Emerson Anderson, "Appeals to the State Commissioner of Education: A Study of Administrative Adjudication," unpublished dissertation, University of Texas at Austin, 1977, p. 218.

130. Mrs. Dora Huston, taped interview by SCA on September 16, 1983, in Austin, Texas, UTOHEC.

131. Dr. Larry Haskew, taped interview by SCA on August 17, 1983, in Austin, Texas. UTOHEC.

CHAPTER 5.   EDUCATOR FOR TEXAS

1. David Tyack, and Elisabeth Hansot, *Managers of Virtue: Public School Leadership in America, 1820–1980*, (New York: Basic Books, Inc., 1982), p. 130.

2. *Ibid.*, p. 169.

3. David Tyack, *Public Schools in Hard Times*, unpublished manuscript, 1984, p. 41.

4. Senator Ottis Lock, taped interview by Stephen C. Anderson (hereafter referred to as SCA) on September 17, 1983, in Burnet, Texas. On file in the University of Texas Oral History Education Collection (hereafter referred to as UTOHEC).

5. J.W. Edgar, "The Edgar Transcripts" [A 325 page transcript of

nine taped interviews with Dr. Edgar by SCA in April, 1983, in Austin, Texas, on file the UTOHEC], April 9, pp. 75–77.

6. Mr. L.P. Sturgeon, taped interview in response to a letter by SCA in August, 1983, from New Boston, Texas. UTOHEC.

7. Dr. Larry Haskew, taped interview by SCA on August 17, 1983, in Austin, Texas. UTOHEC.

8. Dr. Dana Williams, taped interview by SCA on November 17, 1983, in Corpus Christi, Texas. UTOHEC.

9. Mr. Alton O. Bowen, letter to SCA on September 2, 1983, from Bryan, Texas. UTOHEC.

10. Mrs. E.J. Lunz, letter to SCA on July 28, 1983, from Hebbronville, Texas. UTOHEC.

11. Dr. M.G. Bowden, taped interview by SCA on July 13, 1983, in Austin, Texas. UTOHEC.

12. Mrs. Mary Louise Smithheisler, taped interview by SCA on September 17, 1983, in Burnet, Texas, (not on tape). UTOHEC.

13. Mrs. O.D. Weeks, taped interview by SCA on August 6, 1983, in Austin, Texas. UTOHEC.

14. Miss Waurine Walker, taped interview by SCA on August 16, 1983, in Austin, Texas. UTOHEC.

15. Dr. M.L. Brockette, taped interview by SCA on August 4, 1983, in Austin, Texas, (not on tape). UTOHEC.

16. Dr. Robert Mallas, taped interview by SCA on September 9, 1983, in Austin, Texas. UTOHEC.

17. Dr. W.R. Goodson, taped interview by SCA on September 19, 1983, in Austin, Texas. UTOHEC.

18. Dr. James Jeffery, taped interview by SCA on August 3, 1983, in Austin, Texas. UTOHEC.

19. Mrs. Warren Hitt, taped interview by SCA on August 15, 1983, in Austin, Texas. UTOHEC.

20. Mrs. Sally Edgar Ward, taped interview by SCA on September 9, 1983, in Austin, Texas. UTOHEC.

21. Senator Ottis Lock, taped interview by SCA on September 17, 1983, in Burnet, Texas. UTOHEC.

22. Dr. Larry Haskew, taped interview by SCA on August 17, 1983, in Austin, Texas. UTOHEC.

23. Dr. Frank Hubert, taped interview by SCA on August 2, 1983, in College Station, Texas. UTOHEC.

24. Dr. Herbert La Grone, taped interview in a response to a letter from SCA in August, 1983, from Fort Worth, Texas. UTOHEC.

25. *Ibid.*

26. *Ibid.*

27. Mr. C.O. Chandler, letter to SCA on August 2, 1983, from Lufkin, Texas. UTOHEC.

28. Dr. Lee J. Wilborn, taped interview by SCA on October 7, 1983, in Austin, Texas. UTOHEC.

29. *Ibid.*

30. See Appendix F for list of Edgar's awards, life memberships, and honors.

31. Dr. Charles F. Mathews, taped interview by SCA on August 11, 1983, in Austin, Texas. UTOHEC.

32. Dr. Lee J. Wilborn, taped interview by SCA on October 7, 1983, in Austin, Texas. UTOHEC.

33. Dr. Robert Mallas, taped interview by SCA on September 9, 1983, in Austin, Texas. UTOHEC.

34. Dr. Charles F. Mathews, taped interview by SCA on August 11, 1983, in Austin, Texas. UTOHEC.

35. Dr. Herbert La Grone, taped interview in response to a letter from SCA in August, 1983, from Fort Worth, Texas. UTOHEC.

36. Dr. M.L. Brockette, taped interview by SCA on August 4, 1983, in Austin, Texas. UTOHEC.

BIBLIOGRAPHY

ARTICLES

"Board Names New Commissioner." *Texas Outlook.*

"Dr. Edgar Makes Statement on Teacher Loyalty Oath." *The Texas Parent-Teacher,* (June, 1953), 6.

"Duties and Responsibilities of the Commissioner of Education." *Texas Outlook,* (October, 1950).

Edgar, J.W. "Curriculum Improvement in Texas Public Schools." *Senior Scholastic, 75* (8) (November, 1959), 21.

Edgar, J.W. "Curriculum Studies Made of Public Schools in Texas." *East Texas, 33* (11) (August, 1959), 15.

Edgar, J.W. "The State of the Schools in Texas — 1960." *The Texas Parent-Teacher,* (March, 1960), 10.

Edgar, J.W. "Dr. J.W. Edgar Discusses Texas Education: Address to Delegates the Second Evening of the convention." *The Texas Parent-Teacher,* (January, 1961), 18.

Edgar, J.W. "Good Citizenship: Knowledge." *The Texas Parent-Teacher,* (October, 1962), 6.

"Fete Set June 18 to Honor J.W. Edgar." *Texas Outlook* (May, 1974).

Hughes, W.L. "Among Texas Rural Schools." *The Texas Outlook, 12* (2) (February, 1928), 37.

"J. Warren Hitt — He Gave His Life." *Texas School Business, XVI* (5) (February, 1970), 20.

"Just Call Him 'Commissioner'." *Texas Outlook,* (March 1950).

Kliebard, Herbert M. "Education at the Turn of the Century: A Crucible for Curriculum Change." *Educational Researcher,* (January, 1982), 16.

Morehead, Richard M. "Movers and Shapers of Education: J.W. Edgar of Texas." *Saturday Review,* (January, 1961), 88.

Norwood, Pat H. "Work of the Gilmer-Aikin Committee." *Texas Journal of Secondary Education, 1* (Fall, 1948), 1.

Rangle, Jorge C., and Alcala, Carlos M. "Project Report: De Jure Segregation of Chicanos in Texas Schools." *Harvard Civil Rights-Civil Liberties Law Review, 7* (2) (March, 1972), 307.

Salinas, Guadalupe. "Mexican-Americans and the Desegregation of Schools in the Southwest." *El Grito, 4* (Summer, 1971), 36.

Schnepp, Alfred F. "The State and Education in Texas: An Historical Sketch." *The Texas Outlook, 24* (1) (January, 1940), 22.

Sturgeon, L.P. "J.W. Edgar's Contributions Will Be Remembered." *Texas Outlook,* (January, 1974).

Thompson, Fred D. "A Century of Public Schools." *Texas Parade, 14* (January, 1954), 13.
Tyler, Ralph W. "Curriculum Development Since 1900." *Educational Leadership,* (May, 1981), 599.
"The State Board of Education in Texas: A History." *TSAB Journal, 26* (1) (March, 1980), 7.
Vessels, Jay. "One Year After Gilmer-Aikin." *Texas Parade, XI* (6) (November, 1950), 12.

BOOKS

Baum, Willa K. *Transcribing and Editing Oral History.* Nashville: American Association for State and Local History, 1977.
Beach, Richard. *Writing About Ourselves and Others.* Urbana, Illinois: Eric Clearinghouse on Reading & Communication Skills & National Council of Teachers of English, 1977.
Block, Jack. *Understanding Historical Research: A Search for Truth.* Alen Rock, NJ: Research Publications, 1971.
Borg, Walter R. and Gall, Meredith Daminen. *Educational Research: An Introduction.* Longman, NY: 1983.
Brickman, William W. *Guide to Research in Educational History.* New York: New York University Bookstore, 1949.
Campbell, Ronald F., and Mazzoni, Tim L., Jr. *State Policy Making for the Public Schools: A Comparative Analysis of Policy Making for the Public Schools in Twelve States and a Treatment of State Governance Models.* Berkeley, CA: McCutchan Publishing Corporation, 1976.
Caro, Robert A. *The Power Broker.* New York: Alfred A. Knopf, 1974.
Conrad, James H. *Texas Educational History: A Bibliography.* Greenville, TX: Juris Co., 1979.
Davis, Cullom: Back, Kathryn; and MacLean, Kay. *Oral History: From Tape to Type.* Chicago: American Library Association, 1977.
Davis, Gordon B., and Parker, Clyde A. *Writing the Doctoral Dissertation: A Systematic Approach.* Woodbury, NY: Barron's Educational Series, Inc., 1979.
Deering, Mary Joe, and Pomeroy, Barbara. *Transcribing Without Tears.* George Washington University Library: Oral History Program, 1976.
Dexter, Lewis Anthony. *Elite and Specialized Interviewing.* Evanston: Northwestern University Press, 1970.
Donaldson, George W. *School Camping.* New York: Association Press, 1952.
Douglas, Jack D. *Investigative Social Research: Individual and Team Field Research.* Beverly Hills: Sage Publications, 1979.

Gardner, William H. "Title Texan." *The Lake Victor Story.* Edited by Maurice C. Shelby. 1956.

Garraghan, Gilbert J. *A Guide to Historical Method.* New York: Fordham University Press, 1946.

Gittings, Robert. *The Nature of Biography.* Seattle: University of Washington Press, 1978.

Holland, N.S. *Texas Association of School Administrators: A Brief History First Quarter Century 1925–1950.* Henrietta, Texas: Texas Association of School Administrators, 1953.

Kahn, Robert L., and Cannel, Charles R. *The Dynamics of Interviewing.* New York: John Wiley & Sons, Inc., 1957.

Landau, David. *Kissinger: The Uses of Power.* Boston: Houghton Mifflin Company, 1972.

Leedy, Paul D. *Practical Research: Planning and Design.* 2nd ed. New York: Macmillan Publishing Co., 1980.

McCall, George J., and Simmons, J.L. *Issues in Participant Observation: A Text and Reader.* Reading, Mass.: Addison-Wesley Publishing Company, 1969.

Meyer, Agnes E. *Journey Through Chaos.* New York: Harcourt, Brace, 7 Co., 1944.

Miller, Merle. *Lyndon: An Oral Biography.* New York: G.P. Putnam's Sons, 1980.

Ravitch, Diane. *The Troubled Crusade: American Education, 1945–1980.* New York: Basic Books, Inc., 1983.

Sequel, Mary Louise. *The Curriculum Field: Its Formative Years.* New York: Teachers College Press, 1966.

Spradley, James P. *The Ethnographic Interview.* New York: Holt, Rinehart, and Winston, 1979.

Still, Rae. *The Gilmer-Aikin Bills.* Austin: The Steck Co., 1950.

Taylor, Paul Schuster. *An American-Mexican Frontier, Nueces County, Texas.* Chapel Hill: The University of North Carolina Press, 1934.

Turabian, Kate L. *A Manual for Writers of Term Papers, Theses, and Dissertations.* Chicago: University of Chicago Press, 1973.

Tyack, David B. *The One Best System: A History of American Urban Education.* Cambridge, Mass.: Harvard University Press, 1974.

Tyack, David, and Hansot, Elisabeth. *Managers of Virtue: Public School Leadership in America, 1820:1980.* New York: Basic Books, Inc., 1982.

Weinberg, Meyer. "Mexican-American Children: The Neighbors Within." *A Chance to Learn: The History of Race and Education in the United States.* Boston: Cambridge University Press, 1977.

Yoes, E.D., Jr. "Texas: The Texas Education Agency." *Education in the States: Historical Development and Outlook.* Edited by Jim

204 *J.W. EDGAR: Educator For Texas*

B. Pearson, and Edgar Fuller. Washington, DC: National Education Association of the United States, 1969.

DISSERTATIONS AND THESES

Anderson, Thomas Emerson, Jr. "Appeals to the State Commissioner of Education: A Study of Administrative Adjudication." Ph.D. dissertation, University of Texas at Austin, 1977.

Edgar, J.W. "A Study of the Elements and Sources of Public School News." M.A. thesis, The University of Texas at Austin, 1938.

Edgar, J.W. "A Study of Federal Assistance to Schools Under the Lanham Act." Ph.D. dissertation, The University of Texas at Austin, 1947.

Hansen, Jesse Merrell. "Kimball Wiles' Contributions to Curriculum and Instruction: An Analysis Within an Historical Context." Ph.D. dissertation, The University of Texas at Austin, 1971.

Moore, Hollis Andrew. "Equalization of Educational Opportunity and the Distribution of State School Funds in Texas." Ph.D. dissertation, The University of Texas, 1947.

Rowold, Milam C. "The Texas Rural Schools Revisited, 1900–1929." Ph.D. dissertation, The University of Texas at Austin, 1983.

Still, Rae. "The Gilmer-Aikin Bills in the Texas Legislature — A Study in the Legislative Process." M.A. thesis, The University of Texas at Austin, 1949.

INTERVIEWS

Aikin, A.M. Taped interviews by Corrinne E. Crow on July 23, September 19, and November 4, 1975. Archives/Oral History. East Texas State University, Commerce, Texas.

Berry, Pauline. Taped interview by SCA on July 16, 1983, in Burnet, Texas. UTOHEC.

Bowden, M.G. Taped interview by SCA on July 13, 1983, in Austin, Texas. UTOHEC.

Bolton, Paul. Taped interview by SCA on July 25, 1983, in Austin, Texas. UTOHEC.

Brockette, M.L. Taped interview by SCA on August 4, 1983, in Austin, Texas. UTOHEC.

Bynum, Raymon. Taped interview by SCA on August 23, 1983, in Austin, Texas. UTOHEC.

Colvert, Clyde. Taped interview by SCA on August 26, 1983, in Austin, Texas. UTOHEC.

Cowan, S.P. Taped interview by SCA on July 9, 1983, in Seguin, Texas. UTOHEC.

Daniel, Price. Taped interview by Corrinne E. Crow on November 17,

1977. Archives/Oral History. East Texas State University, Commerce, Texas.

Edgar, J.W. Taped interview by Corrine E. Crow on May 28, 1975. Archives/Oral History. East Texas State University, Commerce, Texas.

Edgar. J.W. Taped interview by J. Douglas Caballero on September 30, 1981, in Austin, Texas. UTOHEC.

Edgar, J.W. Taped interviews by SCA on April 6, 7, 9, 11, 12, 13, 15, 16, 17, 18, 1983, in Austin, Texas. UTOHEC.

Edgar, Sue. Taped interview by SCA on July 6, 1983, in Austin, Texas. UTOHEC.

Ferguson, Thomas C. Taped interview July 17, 1983, in Burnet, Texas. UTOHEC.

Galyean. E.L. Taped interview by SCA on August 11, 1983, in Austin, Texas. UTOHEC.

Garcia, Hector. Taped interview by SCA on November 17, 1983, in Corpus Christi, Texas. UTOHEC.

Gilbert, Marie. Taped interview by SCA on August 6, 1983, in Austin, Texas. UTOHEC.

Gilmer, Claud W. Taped interview by Dr. Fred Gantt on April 6, 1968, in Rocksprings, Texas. North Texas State University Oral History Collection.

Gilmer, Claud W. Taped interview by Corrinne E. Crow on November 15, 1976. Archives/Oral History. East Texas State University, Commerce, Texas.

Goodson, W.R. Taped interview by SCA on September 19, 1983, in Austin, Texas. UTOHEC.

Haas, Paul R. Taped interview by SCA on November 18, 1983, in Corpus Christi, Texas. UTOHEC.

Haskew, Lawrence D. Taped interview by SCA on August 17, 1983, in Austin, Texas. UTOHEC.

Hayes, Bascom, Taped interview by SCA on August 15, 1983, in Austin, Texas. UTOHEC.

Hitt, Mrs. Warren. Taped interview by SCA on August 15, 1983, in Austin, Texas. UTOHEC.

Hubert, Frank. Taped interview by SCA on August 2, 1983, in College Station, Texas. UTOHEC.

Hutchinson, P.E. Taped interview by SCA on August 10, 1983, in Austin, Texas. UTOHEC.

Huston, Dora. Taped interview by SCA on September 16, 1983, in Austin, Texas. UTOHEC.

Jeffrey, James. Taped interview by SCA on August 3, 1983, in Austin, Texas. UTOHEC.

Kennamer, Lorrin. Taped interview by SCA on August 24, 1983, in Austin, Texas. UTOHEC.

King, Betty. Taped interview by SCA on August 8, 1983, in Austin, Texas. UTOHEC.

Kocurek, Willie. Taped interview by SCA on July 27, 1983, in Austin, Texas. UTOHEC.

La Grone, Herbert. Taped interview by SCA in August, 1983, in Fort Worth, Texas. UTOHEC.

Lock, Ottis. Taped interview by SCA on September 17, 1983, in Burnet, Texas. UTOHEC.

Mallas, Robert. Taped interview by SCA on September 9, 1983, in Austin, Texas. UTOHEC.

Marshall, J.A. Taped interview by SCA on July 20, 1983, in Austin, Texas. UTOHEC.

Mathews, Charles F. Taped interview by SCA on August 11, 1983, in Austin, Texas. UTOHEC.

McGee, Vernon. Taped interview by SCA on September 9, 1983, in Austin, Texas. UTOHEC.

Ollison, Chester. Taped interview by SCA on August 9, 1983, in Austin, Texas.

Rice, Friendly R. Taped interview by SCA on July 29, 1983, in Austin, Texas. UTOHEC.

Ruhman, Carolyn. Taped interview by SCA on August 16, 1983, in Austin, Texas. UTOHEC.

Shivers, Allan. Taped interview by Corrine E. Crow on November 22, 1976. Archives/Oral History. East Texas State University, Commerce, Texas.

Shivers, Allan. Taped interview by SCA on September 9, 1983, in Austin, Texas. UTOHEC.

Smith, Preston. Taped interview by Corrinne E. Crow on July 31, 1975. Archives/Oral History. East Texas State University, Commerce, Texas.

Smithheisler, Mary Louise. Taped interview by SCA on September 17, 1983, in Burnet, Texas. UTOHEC.

Stockton, John. Taped interview by SCA on August 5, 1983, in Austin, Texas. UTOHEC.

Sturgeon, L.P. Taped interview by Corrine E. Crow on January 15, 1976. Archives/Oral History. East Texas State University, Commerce, Texas.

Sturgeon, L.P. Taped interview from letter in August, 1983, New Boston, Texas. UTOHEC.

Taylor, James E. Taped interview by Corrine E. Crow on March 17, 1976. Archives/Oral History. East Texas State University, Commerce, Texas.

Taylor, James E. Taped interview by SCA on July 30, 1983, in Austin, Texas. UTOHEC.

Thornton, Mary. Taped interview by SCA on September 14, 1983, in Austin, Texas. UTOHEC.

Ward, Sally Edgar. Taped interview by SCA on September 9, 1983, in Austin, Texas. UTOHEC.

Weeks, Mrs. O.D. Taped interview by SCA on August 6, 1983, in Austin, Texas. UTOHEC.

Wilborn, Lee J. Taped interview by SCA on October 7, 1983, in Austin, Texas. UTOHEC.

Williams, Dana. Taped interview by SCA on November 17, 1983, in Corpus Christi, Texas. UTOHEC.

Winston, Mary Frances. Telephone interview by SCA on July 27, 1983, in Austin, Texas. UTOHEC.

Yarborough, Ralph. Taped interview by SCA on October 13, 1983, in Austin, Texas. UTOHEC.

LETTERS

Anderson, Robert V. Letter to J.W. Edgar on July 30, 1956, from New York, New York. UTOHEC.

Baird, Vernon. Letter to J.W. Edgar on July 1, 1974, from Fort Worth, Texas. UTOHEC.

Bowen, Alton O. Letter to SCA on September 2, 1983, from Bryan, Texas, UTOHEC.

Chandler, C.O. Letter to SCA on August 2, 1983, from Lufkin, Texas. UTOHEC.

Edgar, J.W. Letter to Mrs. O.D. Weeks on March 17, 1947, from Orange, Texas. UTOHEC.

Edgar, J.W. Letter to Mrs. O.D. Weeks on March 20, 1947, from Orange, Texas. UTOHEC.

Edgar. J.W. Letter to Robert B. Anderson on August 29, 1956, from Austin, Texas. UTOHEC.

Edgar, J.W. Letter to Paul R. Haas on June 7, 1973, from Austin, Texas. UTOHEC.

Fulbright, J.E. Letter to SCA on June 2, 1983, from Hebbronville, Texas. UTOHEC.

Haas, Paul R. Letter to SCA on October 13, 1983, from Corpus Christi, Texas. UTOHEC.

Haas, Paul R. Letter to SCA on October 25, 1983, from Corpus Christi, Texas. UTOHEC.

Lunz, Peg. Letter to SCA on July 28, 1983, from Hebbronville, Texas. UTOHEC.

Mathews, Paul. Letter to SCA on August 1, 1983, from Greenville, Texas. UTOHEC.

Marcheck, Pete. Letter to SCA on August 9, 1983, from Pawnee, Texas. UTOHEC.

Rosett, Bettina Charles. Letter to SCA on August 1, 1983, from San Antonio, Texas. UTOHEC.

Still, Rae Files. Letter to SCA on August 15, 1983, from Waxahachie, Texas. UTOHEC.

Sturgeon, L.P. Letter to SCA on August 26, 1983, from New Boston, Texas. UTOHEC.

Williams, Dana. Letter to SCA on October 17, 1983, from Corpus Christi, Texas. UTOHEC.

NEWSPAPER ARTICLES

Atterberry, Ann. "Top Officer Looks Both Ways: School Past, Future, Eyed." *Dallas Morning News*, (June 6, 1970).

Bonner, Judy. "Edgar Accepts Harris Award, Gets Plaudits of Educators." *Dallas Times Herald*, (August 5, 1956).

Brewer, Anita. "Edgar Wins State Award." *The Austin Statesman*, (July 17, 1956).

Byers, Bo. "Texas Education Chief Edgar Puts Emphasis on Finance." *Houston Chronicle*, (November 30, 1969).

"Commissioner Edgar Gets Golden Deeds Award." *The Daily Eagle*, College Station, (June 10, 1970).

"Dr. Edgar is Honored." *Austin-American Statesman*, (June 14, 1963).

"Dr. J.W. Edgar is Names 'Educator of the Decade'." *The Burnet Bulletin*, (November 26, 1964).

"Edgar, Mrs. Stinnett Win State Teachers Tributes." *The Austin Statesman*, (December 2, 1955).

"Edgar Gets School Post at $17,000." *The Austin Statesman*, (February 5, 1950).

"Education Commissioner Should be Worth as Much as Grid Coach." *Corpus Christi Caller*, (February 9, 1950).

"Educational Leader." *Beaumont Journal*, (November 14, 1949).

"Ex-Students will Honor Dr. Edgar." *Austin-American Statesman*, (October, 1956).

Gardner, William H. "J.W. Edgar Has Reached Top in Texas Education." *The Houston Post*, (January 20, 1957).

"J.W. Edgar Appointed at $17,500 Yearly Pay." *Fort Worth Telegram*, (February 4, 1950).

"J.W. Edgar of Orange Accepts School Post." *The American Statesman*, (March 24, 1947).

James, Crispin. "UT Session Seeks Way to Insure Sex Equality." *Austin-American Statesman*, (May, 1973).

Lee, Nell. "Meeting Educational Commitment in the Lone Star State." *Austin-American Statesman*, (August, 1972).

Lee, Nell. "Edgar to Retire as Era Ends: 24 Years Were Joyful." *Austin-American Statesman,* (November 18, 1973).

Meyer, Agnes E. "Wartime 'Dream School' Is Found Deep in East Texas." *The Washington Post,* (April 14, 1943).

"Mr. Public Education: Dr. Edgar Quietly Leads Texas School System." *San Antonio News,* (November 20, 1958).

Niven, Jack. "Dr. J.W. Edgar One of Burnet Boys Who Made Good! Burnet-Marble Falls, *The Highlander,* (November 26, 1964).

Olds, Greg. "J.W. Edgar and Texas Education: Noted School Commissioner Looks Back on 50-Year Career of Service." *The Highlander, XVI* (June, 1974).

"Texas Educators Hail Edgar Here: Ovation Is Given by 1,200." *The Austin Statesman,* (January 10, 1963).

REPORTS AND BULLETINS

Board of Education. *The Basic Single Salary Allotment Schedules and Salary Assignments for 1948–49.* Bulletin No. 2, Rules and Regulations, of the Board of Education of the Austin Public School District, 1948.

Board of Education. *Seven Problems Facing the Austin Public Schools: A Report to the People of Austin.* March, 1948.

Board of Education. *Seven Problems Facing the Austin Public Schools: A Report to the People of Austin.* March, 1948.

Citizens of Texas. *Citizens of Texas Recommend A Public School Program to Meet the Needs of Their Children.* Texas State Teachers Association, 1958.

Edgar, J.W. *Report on Study of Graduation Requirements in Accredited School Systems of Texas.* Speech given at a Vocational Education Meeting in Houston, Texas, July 18, 1957.

Gilmer-Aikin Committee on Education. *To Have What We Must.* 1948.

Gilmer-Aikin Committee on Education. *State Management of Education in Texas — Proposals of Sub-Committee No. 1 and the Advisory Committee on State Management.* Austin, Texas: Proceedings of the Gilmer-Aikin Committee, (July 30, 1948).

Governor's Committee on Public School Education. *To Make Texas a National Leader in Public Education: The Challenge and the Change.* 1968.

Hale-Aikin Committee of Twenty-four for the Study of Texas Public Schools. *Tentative Draft of the Final Report,* (November, 1958).

Minimum Foundation School Laws (Gilmer-Aikin Laws). Senate Bills 115, 116, and 117. 316 W. 12th Street, Austin, Texas.

Organization and Functions of the Texas Education Agency. Bulletin of the Texas Education Agency, (April, 1961).

*Petition of the Board of School Trustees for the Independent School
District of Austin to the Austin City Council for a Bond Election.*
Superintendent's Annual Report, 1947–1948. Austin, Texas: Austin
Public Schools, 1948.
*The Texas Way: A Guide for Measuring Progress in the Big Ideas of
Gilmer-Aikin Legislation.* Austin, Texas: October 9, 1950.
Texas Education Agency. *Minimum Foundation School Program.*
Bulletin 564. Austin, Texas: Texas Education Agency, 1955.
Texas Education Agency. *Thirty-six Biennial Report, 1948–49, 1949–
50.* Bulletin 511. Austin, Texas: Texas Education Agency, 1950.
Texas Research League. *Texas Public Schools Under the Minimum
Foundation Program: An Evaluation: 1949–1954.* Report No. 1:
A Summary of a Survey for the State Board of Education. Aus-
tin, Texas: Texas Research League, (November, 1954).
Texas Research League. *School District Structure in Texas.* Report
No. 2: In a Survey for the State Board of Education. Austin,
Texas: Texas Research League, (May, 1955).
Texas Research League. *The Road We Are Traveling: A Statistical
Picture of Selected Public School Trends in Texas.* Report No. 3:
In a Survey for the State Board of Education. Austin, Texas:
Texas Research League, (July, 1957).
Texas Research League. *The Minimum Foundation School Program
in Texas: Its Cost and Financing.* Report No. 4: In a Survey for
the State Board of Education. Austin, Texas: Texas Research
League, (November, 1959).
*Inaugural Program for the Texas Education Agency and Commis-
sioner of Education, Hogg Memorial Auditorium, Monday, Oc-
tober 9, 1950, 8:00 P.M.*

UNPUBLISHED

Edgar, J.W. *"Evidences of Improvement in Texas Public Schools Dur-
ing the Last Ten Years." Paper at TEC, January 1963.*
Edgar, J.W. *"Credentials of J.W. Edgar, Superintendent of Schools,
Orange, Texas." Submitted to the Austin board of Education,
March 17, 1947.*
Edgar, J.W. *Speech in October 1956 as Man of the Year.*
Edgar, J.W. *"What's New in Education?" Speech given at Camp
Waldeman on August 27, 1962, for the Texas Institute on Chil-
dren and youth.*
"J.W. Edgar: School Man for an Era." Unpublished speech.
Hood-Hanchey, Janet L. *"Bobbitt's 1914 San Antonio Survey: Much
Ado About Nothing?" A study completed under the supervision
of Dr. O.L. Davis, The University of Texas at Austin.*

"Minutes of the State Board of Education, Texas Education Agency, Volume I."

Sturgeon, L.P. *"Guidelines for the Minimum Foundation School Program Act." From the State Auditor's Office, June 21, 1949.*

Sturgeon, L.P. *"A Case Study in Public School Administration or An Interim Period in Texas Public School History (June 8, 1949–April 1, 1950)." Unfinished dissertation, UTOHEC.*

Tyack, David; Lowe, Robert; and Hansot, Elisabeth. *Public Schools in Hard Times.* Unpublished book (in press), 1984.

INDEX